INTRODUCTION TO THE CANADIAN LAW OF TORTS

SECOND EDITION

G.H.L. Fridman,
Q.C., F.R.S.C., M.A., B.C.L., LL.M.

of the Ontario Bar, and of the
Middle Temple, Barrister-at-Law

Professor Emeritus, Faculty of Law,
University of Western Ontario

LexisNexis™
Butterworths

Introduction to the Canadian Law of Torts, 2nd edition

July 2003

Members of the LexisNexis Group worldwide

Canada	LexisNexis Canada Inc, 75 Clegg Road, MARKHAM, Ontario
Argentina	Abeledo Perrot, Jurisprudencia Argentina and Depalma, BUENOS AIRES
Australia	Butterworths, a Division of Reed International Books Australia Pty Ltd, CHATSWOOD, New South Wales
Austria	ARD Betriebsdienst and Verlag Orac, VIENNA
Chile	Publitecsa and Conosur Ltda, SANTIAGO DE CHILE
Czech Republic	Orac sro, PRAGUE
France	Éditions du Juris-Classeur SA, PARIS
Hong Kong	Butterworths Asia (Hong Kong), HONG KONG
Hungary	Hvg Orac, BUDAPEST
India	Butterworths India, NEW DELHI
Ireland	Butterworths (Ireland) Ltd, DUBLIN
Italy	Giuffré, MILAN
Malaysia	Malayan Law Journal Sdn Bhd, KUALA LUMPUR
New Zealand	Butterworths of New Zealand, WELLINGTON
Poland	Wydawnictwa Prawnicze PWN, WARSAW
Singapore	Butterworths Asia, SINGAPORE
South Africa	Butterworth Publishers (Pty) Ltd, DURBAN
Switzerland	Stämpfli Verlag AG, BERNE
United Kingdom	Butterworths Tolley, a Division of Reed Elsevier (UK), LONDON, WC2A
USA	LexisNexis, DAYTON, Ohio

National Library of Canada Cataloguing in Publication

Fridman, G.H.L. (Gerald Henry Louis), 1928-
Introduction to the Canadian law of torts / G.H.L. Fridman. — 2nd ed.

Previous ed. published under title: Introduction to the law of torts.
Includes bibliographical references and index.
ISBN 0-433-44015-5

1. Torts—Canada. I. Fridman, G.H.L. (Gerald Henry Louis), 1928- . Introduction to the law of torts. II. Title.

KE1232.F75 2003 346.7103 C2003-903655-3
KF1250.F75 2003

Printed and bound in Canada.

PREFACE

What follows is a revised and reorganized version of the original book that was written a quarter of a century ago. Some parts of the earlier work have been retained, but most has been jettisoned and replaced. In consequence, this may be regarded as a totally new book, the purpose of which is to provide a broad but, it is hoped, comprehensive introductory account of the law of torts in common law Canada.

The undertaking of the revision of the original book after such a long time was the result of discussion with Ms. Caryl Young and Mr. Anand Ablack of LexisNexis Canada Inc. (Butterworths), who received very kindly my suggestion that I do so. I thank them and the publishers for their enthusiasm and support.

When I began the task of revising the original version, I was in some doubt as to how far any such revision should go, apart from the necessity to bring the contents up to date in light of the many developments that had occurred in the intervening period. In this regard I am indebted to Dr. Stephen Pitel, who encouraged me to undertake a complete restructuring of the original contents, thereby obliging me to go beyond merely incorporating new material from the past 25 years. As a result, the scope and character of the book differ greatly from the way the law was explained and discussed in the earlier work — to the advantage, I hope, of this version.

G.H.L.F.
Ash Wednesday 2003
London, Ontario

About the Author

Professor emeritus G.H.L. Fridman, of the Faculty of Law at the University of Western Ontario, is one of the most respected legal writers in Canada. He is a distinguished scholar, and has authored a number of texts that are now in multiple editions, including Butterworths' *Law of Agency*.

TABLE OF CONTENTS

TABLE OF CASES

C

D

M

N

O

T

U

V

PART I: FUNDAMENTALS

Chapter 1

THE NATURE OF TORTIOUS LIABILITY

1. ORIGINS

The law of torts in Canada, except in Quebec, is based on English common law. The history of that law reveals that over the centuries from the Norman Conquest in 1066 there emerged a number of situations in which conduct was held by the courts to create legal liability. In such situations the law characterized the conduct in question as constituting a "tort".[1]

The word "tort", from the old Norman-French, which was the language of the English courts until well past the Middle Ages, means "wrong". What the law recognized for the purposes of giving a remedy were "wrongs", conduct which caused certain types of harm, damages, or loss to another person. The development of the law was closely connected with the kinds of remedies available in the courts, and the circumstances in which such remedies would be granted to an aggrieved party. Whether an aggrieved party could maintain an action against one who was alleged to have committed some wrong to him or her depended upon whether the Chancery (the office which controlled the granting of "writs" by the King's courts) would issue a writ to cover the circumstances, and so permit the aggrieved party to bring the matter before the King's justices and have it determined by whatever procedure was appropriate to the kind of wrong alleged. Sometimes this meant that the issue was tried by means of battle between the parties or their respective champions; sometimes it was by means of rival sets of "compurgators", *i.e.* people who swore to the accuracy, truth, and validity of their respective party's assertions for or against liability; sometimes it was by means of an "ordeal", in which one or other party may have had to undergo some physical trial of his veracity. Only later, from the twelfth century onwards,[2] did the concept of trial by jury creep into the common law. However the issue was tried, it could not begin to be justiciable in any manner until a "writ" was granted to the complainant, the plaintiff, by the Chancery. Such writs were first issued only in certain recognized instances, for example where a trespass to the person of A was alleged to have been committed by B. If the plaintiff could assert that his complaint fell within the confines of an existing writ, so that he could pray in aid the appropriate "form of action", he could at the very least

1 By the eighteenth century Pratt C.J. could say, in *Chapman v. Pickersgill* (1762), 2 Wils. 145 at 146: "Torts are infinitely various".

2 During the reign of Henry II (1154-1189).

have his complaint heard by the court which, in accordance with the principles of the time, had jurisdiction to hear and determine the matter. If the conduct or misbehaviour alleged against the other party, the "defendant" as we would now call him, did not come within the narrow scope of an existing writ, or did not correspond to an existing form of action, then the plaintiff could never get a hearing for his grievance unless and until the clerks of the Chancery were prepared to issue an entirely novel writ to enable the judicial process to begin. Only when an appropriate form of action could be created to cope with a novel fact situation could the courts begin to determine what law governed such cases.[3]

The history of this branch of the common law, therefore, is a tale of gradual evolution and development of instances of liability. Around and from the writs there emerged situations of tortious misconduct. The law did not develop a concept of "tort". Instead it developed individual "torts", based upon fact-situations which were remedied by an action commenced by an appropriate writ. Each writ became identified with a particular type of misbehaviour, wrong, or "tort". In consequence each tort was and still is called after the writ which was appropriate in its instance. Thus we continue to refer to "trespass", "nuisance", "negligence", "conspiracy" and so forth.

"Torts", therefore, became those types of injurious misconduct which were remediable by an action commenced by a particular writ which set out the allegations of fact against the defendant, which he was compelled to deny or to justify or excuse by some available legal principle. He could do this by satisfying the court that the facts proved by the plaintiff did not bring the circumstances within the scope of the writ — leaving the plaintiff to begin again by starting with the proper writ, or by attempting to obtain the creation of a new writ which would cover his case. Failing either of these possibilities, all the defendant could do was rely on his denial that he had committed the acts in question, trusting that the plaintiff would not be able to make out his case, or that he, the defendant, would be able to throw sufficient doubt on the plaintiff's evidence or assertions to convince the court that the plaintiff should not succeed. Thus there were factual defences and technical defences of law and procedure. In the course of working out the details of these, the courts were able to fix the scope and limits of the various writs, and at the same time, the various torts. This development, and this history, we have inherited. The modern law of torts is the result. When we describe today the circumstances in which a particular tort can be committed, and the limits of such a tort, we are describing the present-day effects of several centuries of creation, elaboration, and explanation.

---

3 Where a writ could not be or was not issued to a complainant, the conduct that was the source of the complaint was not, and could not be, termed tortious. Thus some conduct was left outside the scope of the law, even if it was reprehensible and damaging. Not all that was harmful, immoral or antisocial was therefore tortious. However later decisions, as will be seen in appropriate contexts, have dealt with some of the historical omissions, a process that continues.

2. TORTS TODAY

Today "torts" are types of wrongful and harmful conduct redressable by some appropriate legal remedy. This may be a claim for damages, an order from a court requiring a defendant to do or refrain from doing something, or, in certain limited, rare situations, permission for an injured party to engage in self-help, that is rectification of the situation himself by taking appropriate steps without the intervention of a court.[4]

Tortious conduct giving rise to one of the remedies referred to above must have harmed the plaintiff or must threaten to cause him harm. But that in itself will not suffice. In the first place, it must also cause or threaten the sort of harm recognized by the law as being potentially remediable. Second, the conduct must be recognized by the law as coming within the ambit of its concern and displeasure.

The sort of harm potentially remediable has undergone change in recent decades. In the nineteenth century, for example, it was considered that nervous shock suffered by a plaintiff as a result of the defendant's conduct was not the kind of harm that should be recognized as a basis for recovery of damages. That is no longer the case.[5] What is often referred to as "pure" economic loss, for instance, money lost by a plaintiff because of an unsound investment made by the plaintiff in consequence of a negligent misrepresentation made by the defendant to the plaintiff, in the form of inaccurate information or advice, was not a ground for an action unless there was a contractual relationship between the parties. Such loss, in certain circumstances, is now recoverable, where no contract governed the parties' relationship.[6]

The kind of conduct that comes within the scope of the law's concern so as to give rise to an action has also been developed. For example, in the nineteenth century it was accepted that conduct by a defendant amounting to the unjustifiable procuring of a breach of contract between two other persons was actionable at the suit of the contracting party damaged as a consequence. But not conduct which resulted in the failure of parties to conclude a contract or interfered with a contract without causing its breach. Such limitations are no longer applicable.[7]

It is precisely in these ways, by enlarging the kind of harm that is recognized by the law as giving rise to a remedy, and by adding to the list of situations in which an action in tort is permitted, that the courts in the past developed the law of torts and are still carrying on with such development. At the present time, however, it is not possible to state without qualification that any conduct which causes any sort of harm whatsoever will automatically give rise to an action in tort (even if the conduct in question is not lawful or otherwise justifiable or excusable). There are circumstances in which the causing of harm will not involve tortious conduct, however anti-social or morally reprehensible the conduct may be. Moreover, not all harm that is suffered as a consequence of conduct which is

---

4 In cases of nuisance: below pp. 66-67.

5 Below pp. 77-78.

6 Below pp. 102-105.

7 Below pp. 201-204.

bad in the sense of being tortious will be recognized as giving rise to liability. There are categories of unrecognized harm.

Tortious conduct, therefore, is conduct which: (a) has been declared in the past or may be declared in the future to be conduct which is capable of creating liability; and (b) causes harm which is recognized by the law as being redressable by some appropriate remedy, be it damages or otherwise. In determining what is potentially tortious or actionable conduct two concepts are of prime importance: the first is that of "duties"; the second is the concept of "interests". These may be looked upon as two aspects of the same thing.

3. DUTIES AND INTERESTS

(a) Duties

The law of torts, like many other branches of the law, from which the law of torts must be differentiated, is concerned with duties or responsibilities. Indeed one way of defining torts is to state that torts are breaches of duties imposed by the law on people generally. This distinguishes the law of torts from the law of contract and the law of trusts, which deal with duties that are created by the parties themselves, not imposed by the law, and may be limited in their operation to one or several people. However the definition given above does not serve to differentiate tortious conduct from conduct that is criminal. Both involve, or may involve, the breach of a legal duty that is imposed, not voluntarily assumed, and is owed generally. The law of torts, however, is concerned with the redress of harm; criminal law with punishment.[8]

That distinction was not at all clear in the earliest days of the common law. The earliest torts, the various "trespasses", which still exist today,[9] were as much criminal in nature as they were designed to provide a remedy for the victim. The writ by which an action in trespass was commenced set out that the defendant had done such and such, depending on whether the trespass was to land, goods or the person, *vi et armis et contra pacem regis*, by force of arms and against the peace of the King. In other words, the wrongdoing was bad and actionable, in part at least, because it constituted a breach of the peace. Such allegations, in the course of time, became fictitious and not really part of the plaintiff's case or the real basis of his claim. Torts are not actionable because they involve a breach of the peace — even modern-day trespasses. However, there is still an element of this in the law of torts. Clearly if such wrongs were not remedied by an appropriate action in the courts they might lead to violence between individuals, in

---

8 Torts are considered to be *private* wrongs, *i.e.*, wrongs against one or more private individuals. Crimes are *public* wrongs, *i.e.*, wrongs against society as a whole, even though affecting immediately one or more individuals.

The distinction between torts giving rise to compensation and crimes to punishment has become blurred by the rise in importance and scope of awards of punitive or exemplary damages: below p. 216.

9 Below pp. 39-56.

other words a serious breach of the peace of the country. Only by granting an aggrieved party a judicial remedy can the State ensure that society will function harmoniously without constant violence and upset between citizens. However, in accordance with modern thinking, this way of looking at torts as breaches of the peace has been transformed into regarding torts as breaches of duties which are imposed by the law on people so as to prevent breaches of the peace and ensure harmony and peaceful relationships.

(b) Interests

The law of torts can also be regarded as providing the legal framework within which may be described those various interests enjoyed by people generally that are to be treated as worthy of recognition and protection by law. Interference with such interests, at least if it causes harm and sometimes without proof of such harm, merely upon the interference in question, and at least where there is no satisfactory and acceptable reason for permitting such interference, for instance, in cases of necessity such as self-defence from attack, is actionable at the suit of the person whose particular interest has been affected.

Classifying the law of torts in terms of protectable interests, and enunciating such interests, is very much a modern approach to the law of torts. It is a way of looking at this area of the law from a more sociological standpoint, as contrasted with the older, more theoretical attitude of categorizing rights and duties. Various interests have been recognized at different stages in history of the law. Some, for example the interest everybody has in maintaining his or her personal safety, have long been accepted. Others, such as the interest which a person has in maintaining the existence and continuation of his contractual relations with another person, have only been recognized and protected in more recent times. If the law of torts is looked at in this way, we can speak of torts as conduct which invades or harms protectable interests that are recognized by the law and may be enjoyed by people generally. As those interests change or develop, so may the law of torts.

There may be some time-lag between the rise of a particular interest and its recognition and protection by the law; eventually, however, this will take place, whether as a consequence of decisions by the courts or legislation. The history of the law of torts may be viewed as the gradual recognition and protection of various interests as they emerged in society. Hence the impossibility of saying that there is or can be any termination or limit to the nature and scope of torts or the law of torts. As more interests develop in society, so will the law be compelled to decide whether they are to be recognized and protected by the law, particularly by the law of torts.

Such developments will depend on the extent to which the law is prepared to accept that there can be novel interests meriting protection, and is willing and able to adapt or devise a remedy in cases of infringement or interference. One question that can arise in this respect is whether it is legitimate or proper to divide and subdivide interests which have previously been recognized as existing, so as to create new forms of liability. This question has sometimes been raised in connection with the interest which everyone has in regard to his or her personal safety. It has been suggested that there is an interest in physical bodily safety and a distinct interest in mental safety: the former being affected by acts which cause physical harm, the latter by acts resulting in psychological harm. This might lead to recognition of a separate tort of causing nervous shock. It may not be necessary or profitable to atomize the law to such a degree, in that legal policy and the purposes of the law of torts can be served adequately by a more general concept of an interest in personal safety. There may be no advantage to be gained, insofar as the analysis of the law and its development are concerned, to adopt an overly detailed approach based on interests.

4. PURPOSES OF THE LAW OF TORTS

Various aims can be, and have been suggested as being the true purpose behind the creation of tortious liability. One important, and undeniable one is that the law serves to provide ways to compensate victims of tortious conduct for the harm or threatened harm that they have suffered or may suffer as a consequence. Another, broader suggested aim is to set down and maintain certain desirable, if minimal, standards of conduct to be observed by society.

(a) Compensation

In its origins, as noted earlier, the law of torts was not so much concerned with providing a remedy for some injury or harm suffered by one person at the hands of another as with seeking to preclude the possibility of some retaliation by the injured party against the wrongdoer, thereby causing a breach of the peace. An important function of the judicial system and the law imported by the Norman kings into England was to achieve the peaceful settlement of the land. Gradually, however, from being designed to assist in the promotion of peace and harmony, the remedies that became available for what we now term tortious conduct changed their focus and turned into remedies to provide compensation, redress for injuries incurred as a consequence of wrongdoing. Eventually it was recognized that the purpose of such remedies, indeed of the law of torts as a whole, was to restore the injured party to his or her position prior to the occurrence of the damage or loss suffered insofar as money could do so.

In modern times, however, this philosophy of compensation has been called into question in some situations. One is where the victim has been so severely injured by the defendant's wrongdoing, usually in the form of negligence, that any amount of money awarded by way of damages will not be adequate to compensate the victim for his or her injuries, for instance where the victim has become a paraplegic. As will be seen,[10] all the courts can do by way of compensation is to order the payment of such a sum as will provide for the care of the victim for the remainder of the victim's life. This is not truly compensation in the traditional, original sense.

---

[10] Below p. 218.

Another situation causing the questioning of the idea that the law of torts has as its purpose the compensation of victims, not the punishment of wrongdoers, arises where the amount of actual loss suffered by the victim has been small, such that the damages that would adequately compensate the victim for the harm done would not seriously affect the defendant's finances and it has been thought that the defendant's conduct ought to be visited with some greater penalty, not only to indicate the disapproval felt by the law about the defendant's conduct, or the manner in which it was indulged, but also to serve as a warning to other potential tortfeasors to avoid such behaviour. In such instances there has been much discussion, particularly in recent times, of the possibility and purposes of awards of "punitive" or "exemplary" damages, that are not compensatory but are more akin to fines and other penalties imposed on those guilty of crimes than they are to damages normally awarded in actions in tort.[11] The prospect of such awards seems to indicate that the law of torts may have as one, at least, of its aims or purposes either punishment of wrongdoers or deterrence of the future commission of torts.

To the extent to which the remedies available in tort actions go beyond the compensation principle, the law of torts is doing more than merely seeking to provide redress to an injured party. Hence it may be argued that while compensation is an important aim of the law of torts, it does not altogether explain what part of the law is doing. In such situations the law of torts is *quasi*-criminal in character, and serves as an adjunct of the criminal law, providing for punishment as well as compensation. Nonetheless, the primary function, purpose, or aim of the law of torts is to compensate, and awards of greater amounts by way of damages, to the extent to which they may be made are only ancillary.

It must be observed that, as previously mentioned, an award of damages is not the only, and unique, remedy available in cases of tort. Other remedies may be granted to a successful plaintiff, for example, an injunction in cases of nuisance or specific restitution of goods in cases of detinue or conversion. Nor is compensation in the form of damages unique to the law of torts. Compensation, the payment of a sum of money, may be awarded someone who has been affected injuriously by non-tortious conduct, under legislation dealing with workers' compensation, discrimination, compensation of victims of crime, infringement of human rights, or as a result of conduct that is contrary to the *Canadian Charter of Rights and Freedoms*.[12] Finally, the term "damages", which normally refers to the payment of compensation to the victim of a tort, has been used in some courts to denote what is awarded to a successful claimant in an action for restitution based upon unjust enrichment, even though the purpose of such awards is to compel the party who has been unjustly enriched, in circumstances

---

11 Below pp. 216-217.

12 Part I of the *Constitution Act, 1982*, being Schedule B to the *Canada Act 1982* (U.K.), 1982, c. 11.

that do not necessarily amount to the commission of a tort, to disgorge the enrichment that has been achieved at the expense of the claimant.[13]

(b) Standards of Conduct

The earliest function of the law of torts, the maintenance of peace and order, has been noted. The provision of remedies for injuries suffered by one person at the hands of another enabled the law to make a start along the road of setting the standards to be expected of, and observed by, civilized, reasonable people. This aim was not a conscious one, at least in the beginning. At the present time, however, it may be said with more assurance that among the purposes of the law of torts is the maintenance of certain standards of behaviour, below which people generally should not fall if society is to be carried on in an harmonious, efficient, and safe manner.

Thus it is obvious that unless people refrain from striking one another, invading the property of others, taking or destroying their goods, impeaching their characters, deceiving them, and causing them harm in other ways, it will be impossible for life to continue in any civilized, reasonable, and tolerable fashion. The law is desirous of achieving a certain balance between what can and should be done to protect others, and what is permitted to be done in one's own interests and for one's own purposes.

The method employed by the law of torts to achieve this aim is necessarily oblique, and by no means perfect. By making awards of damages in the event of tortious conduct, the law can only hope to deter, not to prevent. Obviously a person who is willing to pay the price of his or her tortious behaviour is, in a sense, at liberty to do what he or she wishes regardless of the harm caused to others. Since monetary awards may be large, not only on basic principles of compensation but also by reason of the possibility, previously mentioned, of punitive or exemplary damages, the requirement that such payments will be made may suffice to deter most people from committing tortious acts. But this is not always so. Moreover, since the advent of liability insurance, it may be that the deterrent effect of the law of torts, at least in relation to liability for negligence, may not be as great as once it may have been.

By way of contrast, however, the modern law of torts has developed, and given greater effect to, older nineteenth century, and earlier decisions which imposed tortious liability on public officials who abused their powers to the damage of persons over and in respect of whom such officials exercised authority. The aim of this form of liability may well be not only to compensate the victims but to deter officials from acting unlawfully and detrimentally.[14] This aspect of the modern law of torts has led some writers to suggest that, in this way, the law of torts performs the role and functions of an "ombudsman". That suggestion, it may be said, is somewhat fanciful. Nonetheless it cannot be

---

13 Note, however, the doctrine of "waiver of tort", below p. 214, by which, in the case of certain torts, the victim can elect to sue in restitution, for unjust enrichment, instead of for damages in tort.

14 Below p. 161.

denied that the evolution of this kind of liability in its modern form is an important development which is capable of providing greater protection to people at a time when governmental activity of all kinds and at all levels has increased and continues to increase, with the consequence that officials charged with the responsibility of carrying out governmental policy are thereby placed in a position to cause harm if they misuse the powers entrusted to them.

5. SOURCES OF THE LAW

The present law of torts in the common law provinces of Canada is derived from the decisions of the courts in England from the time of the Norman Conquest to the present day, as well as from decisions of courts in Canada and other parts of the common law world. The law of torts is for the most part "judge-made" law, that is, it comprises the decisions of the courts and most important, the reasons given for their decisions by those courts. It is in the reasoning as well as in the decisions themselves that the law is to be found, in the sense of the principles underlying those decisions, and the bases for those principles. More recently, in these various jurisdictions legislation has been passed in relation to certain areas of the law of torts for the purposes of eradicating anomalies, rectifying errors, making reforms in the light of recent social and other developments and current thought, and, generally speaking, tidying up the sometimes haphazard, ill-assorted rules and doctrines created by the courts. Such statutory intervention, by and large, has been piecemeal, perfunctory, and interstitial. The greater part of the law of torts is still being developed in and by the courts. It is this which gives the law of torts its fascination, as well as its difficulties. The fact that this area of the law has been and still is a fertile field for the operation of judicial minds, provides it with a flavour and excitement that is almost unique in the modern common law. In the language of the judges, and their employment of the concepts of morality, history, philosophy, economics, social policy and logic, can be discovered the true elements of the common law.

Chapter 2

FOUNDATIONS OF TORTIOUS LIABILITY

1. THE TRIAD

The law of torts, as noted in the preceding chapter, did not emanate from any general, logically structured principles of responsibility or liability but from the more pragmatic requirements of the mediaeval period and the limited possibilities of mediaeval legal procedure. At the present stage in the evolution of the law it is possible to deduce and interpolate from the various instances of liability that emerged in the course of several centuries and are the subject of later chapters some broader, fundamental principles or concepts of liability. These may be considered the foundations of the modern law of torts, the underlying reasons or grounds for imposing liability on someone. These concepts are: intention; negligence; and causation.

In certain circumstances, which will be explained and discussed in due course, a person may be held guilty of tortious behaviour resulting in liability, in the absence of some applicable defence: (a) if he or she has intentionally inflicted harm or loss upon another; (b) if he or she has caused such harm or loss by negligent conduct; or (c) even in the absence of intentional or negligent misconduct, if by reason of otherwise lawful actions harm or loss has been caused to another. This last category of situations entailing liability in tort consists mainly of vestigial instances of so-called "strict" liability, subsisting today long after their justification has disappeared, despite developments which to some degree make it questionable to consider that they involve truly "strict" liability. To these debatable examples of such liability must be added one that, as will be seen, is beyond doubt an instance when liability flows from the fact that harm has been caused for which the defendant can be held responsible although he or she has not physically caused the harm.

The exposition of the different torts recognized by the modern law will reveal how, with the exception of the anomalous instances of "strict" liability, fundamental to each instance of liability will be the defendant's intention to do the act that causes harm or the defendant's negligence that results in harm. Nevertheless, it is not possible, even in the present stage of the law's development, to state that all intentionally or negligently caused harm results in tortious liability, without specifying precisely what "nominate" tort, such as trespass, nuisance, libel, conspiracy, has been committed. There remain situations in which the intention to cause harm or negligence may be shown to have been present, but for various valid reasons the defendant guilty of such conduct is not liable in tort nor is his or her conduct considered to be tortious. We can discuss the fundamental elements of liability that have been referred to above: however the law of torts cannot be reduced to analysis of its content purely in terms of those elements. The law of torts cannot be simplified by stating that a person commits a tort when as a result of intentional or negligent conduct harm or loss results to another. There is no law of tort: there is a law of torts.

2. INTENTION

The idea that liability arises out of an intentional infliction of harm emerged only comparatively recently. It cannot be said, by any stretch of the imagination, that the law of torts began with any settled notion of attributing liability to a wrongdoer who acted in this way. As noted earlier, the law commenced with a number of fact situations, identified and dealt with by an appropriate writ in each instance, giving rise to liability. It so happened that many, if not most of these, at least in origin, were instances of intentionally inflicted harm, *e.g.*, by trespass or nuisance. The essence of liability, however, was not the wrongdoer's state of mind so much as the actual infliction of the injury in the manner which was designated as being wrongful. The relevance of states of mind is a more sophisticated idea, which has grown in importance only in more modern times. It is in the nineteenth century, rather than earlier, that judges begin to theorize about tort liability in terms of such ideas as intentional wrongdoing.

By that time a number of torts had developed in which it had become important to determine, for the sake of deciding upon the issue of liability, whether the defendant intended to harm the plaintiff or had acted in some other manner, even though it resulted in the causing of harm. The problem was that the issue of "intent", in the sense of a deliberate, formulated aim or purpose of causing harm by adopting a certain course of conduct which might thereby make such conduct tortious, was confused with, and bedevilled by, the older and different notion of "malice". The task of modern law has been to disentangle the concept of intention and its effect in the law of torts, from the idea of malice. Both ideas have a role to play. The role of each is different, although the two ideas are interrelated.[1]

Malice is a term which has caused a great deal of difficulty in the law generally, and the law of torts in particular. Originally it meant some kind of ill-will or spite. A person acted maliciously when acting out of some unpleasant, wicked motive, in order to cause harm or damage, and not out of any sense of exercising lawful rights or doing something to advance the actor's own purposes rather than hinder those of another.

This in time became known as "malice in fact". In contrast, there developed or emerged a concept of "malice in law".[2] This referred to the more technical notion that a certain intent, *viz.*, to act unlawfully or improperly, could be attributed to someone by virtue of what that person had done. In many contexts the use of the expression "malice", as a noun, an adjective or an adverb, could mean

1 Fridman, "Malice in the Law of Torts" (1958) 21 Mod. L.R. 484.

2 *Bromage v. Prosser* (1825), 4 B. & C. 247 at 255 *per* Bayley J.

either that the person acting did so out of spite or some improper motive, or had done so with the intention of doing something wrong, in other words, with the intent to commit a tort. Sometimes proof that the person in question was acting spitefully or with an improper motive was material to a question of liability. For example, in cases of defamation it was, and still is relevant in some situations to ask whether the defendant published the defamatory statement maliciously.[3] On other occasions, malice, in that sense, was irrelevant. The fact that the defendant acted in the manner he or she did, and caused damage, would suffice to create liability, as long as it was done with the intent of causing such harm, and not from some other intent which involved the legitimacy of the acts. A simple illustration would be where the defendant deliberately struck the plaintiff. That would be actionable, unless, for example, the defendant acted not simply out of the intention to injure the plaintiff but by way of protection from attack by the plaintiff, or for the purpose of pushing the plaintiff out of the way of some danger which was threatening the plaintiff.

It is not difficult to see how and why the two notions of malice became muddled. To determine whether the defendant's intent was lawful or unlawful there could be no better test than to ask whether the defendant acted spitefully (or from an improper motive).Yet this was to confuse two distinct ideas. It was also to introduce into the law of torts what the courts had refused to admit in the criminal law, namely, the possibility that liability could depend on the motive from which, rather than the intent with which, a party acted. The task of the courts over the past few decades has been to disentangle the law relating to such torts from the earlier operative notions that liability turned on the motive with which a party acted.[4] It has also been necessary to indicate the extent to which malice, in the original factual sense, could provide some evidence of the necessary intent, by establishing that the party whose conduct was in question could not have been acting in a lawful manner, and with a lawful intent, because the aim of the conduct was to cause harm spitefully or otherwise from an improper motive. Thus malice might show that a party acted tortiously. But not all malicious conduct, in the factual sense, is necessarily tortious. Towards the end of the nineteenth century, in the famous case of *Mayor of Bradford v. Pickles*[5] the House of Lords laid down that malice, *i.e.*, an improper motive, could not make an otherwise lawful act into an unlawful, *i.e.*, tortious one. That decision did not, and does not mean, however, that malice in the factual sense is always irrelevant, or that the legality of certain conduct is never tested by reference to the motive of the person whose conduct is in issue.[6] It does mean that, in deciding whether a person's conduct is tortious, in some situations, the legality of that conduct must be determined objectively, without, in the first instance at any rate, appealing to the party's motives to provide the answer.

---

3 Below pp. 141-142.

4 *Cf.* below pp. 201-206, in relation to torts involving interference with economic well-being.

5 [1985] A.C. 587; see also *Allen v. Flood*, [1898] A.C. 1.

6 Fridman, "Motive in the English Law of Nuisance" (1954) 40 Virginia L.R. 585: below pp. 61-62.

In this respect, it must be emphasized, the law is concerned with the intent of the person concerned. The question that should be asked is whether he or she intended to cause harm without having any lawful excuse for acting as he or she did. It is the intention to cause harm which makes the conduct tortious. However, not all intentionally caused harm will give rise to liability. In the first place, if the conduct is justified or excused by the law it will not be actionable. Second, since the law has not developed logically, some situations of this kind are not covered by the law of torts. For example, if A owns a business, and B sets up a rival business next door to A with the intention of driving A into bankruptcy by underselling the same goods as those sold by A, B commits no actionable tort, even though B's intention was to cause economic loss to A. Nor would it matter whether B acted from an improper or an acceptable motive. Some judicial statements in England towards the end of the nineteenth century, suggesting that all intentionally caused harm or injury was actionable unless justified or excluded by law,[7] went too far. Though the law may have developed since then, it is still not accurate to express the scope of the law with such breadth.

In the modern law of torts, as a result of decisions of the past hundred years, there are instances in which the intention of the defendant to cause harm may result in liability for the harm so caused, unless some policy limits that liability in terms of the purpose underlying the infliction of the harm and that purpose comes within the ambit of that limitation. For example, a conspiracy to injure may be actionable.[8] However, it will not be if its purpose is to protect a legitimate interest of the conspirators, such as businesspeople combining to maintain a decent standard of product or trade unionists combining to obtain fair standards of wages. What are legitimate or justifiable purposes, and what excuses certain conduct from being the basis of liability when otherwise it would found an action in tort, are questions of some difficulty. Thus far the limits of legitimacy, justification or excuse have not been settled.[9] The law of torts has not reached finality with respect to torts based upon the intention to cause harm.

Nor can it be said that it is enough to prove an intention to cause harm, subject to the qualification of justification or excuse already mentioned. If it were, then it would be possible to state that there was a general principle of law such that the intention to harm sufficed to establish liability in tort. Neither malice, in

---

7 For example, *Mogul S.S. Co. v. McGregor, Gow & Co.* (1889), 23 Q.B.D. 598 at 615 *per* Bowen L.J. (C.A.).

A similar view was expressed in 1966 by the High Court of Australia in *Beaudesert Shire Council v. Smith* (1966), 120 C.L.R. 145. Although accepted in some later Australian decisions, it was rejected by the House of Lords in *Lonrho Ltd. v. Shell Petroleum Co.*, [1982] A.C. 173 at 187-188, *per* Lord Diplock and by the Court of Appeal in New Zealand: see *Takaro Properties Ltd. v. Rowling*, [1978] 2 N.Z.L.R. 314 and *Van Camp Chocolates Ltd. v. Aulsebrooks Ltd.*, [1984] 1 N.Z.L.R. 354. Ultimately the earlier view was repudiated by the High Court of Australia in *Northern Territory of Australia v. Mengel* (1996), 185 C.L.R. 307; see Dwyer, "Beaudesert: A Spurious Principle After All" (1995) 3 Tort L.R. 165; Fridman "Judicial Independence of a Different Kind", in Mullany, ed., *Torts in the Nineties* (Sydney: LBC Information Services, 1997), 305 at pp. 327-329.

8 Below pp. 184-186.

9 Below p. 187.

the factual sense, nor intent, in the strictly legal sense, will of themselves create liability in tort. There has to be something else. There has to be a fact situation which is recognized by the law as being one in which there can possibly be liability in tort. If the kind of conduct is not capable of being treated as tortious, such as the opening of a rival business in the example given earlier, then neither malice nor intention to injure will produce liability. The instances when the requisite intention, proved or supported by malice in the factual sense, or even in the absence of such malice, will found liability can be listed and discussed both individually and by way of comparison. From them certain common features or elements can be extracted, perhaps the most important being the necessity for an intention to harm as compared with mere negligence. To go further and extrapolate a general principle of intentional wrongdoing is unjustified by the law as it stands at the present time. What can be said is that in certain well-established instances of liability in tort it is not enough to prove that the defendant caused harm, or caused harm by acting negligently. It must be shown that the harm was caused intentionally. It may also have to be shown that this was done without lawful justification or excuse.[10] Certainly the prime element in maintaining an action is proof of the necessary intent. This in turn rests upon knowledge of the facts, the clear intention of acting in the prescribed manner, intention to injure — or at least foresight that this was so likely a result of the conduct in question that it must be concluded that there was an intent to injure.

Thus torts within this category, even apart from the possibility that they may involve in some indirect way the idea of malice in the factual sense of spite or ill-will, reveal an important difference from those within the category of torts based upon negligence. That difference clearly depends upon the relevance of the defendant's state of mind. There is a manifest distinction between a person who desires and intends to harm and one who has no such desire or intention but is treated by the law as guilty and blameworthy because he or she did not do all that was necessary or reasonable to avoid or prevent the causing of some harm.

3. NEGLIGENCE

The expression "negligence" refers to some kind of conduct which involves neglect. It connotes a failure to act with such care as would normally be expected in the circumstances. From the fourteenth century onwards there are to be found in the decisions of English courts and the literature of the common law, references to negligent conduct, to negligent behaviour as being the basis of liability to pay damages. The allegation that the defendant had behaved *negligenter*, *i.e.*, negligently, was held to be sufficient to found an action in certain circumstances. These were situations in which the writ of trespass upon the case, developed in the late thirteenth and subsequent centuries, was available to an injured party. In the earliest times such situations involved negligent performance of their duties by persons who professed a "public" calling, one which meant that they were available to

[10] Or the defendant may have to establish the requisite justification or excuse: below p. 187.

members of the public generally upon payment of a fee, such as carriers, medical men, farriers, those operating a public ferry across a river, and the like. Later the allegation that the defendant had acted negligently was held sufficient to support an action upon the case in other circumstances. Gradually there evolved a list of situations or personalities in respect of which or whom an action would lie if there were negligence, or if they behaved in a negligent fashion.

As yet, however, negligence was conceived of only as a mode of behaviour, as a form of conduct, albeit involving a certain state of mind, namely, careless disregard for consequences and the possibility of causing harm, rather than as something more specific in a legal sense. The idea of negligence, though often referred to in terms of a duty to behave in a certain way, was still not formally or logically connected with any well-developed concept of legal duty. In particular, it was not yet accepted that there was anything more than a list of fact-situations in which a person who acted negligently, in this general sense, might be liable if he caused damage to another. Standing in the way of any more general concept of negligence were some important factors.

In the first place there was the doctrine of privity of contract. By virtue of this doctrine, which is still a vital aspect of the law of contract, it was thought that where there was a contract between two parties which involved some duty to take care on the part of one such party, and that party was in breach of the duty by having acted negligently in some way, the only person who might sue if injured in consequence was the other contracting party, the beneficiary of the duty under the contract. Only if there were fraud might there be any greater scope for liability.[11] This was because in the eighteenth century there emerged a remedy for deceit or fraud, which became recognized as a very general remedy whenever damage, of whatever kind, was caused by deception.[12] In the nineteenth century, however, the doctrine of privity maintained its supremacy, and prevented any extensive application of the original idea of negligence.

Second, the courts were still embroiled in the distinction between direct and indirect injuries. The common law originally only recognized as actionable harm that was immediately and directly caused by an act or acts of the wrongdoer. This idea was enshrined in the concept of a "trespass", an act which immediately and directly caused physical harm to someone, damaged chattels, or constituted an invasion of land.[13] Later there emerged various categories of wrongdoing that involved the indirect harming of the victim by the wrongdoer.[14] A later development was the notion of "negligence", when a careless act or omission by a wrongdoer resulted consequentially in damage or loss to the victim. Until the middle of the nineteenth century this distinction was of the greatest importance

---

11 *Langridge v. Levy* (1837), 2 M. & W. 519.

12 *Pasley v. Freeman* (1789), 3 Term Rep. 51.

13 *Cf.* below pp. 39-56.

14 For example, in cases of *nuisance*, where a wrongdoer blocked a stream on his or her land causing water to flood the victim's land or prevent its flow so as to deprive the victim of access to water.

as far as the substantive law of torts was concerned.[15] Conduct indirectly causing harm was less likely to give rise to liability than conduct which directly affected the victim.

Third, the issue of remoteness of damage, of which more will be said later,[16] had not yet been discussed in depth by the courts. Throughout the nineteenth century the courts were speaking in language that was uncertain and ambivalent on questions relating to causation and the scope of liability for negligent conduct. In a sense it was not necessary for them to be more specific or certain. Given a select group of instances in which negligence could produce liability, and some definition of the circumstances in which even in these instances liability could emerge, it may not have been as vital as it has become subsequently to determine the principles upon which the scope of liability could, and should be based. The very elementary state of the law of torts, in comparison with its state today, meant that the courts did not have to wrestle with anything more advanced or complex than some simple illustrations of neglect causing damage and so creating liability.

The various cross-currents of thought of the nineteenth century were to some extent calmed by the historic decision of the House of Lords in 1932 in *Donaghue v. Stevenson*.[17] That case did two major things. In the first place it summed up the developments of earlier centuries, and made it possible to speak of a more generalized concept of negligence. Second, it opened the way for much greater development of the law and its scope, and led to more sophisticated discussion of some important elements of liability, such as duty, foresight, causation and remoteness.[18] The expression "negligence" took on another meaning after 1932. From having been a term of very general meaning and import, referring to the notion that someone had behaved with less than due care, it also became a technical term of art. As such it denoted that there had been a breach of a duty of care owed by one person to another, by some failure to observe a standard of care set by the law in the circumstances (in accordance with the doctrine of the foresight of consequences to be expected of a reasonable man), and that such breach had caused damage to the plaintiff, in a manner and to an extent which involved the defendant in liability for such damage.

From 1932 therefore, negligence had two meanings. It could still refer or relate to the older idea of carelessness, which might or might not produce liability in tort as an ingredient of liability in torts generally, by being an essential element of the commission of such torts as nuisance or trespass.[19] It was also an independent, separate tort, comprising its own elements, of which negligence,

---

15 Its current relevance lies in the doctrine that torts originally remediable by a writ of trespass are actionable without proof of damage, although the recoverable damages depend on the damage actually suffered, whereas torts originally remediable by the writ of trespass on the case, appropriate where damage was caused indirectly, for instance negligence, are only actionable on proof of damage having been suffered. With respect to such torts "damage is the gist of the action".

16 Below pp. 82-85.

17 [1932] A.C. 562.

18 Below pp. 69-76, 85-87.

19 Below pp. 43, 51, 54, 63.

in the older more general sense, was one. The basis of negligence, in the older more colloquial sense, as well as in the more modern technical one, is the idea that a person is obliged to behave as a reasonable person, given the exact circumstances of the situation and the precise position occupied by the person in question. Thus what is reasonable behaviour in a barber is not necessarily reasonable on the part of a surgeon. Everything depends upon the task that is undertaken, the degree of professionalism or experience of the defendant, the potential danger that is involved, and the extent of the harm that might result from the defendant's conduct. An intrinsic part of this, notably where the tort of negligence is concerned, are questions of legal policy. The law does not operate purely mechanically, by devising concepts and rules and applying them in a logical, theoretical way, regardless of consequences or ultimate social or moral values. On the contrary, as has become more openly recognized in more recent times, the law relating to negligence is very much concerned with advancing certain policies of the law, specifically the need to protect people from the consequences of the acts or omissions of others, and the greater possibilities of harm which can occur in a modern, industrialized, over-populated, sophisticated world, which is more closely integrated than in the past. Not surprisingly, therefore, the courts have been prepared to utilize the notion of negligence which emerged from the medieval and post-medieval world and came to maturity, in some measure, in 1932, to form the basis for the wider action of the law of torts in the creation and maintenance of standards of behaviour as well as the provision of protection and compensation.

At the present time it can be said that underlying much of the content and operation of the law of torts is the idea that negligence, in the sense of the failure to behave with reasonable care, or acting in a manner which indicates an unreasonable disregard for the foreseeable consequences of one's acts or omissions, is the source of much liability. Having regard to modern developments both in relation to the tort of negligence and the relevance of negligence more generally, it may be said that, subject to certain limitations,[20] whenever one person behaves negligently that person will be liable to those injured in consequence. There is a general notion of negligence as a basis of liability in a way that there is not a comparable general notion of the intention to cause harm or injury. The categories of negligence are never closed, as it has been said.[21] That must mean, if it means anything at all, that it is always open to the law to designate negligent conduct as being tortious, whenever the courts consider that the negligent conduct in question is both too serious to be overlooked, and within the scope of the concept of negligence in the narrow technical sense, or the more general wider one. In this way, and to this extent, the courts have the right and the power to regulate conduct, at least by means of imposing liability to compensate an injured party who has suffered in consequence, thereby indirectly attempting to prevent the recurrence of such conduct in the future, by the guilty party or anyone else in a similar position. It means, also, that the courts are free to extend the scope of their intervention and the extent of the

---

20 Stemming from doctrines such as assumption of risk or remoteness of damage: below pp. 82, 92.

21 Lord Macmillan in *Donaghue v. Stevenson*, [1932] A.C. 562 at 619.

law's operation. Negligence is not a totally finite concept: it is more flexible. As such it is a more useful tool with which to construct legal policy.

4. CAUSATION: STRICT LIABILITY

Unlike the criminal law, the law of torts does not stress the need for showing *mens rea*, a guilty mind. In the case of certain torts some form of guilty or reprehensible mentality, in the form of an intention to cause harm or a failure to foresee and use reasonable care to avoid causing harm, may be an ingredient of actionability. However there are situations in which even a totally innocent person may be guilty of tortious conduct for which liability will ensue. In those situations the fact that the person concerned lacked any intention of causing harm, nor could be described as having been negligent or otherwise blameworthy, will not operate as an excuse so as to exempt the person in question from liability. Such examples of what has sometimes been called "absolute" liability, but is more appropriately termed "strict" liability, are anomalous: they remain as vestigial reminders of the older medieval approach to liability, which was based on causation rather than fault.[22] That may have altered in the nineteenth century.[23] Nonetheless there are still instances of tortious liability where the fact that the defendant's acts or omissions have resulted in, or caused harm to a victim suffices to make the defendant liable. Three important instances of tortious liability being imposed "strictly", without proof of either an intention to harm or negligence, are: (i) some examples of nuisance;[24] (ii) liability under the doctrine first laid down in *Rylands v. Fletcher*;[25] and (iii) where a defendant is held responsible vicariously for the tortious behaviour of a servant, agent or, in some circumstances, an independent contractor.[26]

Two major developments have occurred in relation to all these forms of strict liability. In the first place, some, for example, liability under *Rylands v. Fletcher*,[27] may no longer be quite as strict in their nature as once they were. The idea of nuisance has also been developed in such a way as to suggest that for there to be liability, some nuisances may involve more than mere proof of interference with the plaintiff's property or convenience.[28] In these and other instances the courts have been willing to accept that there are limitations upon the scope and application of "strict" liability. They have made it clear that proof of negligence (at the very least) will be required before liability can exist. Secondly, statutes have provided for some limitation on the liability of an "innocent" party

---

22 Kretzmer, "Transformation of Tort Liability in the Nineteenth Century: The Visible Hand" (1984) 4 Ox. J. Leg. St. 46.

23 *Ibid.*

24 Below pp. 59-62.

25 (1866), L.R. 1 Ex. 265, affirmed (1868), L.R. 3 H.L. 330: below pp. 111-115.

26 Below pp. 31-36.

27 Below p. 113.

28 Below p. 61.

in cases of what would otherwise be strict liability.[29] That concept may be breaking down, to be replaced by a concept of liability based upon "fault", *i.e.*, the intention to cause harm or negligence.

This suggestion cannot be taken too far. Undoubtedly, there remain in the modern law of torts, apart from the three instances referred to earlier, other examples of liability that is not dependent upon fault. The person who deals with the title to goods belonging to another when he or she is not authorized to do so, may be liable to the true owner even where the one guilty of interference never intended to act wrongfully, as, for example, where he or she bought the goods from a thief and did so in good faith, believing that the thief was the true owner.[30] The keeper of a wild animal may be liable if the animal does harm, *e.g.*, by escaping from control and attacking another person, even if the keeper of the animal had done everything in his or her power, as a reasonable person, to ensure that the animal was unable to escape.[31] The person who publishes a defamatory statement about another may be liable for the libel or slander in question even if he or she did not know it was defamatory, had no reason to believe that it was, and possibly was ignorant of the existence of the person defamed.[32] Of course there are limitations upon the liability of the party alleged to be liable in tort in the above instances and in many others. However, it is still correct to say that, unless some appropriate defence is available,[33] the "innocence" of the defendant is not an excuse. Nevertheless, the movement of the law in modern times has by and large been towards making liability in tort rest upon some basis of fault on the part of the alleged tortfeasor. That the law cannot go the entire way towards an eventual adoption of such a view without qualification is the result of historical inheritance and modern necessity. The former is seen in operation in those instances which came down to modern law from earlier times, even though courts, as suggested, have been able to make some changes. The latter is seen in operation in those instances in which the ultimate policy of the law of torts, namely, to provide compensation for injured parties, would be frustrated if such doctrines as vicarious responsibility, strict though they may have become in their approach, had not been invented and developed.

---

29 Below p. 134.
30 Below p. 126.
31 Below p. 121.
32 Below p. 131.
33 Such as an act of God or privilege: below pp. 113, 139-142.

Chapter 3

THE SCOPE OF TORTIOUS LIABILITY

1. THE AMBIT OF PROTECTION

Torts are wrongs against persons. Whatever be the particular tort that is involved, the essence of tortious liability is that someone has been harmed by the conduct of the defendant. As will appear in later chapters, such harm takes various forms. These include physical or mental injury: death (including the death of another); loss of, damage to, misuse of, or interference with real or personal property; loss of reputation; invasion of privacy; economic loss; and interference with a legal right. To determine the identity of the plaintiff who may sue in respect of such harm, it is vital to clarify who, in the eyes of the law, is a person. Those who may sue in respect of a tort fall within one of two groups: they are either natural or juristic persons.

(a) Natural Persons

This expression refers to all human beings, male or female,[1] adults or infants, married and single, citizens and aliens. The law of tort protects all within the jurisdiction of the law. None are outside its scope, although special procedural rules can apply in individual instances. For example, if an infant has been injured, any action in law must be brought by someone "on behalf" of the infant. The action, however, is that of the infant, and any damages recovered are recovered for, and on behalf of the infant.[2] An alien may be deprived of the right to sue during a war in which the country of which the alien is a national is at war with Canada. Such procedural rules and requirements, however, do not affect the substantive principles of the law of liability in tort.

The protection of the law extends even to those who have offended against the law. The ancient common law concept of the "outlaw", which existed in very early times, is no longer a part of the law. Thus a criminal, before or after

---

1 Until recently actions in tort between husband and wife were not allowed. This has been changed by statute in most Canadian provinces. Where no such legislation has been enacted, the provisions of the *Canadian Charter of Rights and Freedoms*, Part I of the *Constitution Act, 1982*, being Schedule B to the *Canada Act 1982* (U.K.), 1982, c. 11 against discrimination will probably have the same effect.

2 So, too, the right of a bankrupt to sue may depend upon the nature of the alleged wrong. In some circumstances the right of action passes to, or is vested in, the trustee in bankruptcy for the benefit of the bankrupt's creditors.

conviction, is equally entitled to the protection of the law of tort, and to maintain an action if he or she has been injured tortiously by another. For example, a convicted person in prison may sue someone who unlawfully injures him or her, whether personally or otherwise, while he or she is serving his sentence. The prisoner may even be entitled to maintain an action against a jailer or other officer who injures him or her without lawful excuse, such as in the event of an unwarranted, unprovoked attack by the jailer upon the prisoner. The same would certainly be true if one prisoner attacked another in circumstances which would be tortious if the attack had been made by one person upon another outside the prison. So too, there may be duties of care owed to a convicted prisoner, *e.g.*, by the prison authorities, such that, upon proof of a breach, such as a failure to exercise the appropriate degree of care, leading to the injury of the prisoner, the latter may sue.[3]

Once a human being is born, therefore, and for as long as he or she lives the law of torts maintains its protection and permits him or her to sue in respect of a tort that is committed against him or her during his or her lifetime. Recent developments, however, now extend the concept of a natural person, for the purposes of permitting an action in tort to be brought, to include those who have not yet been born as well as those who have ceased to live. Thus it may now be possible for liability to arise in respect of a tortious act that injures a child before it has been born, while that child is in its mother's womb.[4] Second, legislative change has abolished the ancient principle that the death of a human being does not give rise to a cause of action and that a personal action, that is to say an action for tort,[5] dies with the person. Now, with some exceptions, the estate of a deceased person, representing the deceased, may sue in respect of a tort that brought about that person's death or for a tort committed against the deceased prior to his or her death.[6]

Moreover, another effect of such legislation is that where death has been caused a right of action is given to certain family members who are harmed economically by such death.[7] In Ontario, that cause of action also arises where injury but not death has resulted from the tort and enables the family members to recover not merely for economic, but also for loss of guidance, care and companionship suffered as a result.[8]

---

3 See, *e.g.*, *MacLean v. The Queen* (1973), 27 D.L.R. (3d) 365. A lawfully convicted prisoner may even be able to sue for false imprisonment, below p. 42, if he or she has been dealt with improperly, for example, by being put in solitary confinement unjustly: *Brandon v. Canada (Correctional Service of Canada)* (1996), 131 D.L.R. (4th) 761 (F.C.T.D.).

4 Below p. 78.

5 That did not necessarily apply to actions for breach of contract: Fridman, *The Law of Contract in Canada*, 4th ed. (Toronto: Carswell, 1999), at p. 731.

6 See *e.g.*, *Trustee Act*, R.S.O. 1990, c. T.23, s. 38(1).

7 For example, under the *Fatal Accidents Acts* of Alberta, R.S.A. 2000, c. F-8; Manitoba, R.S.M. 1987, c. 50; and Saskatchewan, R.S.S. 1978, c. F-11; the *Fatal Injuries Act* of Nova Scotia, R.S.N.S. 1989, c. 163; and the *Family Compensation Act* of British Columbia, R.S.B.C. 1996, c. 126.

8 *Family Law Act*, R.S.O. 1990, c. F.3, ss. 61-63.

(b) Juristic Persons

Legal personality has been conferred on entities that, in point of fact, are comprised of one or more human beings. When this is done, the "person" that exists artificially, as a consequence of the conferment of that status on the entity, is a distinct legal person from the human being or beings involved.[9] The entities in question are called "corporations".

These are either corporations sole or corporations aggregate. A corporation sole is a human being who is regarded as having a distinct legal personality quite apart from his or her personality as a human being. The prime example of such a corporation is the Crown. The human individual who occupies the throne at any given time is treated by the law as someone different from the constitutional concept of the sovereign, which has been personified by the law. The personality in law of the sovereign is a complex matter in a federal state such as Canada. Suffice it to say that within Canada there are several sovereigns, *i.e.*, the sovereign of each individual province and the Queen of Canada. Each of these is an individual for the purposes of the law and in particular the law of torts. A tort may be committed against any of these sovereigns, and by one of them against another. Special procedural as well as substantive problems arise from the nature of this personality, and constitutional law has recognized the need for special rules. For the moment, it is enough to state that a tort may be committed against the Queen in one of her various capacities, for example, where a defendant has stolen or damaged property belonging to the Crown, such as a car which is owned by the province of Ontario and used for government purposes.

Corporations aggregate are corporations comprised of a collection of human beings, or other juristic persons, and treated as a separate person by the law. The chief example is a limited liability company, a business corporation as modern statutes term it.[10] There is no doubt that such corporations can be harmed tortiously, and may sue in respect of such torts. Some torts can probably not be committed against a corporation, for example, trespass to the person. Others, even more personal ones such as defamation, may be.[11] Insofar as it is possible, the law tends to assimilate artificial persons, such as corporations aggregate, with natural ones. There may be technical problems of a procedural kind, or even of a substantive kind emanating from the lack of corporeality of the corporation. Taking such matters into account, however, it is fair and accurate to state that, legally speaking, there is no difference between these two classes of persons.

Other organizations or groups, however, may not be incorporated, and as a consequence may not possess sufficient independent personality in law to permit them to be regarded as being within the protection of the law of tort as a group,

---

9 *Salomon v. Salomon & Co.*, [1897] A.C. 22.

10 See *e.g.*, the *Canada Business Corporations Act*, R.S.C. 1985, c. C-44; the Ontario *Business Corporations Act*, R.S.O. 1990, c. B.16. Another important group of corporations aggregate are *municipal corporations*, which are the bodies that govern towns and cities.

11 As long as the defamatory matter reflects on the reputation of the corporation *and* causes monetary damage.

even though the individual members of the group undoubtedly possess personality and are so protected. A private members' club, a trade union, an investors syndicate comprised of a number of individuals who pool their resources to invest in stocks and shares, are examples of such groups. While they are not equated with corporations (except certain trade unions, for certain purposes under federal and provincial legislation), the law has developed to a certain extent towards recognizing that they may have a common interest in maintaining an action as a group rather than as individuals, since the wrong may have been committed against them as such a group. In consequence, procedural changes in the law have been made to permit what are called "representative" actions to be brought by and on behalf of the group by some select representatives such as the committee of the club.[12]

2. THE REACH OF LIABILITY

Just as persons are the subject of the protection of the law of torts, so the scope of tortious liability is founded upon the idea of personal responsibility for tortious acts or omissions.[13] Only natural or juristic persons can be held guilty of tortious conduct, although the harm suffered by the victim may have been caused by an animal or some inanimate object such as an automobile. With respect to both classes of persons, however, there are limitations on the extent to which certain members of those classes can be held liable. For various reasons, stemming from a particular purpose of policy, the law deviates from the normal doctrine of imposing liability upon a person who or which has caused harm to the plaintiff.

Some human beings, for particular reasons, are not amenable to the jurisdiction of the courts, and so cannot be held liable for what otherwise would be tortious acts. The sovereign, in her personal capacity, for instance, is one such. Formerly, this meant that no action in tort could be brought against the Crown in respect of any tort committed not by the sovereign personally, but by some servant or agency of the Crown, such as a government department, a civil servant, or the driver of a Crown vehicle. The maxim of the common law was: "The King can do no wrong". It had the effect of immunizing from liability not only the Crown but also all who worked for and on behalf of the Crown, at least as long as, and in respect of when they were acting, in the course of such employment. Legislative change in the various provinces, as well as in relation to the government of Canada, has resulted in provisions whereby in appropriate circumstances, and subject to certain qualifications and restrictions, the Crown, in its symbolic sense, whether federally or provincially, may now be held as liable in tort as any private citizen or corporation.[14] The immunity from liability or suit

---

[12] See, *e.g.*, Rules of Civil Procedure, R.R.O. 1990, Reg. 194, as am., r. 12.08.

[13] The exception to this is provided by the law of vicarious liability, under which a person may be liable although that person has not personally acted tortiously: below pp. 31-36.

[14] Federally, see the *Crown Liability and Proceedings Act*, R.S.C. 1985, c. C-50. A typical provincial statute is the Ontario *Proceedings Against the Crown Act*, R.S.O. 1990, c. P.27. Despite this

of the Crown, however, still continues with respect to foreign sovereigns and their diplomatic representatives.[15] The dictates and necessities of international law and diplomacy require that the policy of immunity remains in force, despite alterations which have been found necessary with regard to the national sovereign. Hence no ambassador, or similar representative may be guilty of a tort, although such immunity does not extend downwards to lower categories of diplomatic personnel. These are matters of international law rather than of the law of torts, and require nothing more than mention at this juncture.

Except for those regarded by the law as incompetent, all others are equally regarded by the law. However, some particular quirks of the law are to be noted in this regard. Thus, whereas the outbreak of war may result in an enemy alien's being unable to enforce any right of action he or she might have had against a citizen or anybody else, it will not prevent an action *against* such an alien in respect of a tort committed by him or her. As seen earlier, the death of a wrongdoer will not determine liability for a tort committed by the deceased prior to his or her death (with certain exceptions).[16] The estate of the deceased will remain liable to the injured party, as a result of legislative changes which have been made with respect to the old common law rule about personal actions. Certain procedural requirements have to be met, but if they are followed, liability in tort continues beyond the grave, in the same way as rights of action may survive the death of the victim of a tort. Another important change which has occurred in modern times, is the abolition by statute of the doctrine that if a wife committed a tort her husband was liable, rather than the married woman herself. In the modern law of torts, each spouse is individually responsible for a tort committed by himself or herself.

The category of those who may be considered incompetent remains to be considered. This comprehends all those natural persons who, for one reason or another, might be regarded as in some way not truly responsible for their acts or omissions, so as to relieve them of guilt of, or liability for tortious conduct. Such persons are infants, those who are below the legal age of majority, whether children or young persons, and the insane, including for this purpose those who may be less mentally competent than others without actually being insane within the usual legal definition of insanity. In the criminal law, since the object of the law is to punish those who ought to be held culpable, some exemption from, or limitation upon liability is found in most systems of law, and notably in the common law world. With respect to torts, however, in regard to which, as already seen, compensation of victims rather than punishment of violators of the law is the major objective or purpose, there seems to be lacking the same motive for creating or admitting any equivalent exemption or limitation. Theoretically,

---

legislation the Crown might be immune in respect of, "acts of state", *i.e.*, certain acts of the Crown or its servants or agents against *foreigners*, performed outside the jurisdiction. This is a matter of the prerogative and, perhaps, is an example of the application of the doctrine of *necessity*.

15 And even to other agencies of a foreign state: see *Trendtex Trading Corp. v. Central Bank of Nigeria*, [1976] 3 All E.R. 437 (Q.B.); *cf. Phillipine Admiral (Owners) v. Wallem Shipping (Hong Kong) Ltd.*, [1976] 1 All E.R. 78 (P.C.).

16 *Viz.*, actions for libel and slander.

therefore, no distinction should be drawn for the purposes of the law of torts, between an adult and an infant, nor between a sane and an insane or mentally incompetent person. However, in some respects infancy or mental incompetence is not irrelevant to issues of liability. Wherever a state of mind is an essential ingredient of any form of liability in tort, for example where the intention to assault is required to establish liability in trespass, or where negligence is in issue, it may well be that the inability of a person to formulate such an intention, or to exercise reasonable care, because of lack of years or mental comprehension, will result in the immunity or non-liability of such a person.[17] So, too, where contributory negligence on the part of the plaintiff is relevant to questions of liability and damages, the fact that the plaintiff was young, or insane, might affect the ultimate decision as to his or her guilt of such conduct.[18] Thus, indirectly, as contrasted with the attitude of the criminal law, where such matters are directly relevant, the law of torts takes notice of, and gives effect to, such matters as infancy and insanity.

The aim of the law of torts is to make wrongdoers responsible for their wrongful conduct; only the *actor*, the one personally guilty, is liable. This includes within its scope juristic persons, *i.e.*, corporations,[19] even though, in fact, such corporations cannot act personally, but perform wrongful acts or are guilty of wrongful omissions through the medium of natural persons. The acts or omissions of such persons, as long as they fall within certain categories, *viz.*, agents or servants, as will be more closely examined later in connection with the notion of vicarious liability or responsibility,[20] are considered in law to be the acts or omissions of the juristic person, provided they take place when the natural person is acting for and on behalf of the juristic person. When such a natural person is so acting, the juristic person will be treated as the one guilty of, and responsible for any tort that is thereby committed. Theoretically, therefore, it would seem that there is no limit to the kind of wrongdoing for which a juristic person can be liable (as contrasted with the situation in the criminal law, under which such persons may not be liable for certain crimes, such as murder, and rape, even if perpetrated by an agent or servant of the juristic person and allegedly on behalf of, or for the benefit or purposes of such person). One reason for this is that tort law is designed to provide compensation for injuries, whereas criminal law has as its aim the punishment of the guilty, and it is impossible to inflict the appropriate punishment, *viz.*, imprisonment now that the death penalty is no longer available, upon a juristic person such as a business corporation. It follows that whatever tort is committed by the agent or servant of the juristic person,[21]

---

17 *Walmsley v. Humenick*, [1954] 2 D.L.R. 232 (B.C.S.C.); *Nespolon v. Alford* (1998), 40 O.R. (2d) 355 (C.A.); *Morriss v. Marsden*, [1952] 1 All E.R. 925; *Lawson v. Wellesley Hospital* (1975), 9 O.R. (2d) 677 (C.A.); *Fiala v. Cechmanek* (1999), 246 A.R. 120 (Q.B.); Fridman, "Mental Incompetency" (1963) 79 L.Q.R. 502, (1964) 80 L.Q.R. 84; below p.

18 *Yachuk v. Oliver Blais*, [1949] A.C. 386 (P.C.); *Hnatuk v. Trapp* (1976), 10 N.R. 97 (Fed. C.A.).

19 But the *members* of the corporation are not *as such* liable for torts committed by the corporation.

20 Below pp. 31-36.

21 Including torts involving malice or fraud: the fact that a state of mind is relevant to liability will not exclude the corporation from possible liability. The mind of the servant or agent is the mind of the corporation for this purpose.

the latter can be made to pay the appropriate compensation, provided the circumstances justify holding the artificial person liable.

However, there appears to be an important limitation upon the extent of a juristic person's actual or potential responsibility in tort. This is the doctrine of *ultra vires.* Whereas there are no theoretical limits upon the capacity of a natural person to act, such that, whenever such a person behaves in what is a tortious manner, he or she will be liable, the legal nature of juristic persons is such that their legal capacities are not as extensive as those of natural persons. A juristic person owes its existence, and its legal powers, to the law. It is the legal system which sets out the ways in which such persons can come into being, and what powers such persons may enjoy. Into the details of these matters it is not necessary to go for present purposes. The law relating to corporations makes it clear that their powers are defined by, and limited to: (i) the precise nature of the corporation; and (ii) the purposes for which the corporation was created. Thus it will make a difference whether the corporation is one that has been chartered by the Crown, such as the Hudson's Bay Company, as it was originally founded; or is formed under the provisions of some relevant legislation, such as the Ontario *Business Corporations Act.* The scope of liability of chartered corporations is wider, at common law, than that of statutory ones.[22] Secondly, the objects or purposes of the corporation, where it is created under statutory powers, will fix or determine what kinds of activities it may perform, and this in turn will affect the question of whether something done by a servant or agent of the corporation will result in the latter's liability. Where the corporation has no express or implied legal power to act in a certain way, *e.g.*, to arrest a person travelling without paying his fare in the case of a corporation created to run a railway, then under no circumstances can the corporation be held liable for any false arrest.[23] Thus the *ultra vires* doctrine, to the extent to which it has not been affected by statutory provisions widening the scope of a corporation's liability,[24] will raise an artificial, some might say an illogical, barrier to the operation of what would otherwise be normal principles of liability.[25]

Some mention should also be made here of the situation with respect to unincorporated associations. Since these are not granted the privilege and status of a legal personality, they may not normally be liable if a member of such an association, or an employee, commits a tort. Such organizations, as already noted, are not separate entities in law from their constituent members.

---

22 *Sutton's Hospital Case* (1612), 10 Co. Rep. 23a (Ex. Ch.).

23 *Poulton v. London & South Western Ry. Co.* (1867), L.R. 2 Q.B. 534. So too, if the corporation had no power to employ the servant or agent in question. The relationship of master and servant or principal and agent will not arise, therefore there can be no vicarious responsibility.

24 See *e.g.*, *Canada Business Corporations Act*, R.S.C. 1985, c. C-44, s. 15, which gives to corporations within that statute the rights and capacities of a natural person. Compare also the Ontario *Business Corporations Act*, R.S.O. 1990, c. B.16.

25 Unless it can be said that the corporation is not acting vicariously, but directly, through its guiding mind or will, in which event the doctrine would be inapplicable: see *e.g.*, *Campbell v. Paddington Corp.*, [1911] 1 K.B. 869 (D.C.). In England changes have come about by virtue of the admission of the United Kingdom to the Common Market: see *the European Communities Act 1972*, c. 28, s. 9(1).

However, procedural developments have lead to the possibility of maintaining a "representative" action against some members of a group, such as the committee of a club, so as to remove the difficulty of having to sue and make liable each and every individual who makes up the association, and so as to permit the easier recovery of whatever amount is awarded the injured party by way of damages. Moreover trade unions, which, generally speaking, are examples of such unincorporated associations, have been rendered subject to special rules, at least in some circumstances and for some purposes, by various provincial statutes, with the results that, certainly under statutes, and possibly even at common law, a trade union may be liable, as an entity distinct from its members, if the union, its officials, members or employees committed a tort.[26]

---

26 See, for example, the Rules cited above at note 12; *Taff Vale Ry. Co. v. Amalgamated Society of Railway Servants*, [1901] A.C. 426. Unless the trade union has been given immunity in regard to a tort committed in the course of, or for the furtherance of a trade dispute, as originally provided for in English legislation enacted after the *Taff Vale* case: as in Ontario, under the *Rights of Labour Act,* R.S.O. 1990, c. R.33, s. 3(1), or in Saskatchewan under the *Trade Union Act*, R.S.S. 1978, c. T.17, s. 28.

Chapter 4

VICARIOUS LIABILITY

1. THE DOCTRINE STATED

In a previous chapter it was observed that there are circumstances in which someone who would otherwise be guilty of, and liable for tortious behaviour may be excused or exempted from responsibility, for example because of infancy or insanity.[1] By contrast there are situations in which a natural or juristic person not personally guilty of tortious conduct may be held liable for the tortious conduct of another. Such instances involve vicarious liability. Such liability must be differentiated from the "direct" liability of the actual tortfeasor who is liable for his or her own personal commission of the tort in question. Where vicarious liability occurs, the actual tortfeasor[2] makes someone else liable for his or her act by virtue of the relationship between them. The relationships that are relevant in this context are those between: (i) master and servant (or, in more modern parlance, employer and employee); and (ii) principal and agent. However the fact that such a relationship exists between the parties will only give rise to the vicarious liability of the master or principal when the servant or agent committed the tort while performing something the latter was "authorized" to do.

Vicarious liability is of especial importance where juristic persons are concerned. Since such persons, notably business corporations, can only act through the medium of human beings employed as servants or agents, or through other such corporations which act by means of human beings employed as servants or agents, the tortious liability of such persons is usually vicarious rather than direct. This raises a difficulty that is peculiar to the application of the doctrine of vicarious liability to business corporations: the need to determine whether the conduct of the servant or agent of the corporation occurred while that servant or agent was doing something that was within the powers of the corporation to do.[3] If it was not, then the corporation may not, although the servant or agent will, be liable in tort.

---

1 Above pp. 27-28.

2 Who may not be liable to the injured party, for example, because he or she is immune from suit, which was the case, formerly, where the tortfeasor was the spouse of the injured party: *Broom v. Morgan*, [1953] 1 Q.B. 597 (C.A.). This would not be the case today: above p. 23.

3 *Cf.* above p. 29.

The principle of vicarious liability that has been stated above may be said to have been extended to apply where the party whose act amounts to a tort is neither a servant nor an agent but is employed as an independent contractor, acting for another under an agreement to perform a certain task.[4] However, where the law holds an employer liable for the torts of such a contractor it is because the employer was under a personal duty of care which was breached by the wrongful act of the independent contractor (or the latter's servant or agent). In such instances the employer may be liable in a sense vicariously for the wrongful act of another. But this is because the employer is considered to have broken his, her or its personal duty towards the victim. Under the general principle of vicarious liability one person is vicariously liable for the "tort" of another. In respect of independent contractors, however, the employer is vicariously liable for the "act" of another. Perhaps it would be more correct, analytically, to consider such liability direct, rather than truly vicarious. Traditionally, however, the liability of employers of independent contractors has been discussed alongside and together with the vicarious liability of masters and principals.

2. JUSTIFICATIONS OF THE DOCTRINE

Two different ideas have frequently been cited and provided as reasons for the imposition of vicarious liability. One is contained in the maxim *qui facit per alium facit per se*. In other words, the reason for such liability is that the person who is held vicariously liable is treated as if he or she had committed the act or omission in question, even though it was committed by someone else. The latter is regarded as a physical extension of the former. This would still be a satisfactory explanation of the early instances of vicarious liability, which concerned the responsibility of the head of the household for the acts of members of his family or his immediate household or agricultural servants. So, too, it will explain those cases where the actual tortfeasor has been expressly commanded or ordered to commit the act in question by the person who is subsequently held vicariously liable. It does not explain the cases in which the doctrine has been extended, where there was never any express command, order, or authority to act in the manner in question, nor could it be said that such command, *etc.*, was implied, but, nonetheless, the actual tortfeasor makes the vicariously liable tortfeasor responsible.

In such instances the better explanation would appear to be that it is desirable to make someone else liable for the sake of ensuring that the injured party has a financially competent defendant to sue, and the relationship between the defendant and the actual tortfeasor was such that it is not unreasonable to say that the defendant enabled the actual tortfeasor to perpetrate the tort and inflict the damage or loss, by reason of the fact that the defendant provided the tortfeasor with the means or opportunity to do so. Thus the principal who entrusts a certain undertaking to an agent, or the master who instructs his servant to

---

4 Below p. 36.

perform a certain act, puts the agent or servant into a situation and gives him the opportunity to cause the harm in question, even if the principal or master has not instructed the agent or servant to commit the harm, may even have prohibited the acts in question, and quite possibly may not benefit from what the agent or servant has done. The maxim that incorporates this reasoning is *respondeat superior*. In other words, the party to the relationship who is regarded as being the superior is answerable in law for what has been done by the party who is the inferior in such relationship.

Neither superficially explicatory maxim truly represents how and why the modern law of torts views and understands the, sometimes anomalous, doctrine of vicarious liability. Nevertheless, the doctrine is an integral part of the common law of torts. Its effect is to modify the basic conception of that law as being a system of rules to make a wrongdoer compensate an injured party, and, thereby, to attempt to lay down standards of behaviour for people generally. If liability is based on true vicarious liability for the torts of others, and not on personal liability for one's own torts, it seems illogical to state that the law of torts visits responsibility for the compensation of an injured party upon a tortfeasor. Nor can it be said that the imposition of vicarious liability supports the idea that one purpose of the law of torts is to ensure the maintenance of proper standards.

3. LIABILITY FOR SERVANTS AND AGENTS

(a) To Whom the Doctrine Applies

The former distinction between servants and agents, which depended on various factors such as the degree of control exercised by the master or principal, the kind of task on which the person concerned was employed, and the duration of that employment, was rendered inapplicable after the decision of the House of Lords in *Lloyd v. Grace, Smith & Co.*[5] in 1912. In the modern law of torts both categories are treated alike, although the courts use different terminology when discussing the circumstances under which the master or principal will be vicariously liable. The distinction between servants and agents remains relevant, however, in the context of the law of contract.[6]

The traditional test of service or agency was "control".[7] To qualify as a servant or agent the person in question had to be subject not only to direction as to what was to be done for the "employer" but also with respect to the manner in which it was to be done. Even if the servant or agent was a skilled professional, and the master or principal was incapable of being regulated by the unprofessional master or principal, the relevant relationship could exist. The essential factor was whether the "employee", whether servant or agent, was employed under a contract of service, rather than a contract to provide services, which was the hallmark of the relationship between an employer and an independent

---

5 [1912] A.C. 716.

6 Fridman, *The Law of Agency*, 7th ed. (London: Butterworths, 1996), pp. 31-37.

7 *Quarman v. Burnett* (1840), 6 M. & W. 499.

contractor. However, there was no need to prove that there was an actual "contract" between the parties, in the sense that the servant or agent was paid for the service. A volunteer, acting gratuitously, could, and still can be a servant or agent for the purposes of vicarious liability, provided the requisite degree of control, as defined above, was present.[8] Hence the suggestion, in modern times, that the true test for this purpose is whether the one whose tortious conduct is in issue was an integral part of some "organization", to be held responsible for the tortfeasor's acts or omissions.[9] However, it would appear that control, as traditionally understood, may remain the chief test of whether someone is to be treated as a servant or agent.

Problems emerged, *inter alia*, with regard to the position of hospitals, in which doctors had the privilege of performing operations without being employees in the strict sense of the hospital, and made use of, and controlled the performance of nurses who were employees of the hospital;[10] and where the servant of one master or employer was "transferred", for a time, either with or without tools or equipment belonging to the employer who "lent" the servant to another employer.[11] These were resolved by various applications of the idea of control, sometimes adapted to fit the particular circumstances.

One striking development in the last 50 years, during which time the automobile has become more prevalent and more dangerous, has been the rise of common law and statutory doctrines by which the concept of vicarious liability, in relation to the use of automobiles, has been even more extended, and has resulted in more stringent liability. This is particularly true in Canada, where many provinces have statutory enactments under which the owner of a motor vehicle may be responsible for injury or damage caused by its use even where the actual driver at the time the injury or damage was inflicted was not an agent or servant of the owner in the strict legal senses of those terms.[12] Sometimes this is based upon some family relationship between the owner and the driver (a development that has been most pronounced in the United States as a result of judicial determinations even before there were any statutes).[13] Other times, it is based upon consent to the use of the vehicle, even if that use was for the purpose and benefit of the driver only, and not the owner in any way.

(b) When the Doctrine Applies

A master will be liable for a tort committed by a servant while that servant was acting in his or her "course of employment". A principal will be liable for tortious

---

8 *Cunningham v. Grand Trunk Ry. Co.* (1871), 31 U.C.Q.B. 350.

9 *Montreal v. Montreal Locomotive Works Ltd.*, [1947] 1 D.L.R. 161 (P.C.).

10 *Hillyer v. Governors of St. Bartholemew's Hospital*, [1909] 2 K.B. 820; *Fleming v. Sisters of St. Joseph of the Diocese of London*, [1938] S.C.R. 172; *Ypremiam v. Scarborough General Hospital* (1980), 110 D.L.R. (3d) 513 (Ont. C.A.); *Vancouver General Hospital v. Fraser*, [1952] 2 S.C.R. 36; *Hôpital Notre-Dame de l'Espérance v. Laurent*, [1978] 1 S.C.R. 605.

11 *Mersey Docks & Harbour Board v. Coggins & Griffith*, [1947] A.C. 1; *Marine Pipeline & Dredging Ltd. v. Canadian Fina Oil Ltd.* (1964), 46 D.L.R. (2d) 495 (Alta. C.A.).

12 See, *e.g.*, *Highway Traffic Act*, R.S.O. 1990, c. H.8, s. 192.

13 Fridman, "The Doctrine of the Family Car" (1976) 8 Texas Tech. L.R. 323.

acts committed by an agent acting within "the scope of the agent's authority". Once these expressions were interpreted differently. Since 1912[14] they have come to have the same connotation. If the master or principal has expressly commanded the commission of the wrongful act, vicarious liability will be clear. In the, more usual, absence of such express statement, it is necessary to determine whether what has been done by the servant or agent can be held to have been authorized or commanded impliedly by the master or principal,[15] as being implicit in the performance of the acts for which the servant or agent has been employed. Beyond even that extension, there come situations where the liability has been imposed on a master or principal on other grounds.

Recent cases involving the vicarious liability of the Crown and various other employers for sexual assaults by employees on children within their care have resulted in an attempt by the Supreme Court of Canada to set out the parameters of what is meant by the course of employment or scope of authority.

"The fundamental question", said McLachlin J., now Chief Justice of Canada,[16] "is whether the wrongful act is sufficiently related to conduct authorized by the employer to justify the imposition of vicarious liability. Vicarious liability is generally appropriate where there is a significant connection between the creation or enhancement of a risk and the wrong that accrues therefrom, even if unrelated to the employer's desires". This approach to the issue of when vicarious liability arises was founded on the two policy considerations, which have been referred to in an earlier chapter, of providing a remedy in the form of compensation and ensuring standards of behaviour by deterring others from acting wrongfully.[17]

This exposition of the applicability of vicarious liability was given in the context of acts performed for the benefit solely of the servant or agent. Many leading cases establish that such behaviour, which includes the commission of sexual and non-sexual assaults on someone,[18] and the perpetration of fraud against a third party,[19] even the doing of something that was expressly forbidden by the master or principal,[20] can nonetheless involve such master or principal in

---

14 *Lloyd v. Grace, Smith & Co.*, [1912] A.C. 716.

15 Or the master or principal has "held out" the servant or agent as having the authority to perform the act in question: *Kooragang Investments Pty. Ltd. v. Richardson & Wrench Ltd.*, [1981] 3 All E.R. 65.

16 *B. (P.A.) v. Curry* (1999), 174 D.L.R. (4th) 45 (S.C.C.) at 64. The whole passage at 64-65 should be consulted for the details of what will be a sufficient relation or connection for this purpose.

17 Above pp. 8-11.

18 See, *e.g.*, *B. (P.A.) v. Curry* (1999), 174 D.L.R. (4th) 45 (S.C.C.); *T. (G.) v. Griffiths* (1999), 174 D.L.R. (4th) 71 (S.C.C.) (sexual assaults); *Fagnan v. Monaghan* (1996), 105 Man. R. (2d) 208 (C.A.); *Verbeck v. Stefura* (1981), 26 A.R. 497 (Q.B.) (non-sexual assaults).

19 *Lloyd v. Grace, Smith & Co.*, [1912] A.C. 716. The same will apply if the employee is guilty of theft: *Purdy v. Ryan* (1993), 136 N.B.R. (2d) 1 (Q.B.). Contrast with these cases, *Armagas Ltd. v. Mundogas SA.*, [1986] 2 All E.R. 385; *Keddie v. Horne* (2000), 179 D.L.R. (4th) 1 (B.C.C.A.); *Layden v. Scotia McLeod Inc.* (1997), 186 N.B.R. (2d) 241 (Q.B.).

20 *Limpus v. London General Omnibus Co.* (1862), 1 H. & C. 526; *B.C. Ferry Corp. v. Invicta Security Service Corp.* (1997), 35 B.C.L.R. (3d) 41 (S.C.), affirmed (1998), 58 B.C.L.R. (3d) 80 (C.A.).

responsibility in law of the harm that has been done. As an English judge said in 1981,[21] where vicarious liability is concerned, "the tendency has been toward more liberal protection of innocent third parties".

4. LIABILITY FOR INDEPENDENT CONTRACTORS

In general an employer of an independent contractor, who is neither the servant or agent of the employer, will not be liable vicariously for a tort committed by such contractor (or the servants or agents of the contractor).[22] To this there are two exceptions or qualifications. The employer of an independent contractor will be vicariously liable for the acts of the contractor (i) if the employer is under a personal duty towards the victim, which duty may not be delegated to an independent contractor to fulfil: (ii) where the contractor is employed to perform an extra-hazardous or ultra-hazardous activity, which entails grave danger of injury or damage to others.[23] In both instances the act or acts of the contractor that cause the injury or damage must not be casual or collateral to the performance of the task entrusted to the contractor, but an integral part of such performance.[24]

The duty that is breached by the contractor, for which the employer will be liable, can arise under statute or at common law.[25] Liability where an extra-hazardous or ultra-hazardous activity is involved may arise under the doctrine of *Rylands v. Fletcher*,[26] where fire is involved,[27] or where something being done is necessarily or inherently dangerous.[28]

---

21 Lord Wilberforce in *Kooragang Investments Pty. Ltd. v. Richardson & Wrench Ltd.*, [1981] 3 All E.R. 65, at 68.

22 *Quarman v. Burnett* (1840), 6 M. & W. 499; *Dalton v. Angus* (1881), 6 App. Cas. 740.

23 *Bowaters Newfoundland Ltd. v. Lundrigans Ltd.* (1970), 1 Nfld. & P.E.I.R. 223 (Nfld. S.C.).

24 *Kitchener (City) v. Robe & Clothing Co.*, [1925] S.C.R. 106.

25 See, *e.g.*, *Piercy v. Board of Education of Lunenburg County District* (1998), 167 N.S.R. (2d) 68 (C.A.); *Schoeni v. King*, [1944] 1 D.L.R. 326 (Ont. C.A.).

26 (1868), L.R. 3 H.L. 330: below p. 111.

27 *Balfour v. Barty-King*, [1957] 1 Q.B. 496 (C.A.); *Aga Heat (Canada) Ltd. v. Brockville Hotel Co.*, [1945] S.C.R. 184.

28 *Aiello v. Central Gas Ontario Inc.* (2000), 47 C.C.L.T. (2d) 39 (Ont. S.C.J.).

PART II: SPECIFIC TORTS

Chapter 5

TRESPASS

1. INTRODUCTION

The pristine essential idea underlying the old writ of trespass was that the defendant had committed a wrong to the victim *vi et armis et contra pacem regis*, by force of arms and against the peace of the King. Trespass was conceived of as involving acts of violence against a person, goods or land. Hence there were three variations of the writ: (a) trespass *vi et armis*, which was appropriate in cases of trespass to a person; (b) trespass *de bonis asportatis*, for wrongdoing to the personal property or chattels of another; and (c) trespass *quare clausum fregit*, where the wrong alleged was the unlawful invasion by the defendant of the victim's land. Although the old writs have disappeared, the law still distinguishes between trespass to the person, trespass to goods, or and trespass to land, to all of which the following are common.

First there is the notion of *force*. Trespass, historically, and today, involves the use of force. Unless the amount of force used by the defendant is so slight or trivial that it would almost be absurd to deem what has been done a trespass, any degree of force will suffice. However the wrongdoer must have acted consciously, with awareness of what he or she was doing. Hence, as will be seen, where the defendant does not know, or is incapable of knowing, what he or she is doing, no actionable trespass will have been committed.[1]

Second, the relevant force must have been applied by the defendant *directly* against the person, goods or land of the victim. Force will be considered to have been applied directly. However, where the defendant uses something to that end, for example, an implement such as an axe with which the plaintiff is struck, a crane which seizes another's goods, or an automobile that is driven onto another's land. The distinction that is vital here is between such acts that immediately and directly have an effect on a person, goods or land, and an act which indirectly does so. To hit the plaintiff with a log will be a trespass: to leave a log on the highway so that the plaintiff later trips over it and is injured will not be. The indirect infliction of harm or damage was formerly remedied by other writs, such as the action on the case for negligence.[2] In modern times, while the old distinction between direct and indirect infliction of injury does not have the

---

1 Below p. 46.

2 See the old case of *Scott v. Shepherd* (1773), 2 W. Bl. 892; see also *Leame v. Bray* (1803), 3 East 593; *Non-Marine Underwriters Lloyds of London v. Scalera* (2000), 185 D.L.R. (4th) 1 (S.C.C.).

same procedural importance, it remains to mark the difference between what is a trespass and what may be some other tort for which the victim may bring an action, in respect of which the essentials of liability are different from those which apply where a trespass is alleged. Such differences may also be important from the point of view of the possible defences that may be raised to an action.

Third, there is the question of the defendant's state of mind. Trespass was, and, to a certain extent remains, a tort of strict liability. What that means is that, to establish a *prima facie* case of trespass, it is not necessary for the plaintiff to prove "fault" on the part of the defendant, in the sense that the defendant acted with the intent to cause harm or with negligence. The fact of the relevant interference with the plaintiff's person, goods, or land suffices to make the perpetrator liable in the absence of some applicable defence. Where trespass to the person is concerned, in addition to the various limitations on liability that may be raised by way of defence, the person guilty of the trespass can also establish that what happened was "accidental", by proving that he or she acted without any intent to cause harm and without any negligence. In other kinds of trespass, however, it is questionable whether the defendant may escape liability by establishing such lack of intent or negligence.[3]

Fourth, in cases of trespass, unlike torts where the conduct of the defendant indirectly caused injury or damage to the plaintiff, actual damage to the plaintiff is presumed to have occurred. Trespass, it is said, is actionable *per se*. Of course, if no such damage has occurred the plaintiff will be entitled to no more than nominal damages, in recognition of the fact that his or her rights have been infringed by the defendant (and this may result in an award of costs against the plaintiff). For substantial damages to be recovered, the plaintiff must prove what has been suffered or lost.

2. TRESPASS TO THE PERSON

(a) Acts Amounting to Trespass

A trespass to the person is committed when someone makes a direct attack on another so as to cause the latter physical or mental injury or does something that affects the personal liberty, *i.e.*, freedom of action, of another. The law distinguishes three forms of trespass to the person: battery, assault, and false imprisonment. However, although the term "assault" is frequently used, particularly in the criminal law, to denote both "assault" in the correct sense and battery, there is an important technical difference between the two.[4]

Battery involves the actual application of violence against the victim by the defendant.[5] The violence need not be substantial. As it was said in the 18th century:[6]

---

[3] Below pp. 51, 54.

[4] *Hurley v. Moore* (1993), 112 Nfld. & P.E.I.R. 40 at 46 (Nfld. C.A.), *per* Steele J.A.

[5] Even if the plaintiff is unaware of this: *Malette v. Schulman* (1990), 72 O.R. (2d) 417 (C.A.).

[6] *Cole v. Turner* (1704), 6 Mod. Rep. 149 *per* Holt C.J. See, generally, Handford, "Tort Liability for Threatening or Insulting Words" (1976) 54 Can. Bar Rev. 563.

"The least touching of a man in anger is a battery". Any physical act by one person against another, in circumstances which do not excuse or justify such conduct, such as accident, mistake, necessity or lawful authority,[7] will be actionable. Physical contact which goes beyond acceptable boundaries of everyday behaviour may be an actionable battery not only where it results in bodily injury but also if it violates the plaintiff's bodily integrity or offends the plaintiff's sense of dignity.[8] The latter is exemplified by spitting at the plaintiff, or kissing a woman against her will.

The latter act would amount to a sexual battery. Recently it was suggested by at least one member of the Supreme Court of Canada,[9] that sexual battery was a distinct form of trespass to the person, not merely one form of the tort. That suggestion was rejected by other members of the court,[10] and there seems to be no valid legal justification for any such distinction to be drawn. Whether there is a sexual content in the defendant's act, the misconduct in issue will constitute a trespass to the person of the victim. No substantive legal significance is involved in the fact that a sexual element is also involved.

Assault, in some respects, is an incomplete battery. In cases of assault the wrongdoer does not actually strike the victim. What the wrongdoer does is instil in the victim the fear that he or she will be struck or otherwise physically attacked. Two important features must be noted. In the first place, whereas a battery can occur without any prior knowledge on the part of the victim that it is going to take place (and perhaps even without any realization by him or her that it has occurred), an assault can only take place when the victim is aware that something is happening, *i.e.*, that a battery is about to occur, or may occur. Hence, if for some reason the alleged victim is ignorant of what the supposed assaulter is doing, *e.g.*, as where the latter raises his or her fist in a threatening manner behind the victim's back, or the alleged victim knows or ought to appreciate that no actual battery will take place, as in the old English case in which the defendant put his hand on his sword hilt and said, "If this were not Assize time I would run you through",[11] then, in such circumstances, no assault is committed. Second, for an assault to take place, the threat of violence must be such as would put a reasonable person of ordinary courage in fear of an attack.[12] Hence if the threat is one that the defendant is incapable of carrying out in the circumstances, or is of the kind of attack that would not ordinarily frighten a reasonable person, *e.g.*, "I will throw my table-tennis ball at you", then, presumably, there is no assault. This marks another difference between assault and battery. *Any* improper handling of the victim is a battery. Only threats of attack which are truly capable of putting a reasonable person in fear of being injured will amount to assaults.

---

7 Below pp. 43-46, 47-50.

8 *Non-Marine Underwriters Lloyds of London v. Scalera* (2000), 185 D.L.R. (4th) 1 (S.C.C.).

9 *Ibid.*, at 40 *per* Iacobucci J.

10 *Ibid.*, at 17 *per* McLachlin J.

11 *Tuberville v. Savage* (1669), 1 Mod. Rep. 3.

12 *Bruce v. Dyer*, [1966] 2 O.R. 705 (H.C.), affirmed [1970] 1 O.R. 482*n* (C.A.).

The conduct of the defendant may amount to both an assault and a battery,[13] as where the defendant first threatens the victim with physical harm and then carries out the threat. However the distinction between the two should be recognized because there can be a battery without an assault, for example, where the defendant strikes the victim from behind without warning, and there can be an assault without a battery, for example, where the defendant threatens harm but does not carry out the threat.

The concept of trespass to the person has been extended to include not only the causing of physical injury to someone but also the intentional infliction of mental harm, in the form of nervous shock, resulting in physical consequences, on the victim.[14]

False imprisonment or false arrest, as noted earlier, involves the unlawful restraint of another's freedom of movement. This means that the victim is *totally* prevented from going as and where he or she pleases. If all that occurs is some regulation of movement, *e.g.*, by preventing the victim from going in a certain way, or to a certain place, without complete interference, then this form of trespass is not committed. The term "false" in this context does not denote that the defendant has acted dishonestly or fraudulently, but that he or she acted without any lawful excuse or justification. The imprisonment or arrest in question must have been *wrong*.[15] Hence, even if the defendant makes an honest mistake, he or she may still be guilty. However, an erroneous defendant may escape liability in some circumstances. This is an issue which frequently arises, as do many questions relating to false imprisonment or arrest, in connection with the activities of police officers, and similar personnel, and sometimes, of citizens who are not police officers acting under powers which now, in Canada, are derived from the *Criminal Code*, though, formerly were common law in origin. Of these more will be said later.[16] It should be noted, however, that questions as to the commission of this tort, including issues of lawfulness of the arrest, can also arise in other contexts, *e.g.*, keeping a schoolboy in school after the end of term because of non-payment of his fees, refusing to bring miners up from the coal face when they stated that they were on strike, refusing to let someone off a ferry unless he or she paid the fare, *etc.*[17] This form of trespass can occur when the defendant takes hold of the victim and prevents him or her from escaping from such con-

---

13 *Nurse v. Canada* (1997), 132 F.T.R. 131 (T.D.); *Swanson v. Mallow* (1992), 97 Sask. R. 202 (C.A.).

14 *Wilkinson v. Downton*, [1897] 2 Q.B. 57; *Janvier v. Sweeney*, [1919] 2 K.B. 316; *Bell-Ginsburg v. Ginsburg* (1993), 14 O.R. (3d) 217 (Gen. Div.). Note also the possibility of an action for conduct which falls short of trespass but amounts to *harassment* of the plaintiff: Fridman, "The Judicial response to Non-Sexual Harassment Claims", (1998) 77 Can. Bar Rev. 299.

15 The defendant must personally bring about the imprisonment. Hence initiating a prosecution which, wrongfully as it turns out, results in the imprisonment of the plaintiff will not be false imprisonment, athough it might amount to the tort of malicious prosecution (below pp. 151-156): *Davidson v. Chief Constable of North Wales*, [1994] 2 All E.R. 597; *Pigeau v. Cromwell P.C.J.* (1990), 96 N.S.R. (2d) 412 (C.A.).

16 Below p. 48.

17 *Bird v. Jones* (1845), 7 Q.B. 742; *Robinson v. Balmain New Ferry Co. Ltd.*, [1910] A.C. 295; *Herd v. Weardale Steel, Coal & Coke Co. Ltd.*, [1915] A.C. 67.

trol, or the victim is locked in a room (without having been touched by the defendant), or is wrongly incarcerated in an asylum for the insane. In most instances, the victim will know or appreciate what is happening. Is it necessary that he or she should? There are indications in the cases that it is enough if the imprisonment occurs and is unlawful, and that if the victim is unaware at the time that he or she is being imprisoned, it will make no difference to the issue of liability.[18] This appears somewhat illogical. Can it be said that a person is imprisoned, *i.e.*, deprived of liberty of action and movement, if that person does not know that he or she is being imprisoned? Has the person suffered any harm? Assault, as seen, involves knowledge of what is happening. Battery usually occurs to the knowledge of the victim (though this is not the case where the victim has been rendered unconscious first, perhaps with his or her consent, *e.g.*, where a doctor obtains the patient's agreement to anaesthesia prior to an agreed operation, and then proceeds to cut off a limb which was not intended by the victim to be touched — a bizarre, but possible set of events). False imprisonment, therefore, ought to involve similar understanding of what is happening, and appreciation of loss or injury, on the part of the victim. So strong is the law's antagonism to such conduct however, because it is a gross infringement of an elementary and vital freedom, that it would seem that the courts are prepared to penalize acts which amount to the commission of the tort even where the victim is ignorant of what has taken place (though this might have an effect upon the damages recoverable). And even though no force is used, for example where the plaintiff consents to the restraint.[19] False imprisonment can also be committed where the plaintiff is already being legally confined, for example, as a convicted prisoner in jail, if such prisoner is treated improperly and unlawfully while being incarcerated after sentence. Such will be the case if a prisoner is wrongfully given solitary confinement or is put into segregated custody.[20]

(b) The Relevance of Mental States

(i) Accident and Mistake

In the mediaeval common law trespass to the person was what would now be considered a tort of strict liability, because the court was not concerned with whether the defendant committed the trespass intentionally, negligently, or accidentally but only with whether he committed the act of trespass. In the 17th century[21] it was stated that where a trespass was committed the defendant would not be excused unless he could show that which occurred was "utterly

---

18 *Meering v. Grahame-White Aviation Co. Ltd.* (1919) 122 L.T. 44 at 53 *per* Atkin L.J. : *Hussey v. Ministry of Defence*, [1988] 1 W.L.R. 692.

19 *Chaytor v. London, New York & Paris Association of Fashion Ltd.* (1961), 30 D.L.R. (2d) 527 (Nfld. S.C.); *Kavanagh v. Canadian Tire Corp.* (1989), 74 Nfld. & P.E.I.R. 205.

20 *Brandon v. Canada (Correctional Services of Canada)* (1996), 131 D.L.R. (4th) 761; *Hill v. British Columbia* (1997), 36 B.C.L.R. (3d) 211 (C.A.). The law is different in England: *Weldon v. Home Office*, [1991] 3 All E.R. 733. But it is the same in Australia: *Cowell v. Correctional Services Commission of New South Wales* (1988), 13 N.S.W.L.R. 714.

21 *Weaver v. Ward* (1616), Hobart 134.

without his fault" — a phrase which seems to have meant that it was not reasonably possible for him to have avoided what happened, and he had not intended it to happen. This was the case in that instance, where the plaintiff was injured when he walked directly in front of where the defendant was, quite lawfully, training to shoot. The attitude of the common law, therefore, was that a man "acted at his peril". If his conduct resulted in the commission of an act of trespass, then he would be liable accordingly. Only where he could establish some lawful excuse for so acting would he escape such liability.

Towards the end of the 19th century, in the case of *Stanley v. Powell*,[22] it was suggested that in cases of trespass to the person, as in that instance in which the plaintiff was accidentally injured by a shot from a gun which was fired by the defendant while out shooting birds, it was open to the defendant to prove that he had not intended to injure the plaintiff, nor had he behaved negligently and so caused the injury in question. The onus was on the defendant. He had to establish that what had occurred was the result of what was termed an "inevitable accident". By this was meant that what had occurred was unforeseen and was indeed unforeseeable as a consequence of the totally lawful conduct of the defendant, and of course, had not been intended by him. In that case, for example, the shot had ricochetted from a tree, and thus had struck the plaintiff. In these circumstances, as the defendant had proved that he was not negligent, he was held not liable in trespass.

The effect of this decision was that trespass to the person ceased to be a tort of strict liability, because the defendant could excuse himself or herself by pleading and proving that the injury was unintended and was not the result of any negligent behaviour on his or her part. In other words an accidental trespass to the person was no trespass. The problem that emerged, however, was whether it was for the defendant to excuse himself or herself by a plea of no intention to injure or negligence or for the plaintiff to establish, as part of his or her case against the defendant, that the latter knew what he or she was doing and intended to cause harm, or at the very least was negligent in the way he or she acted, and could have avoided the accident if the defendant had taken reasonable care. In this respect a divergence of opinion has arisen between the courts in Canada and those in England.

In England the decision of Diplock J. in *Fowler v. Lanning*,[23] followed by the statements by members of the Court of Appeal in *Letang v. Cooper*,[24] indicate that, in modern times, in England, to establish a good cause of action in trespass, the plaintiff must prove that the defendant acted negligently or with intent to injure. Canadian cases, however, favour the opposite approach.[25] This may clearly be seen in operation in the decision of the Supreme Court of Canada in

---

22 [1891] 1 Q.B. 86.

23 [1959] 1 Q.B. 426.

24 [1965] 1 Q.B. 232.

25 See *e.g.*, *Dahlberg v. Naydiuk* (1970), 10 D.L.R. (3d) 319 (Man. C.A.); *Goshen v. Larin* (1975), 10 N.S.R. (2d) 66 (C.A.).

Cook v. Lewis,[26] in which the facts very closely resembled those in *Stanley v. Powell*, save that in the Canadian case there were "two" hunters who were shooting at the same time, and "either one" could have been the person whose shot caused the plaintiff's injury. If the plaintiff had been forced to establish the actual culprit, by proving which had intended to harm him or had been negligent, he would probably have failed in his action. The Court held that the onus was on "both" defendants to excuse themselves, and if they could not, they would be jointly liable to the plaintiff. It must be said that this decision seriously undermines the principle that a plaintiff must establish, among other things, as seen in an earlier chapter, that the defendant "caused" his or her injury. This the plaintiff could not do with respect to either defendant in *Cook v. Lewis*. It is possible to accept the decision solely on the ground that, otherwise, the plaintiff would have been deprived of a remedy when clearly he was entitled to one against someone, namely one or other of the defendants. The choice for the Court was to make both liable or else enable the guilty party to evade or escape responsibility. In those circumstances, the decision is not an unreasonable one. Later cases in Canada reveal support for the proposition that trespass is actionable unless the defendant succeeds in proving his or her lack of the necessary mental state, *i.e.*, intention or negligence.

The result of this difference is that in Canada a trespass to the person is either intentional or negligent,[27] whereas in England such a trespass can only occur intentionally. An unintentional, but negligently caused personal injury will be remediable only by an action framed in negligence, the onus of which, as will be seen, lies on the plaintiff. A consequence of this is that in Canada a person guilty of trespass to the person will be liable for unforeseeable, as well as intended or foreseeable consequences of the trespass,[28] whereas in England a defendant will only be liable for intended or foreseeable consequences of the act of trespass to the person.

In contrast to the situation where it is alleged that the trespass was the result of an accident, where the defendant seeks to argue that it was the result of a mistake, that argument will not operate to excuse the defendant from liability, though it may mitigate such liability and reduce the damages that are payable to the plaintiff.[29] Mistake, however, may be relevant where the defendant seeks to justify the trespass on the ground that the defendant was entitled under the law to effect an arrest of the plaintiff.[30] However it is doubtful whether the defendant's mistaken belief that the plaintiff had consented to the trespass or that the defendant was entitled to commit the trespass in self-defence will enable the

---

26 [1951] S.C.R. 830, with which compare and contrast *Woodward v. Begbie*, [1962] O.R. 60 (H.C.); *Lange v. Bennett*, [1964] 1 O.R. 233 (H.C.).

27 If the trespass is the result of negligence, the plaintiff's contributory negligence (below p. 90) will affect the question of damages: *Parmley v. Parmley*, [1945] S.C.R. 635; *Dempsey v. Primeau* (1995), 144 N.S.R. (2d) 275 (S.C.).

28 *Bettel v. Yim* (1978), 20 O.R. (2d) 617 (Co. Ct.).

29 *Hodgkinson v. Martin*, [1928] 3 W.W.R. 763.

30 Below p. 49.

defendant to rely on the defences of consent or self-defence that are available in otherwise appropriate circumstances.[31]

(ii) Infancy and Insanity

Since an intent to harm or negligence are material factors in liability for trespass to the person, the age of the perpetrator of such a trespass may be relevant. For liability to ensue the wrongdoer must have been old enough to have the intelligence to know what he or she was doing, that is, to formulate the requisite intent to injure or to be capable of being held negligent. The category of infants, or minors, comprises those who are under the age of majority, in modern times 18. Although all persons under that age are considered to be infants or minors, it is obvious that they will not all be incapable of forming the required intent or of being negligent so as to be relieved from liability. The closer in age the wrongdoer is to 18 the more likely is it that he or she will be held liable: the younger a person is, the less likely. Hence in some decided cases which illustrate the application of this doctrine a five-year-old child[32] and a three-year-old child[33] were held not liable. It should be noted, however, that if the infant is exempt from responsibility, a parent may be, if the parent, by a negligent act or omission, enabled the infant to commit the tort, for example, by allowing a very young child to have an airgun the use of which injured the plaintiff.[34]

Someone who is mentally impaired may also not be liable for what would otherwise be a trespass. However the extent to which a defendant's insanity can be raised so as to exempt the defendant from liability is not clear. It would appear to be accepted that if the defendant's mental incapacity is such that he or she could not have formed any intent to injure the victim,[35] or to appreciate that he or she was acting negligently,[36] then the defendant cannot be held liable, for example, if the defendant physically attacked the plaintiff. The question that remains unanswered, however, is whether a similar exemption from liability operates where the defendant knew what he or she was doing but, by reason of mental illness, could not understand the effect of what he or she was doing. The cases have never decisively dealt with this issue.[37] It is probable that insanity will only excuse someone from liability for trespass if the effect of the illness is to establish that the defendant had not acted truly voluntarily, for example, if the illness causes the defendant to lose control of his or her actions.

---

31 Below pp. 47-48.

32 *Walmsley v. Humenick*, [1954] 2 D.L.R. 232 (B.C.S.C.).

33 *Tillander v. Gosselin*, [1967] 1 O.R. 203 (H.C.), affirmed 61 D.L.R. (2d) 192*n* (Ont. C.A.).

34 *Newton v. Edgerley*, [1959] 1 W.L.R. 1031; *Ryan v. Hickson* (1974), 55 D.L.R. (3d) 196 (Ont. H.C.); *B. (D.C.) v. Arkin* (1996), 138 D.L.R. (4th) 309 (Man. Q.B.).

35 *Tindale v. Tindale*, [1950] 4 D.L.R. 363 (B.C.S.C.); *Phillips v. Soloway* (1956), 6 D.L.R. (2d) 570 (Man. Q.B.).

36 Hence a defendant may not be liable in negligence on account of a mental disorder, but liable for trespass to the person, battery, because he knew he was applying force to the plaintiff: *Canada (Attorney-General) v. Connolly* (1990), 64 C.C.L.I. 301 (B.C.S.C.), affirmed (1992), 72 B.C.L.R. (2d) 166 (C.A.).

37 See, *e.g.*, *Beale v. Beale* (1982), 24 C.C.L.T. 101 (N.S.T.D.).

(c) Defences

There are various circumstances under which an act that otherwise would be actionable as a trespass against the person will not lead to liability. This will be the case, for example, where the defendant acted: (i) in self-defence;[38] (ii) to recover his or her goods; (iii) to eject a trespasser on his land;[39] (iv) to effect discipline, for example, as a parent, teacher or master of a ship.[40] In such instances, however, the defendant must not exceed the use of force that is reasonable for the particular purpose. If the force used is excessive, the appropriate defence will not be available.[41] But probably the most important defences that may be raised to counter an allegation of trespass to the person are: (a) that the plaintiff consented to the act in question; and (b) that the defendant was arresting the plaintiff in the exercise of powers conferred on the defendant by the *Criminal Code* or some other statute.

An important maxim of the common law is: *volenti non fit injuria*, no wrong is committed against one who consents. This idea, as will be seen in a later chapter,[42] figures conspicuously in the law of negligence, in which context it is sometimes referred to as "assumption of risk". In relation to trespass to the person it means that no action will lie against the one who has committed a battery or assault against, or has wrongfully imprisoned another if the victim consented to such action in advance. For this to result, however, the act which amounts to the trespass must not be a criminal act.[43] The consent must have been given freely, not induced by fraud or duress, and the victim must have been able to realize the consequences of his or her consent.[44] This means that the defence will not be applicable where the victim was too young or too mentally disordered to appreciate what was happening. Nor can it be raised against a victim unconscious at the time of the trespass, for example, a patient anaesthetized at the material time.[45] Such a person cannot in law give a valid consent to a trespass. However, a person who can in law validly consent may agree prior to a medical or dental procedure that would otherwise amount to a trespass, although if the doctor or dentist does something outside the scope of such consensual procedure, for example, by amputating the wrong limb, a trespass will be committed.[46] Should the doctor or dentist not go beyond the scope of the consent, but cause

---

38 *Bruce v. Dyer* (1966), 58 D.L.R. (2d) 211 (Ont. C.A.); *Landry v. Godin* (1990), 105 N.B.R. (2d) 271 (Q.B.). But the provocation of the defendant by the plaintiff will not excuse the former from liability, although it might lead to a reduction in damages: *Peck v. Chomyc Hotels Ltd.* (1989), 101 A.R. 65 (Q.B.); *Hurley v. Moore* (1993), 112 Nfld. & P.E.I.R. 40 (Nfld. C.A.).

39 *Ball v. Manthorpe* (1970), 15 D.L.R. (3d) 99 (B.C. Co. Ct.).

40 *Hook v. Cunard S.S. Co.*, [1953] 1 W.L.R. 682.

41 *De Fosse v. Wille* (1999), 170 Sask. R. 156 (Q.B.); *Arseneau v. Albert* (1980), 32 N.B.R. (2d) 235 (C.A.); *Paull v. Ferris* (1997), 153 Sask. R. 216 (C.A.).

42 Below p. 92.

43 *R. v. Donovan*, [1934] 2 K.B. 498.

44 *Norberg v. Wynrib* (1992), 92 D.L.R. (4th) 449 (S.C.C.); *Campbell v. S.S. Kresge Co.* (1976), 74 D.L.R. (3d) 717 (N.S.T.D.).

45 *Malette v. Shulman* (1990), 72 O.R. (2d) 417 (C.A.). Except, possibly, in cases of emergency.

46 *Mulloy v. Hop Sang*, [1935] 1 W.W.R. 714.

harm to the patient by negligence, however, this will not be a trespass, but may entitle the patient to sue for negligence.[47] Consent is also a possible defence to an action for trespass to the person where the injury to the plaintiff has been caused by another player in the course of participation in a sport. However this will only be true if the sport was a lawful one and the act of the defendant was something that was within the rules of the sport, that is to say, an accidental injury inflicted in the course of the game as opposed to a deliberate attack on another player.[48]

The *Criminal Code*,[49] which replaces the common law insofar as criminal offences are concerned, governs powers of arrest. While its main purpose is to protect those within its scope from criminal liability for the use of force in certain circumstances, it would seem that at the same time whatever is justified under the criminal law would be justified with regard to possible civil liability in tort. Thus it is vital to note the conditions under which the use of force or restraint is permitted and justified under the Code.

Thus every one, whether private citizen, peace officer, or otherwise, may use whatever force is reasonably necessary to do what he or she is required or authorized to do in regard to the administration or enforcement of the law, as long as he or she is acting on reasonable and probable grounds.[50] This does not go to the extent of permitting the use of force that is intended or likely to cause death or grievous bodily harm, unless such force is believed on reasonable and probable grounds to be necessary to preserve oneself or anyone under one's protection from death or grievous bodily harm. But in the case of a peace officer (not a private citizen) who is lawfully arresting someone with or without a warrant, as much force as is necessary to prevent the escape of the person to be arrested may be used, unless the escape can be prevented by reasonable means less violently.[51] But everyone, peace officer or otherwise may use reasonable force to prevent the continuance or further commission of a breach of the peace which he or she witnesses, and may use reasonable force to prevent the commission of offences for which the criminal may be arrested without warrant, and which are likely to cause immediate and serious injury to another person or his or her property. It should also be noted that so far as criminal liability is concerned, an honest and reasonable mistake about the person who is arrested, where the arrest, though of the correct person, was authorized by warrant, will not involve

---

47 Unless the patient has given an "informed consent" to the procedure: *Reibl v. Hughes* (1981), 114 D.L.R. (3d) 1 (S.C.C.): below p. 93.

48 Compare *Knockwood v. Cormier* (1995), 167 N.B.R. (2d) 147 (Q.B.) with *Agar v. Canning* (1965), 54 W.W.R. 302.

49 R.S.C. 1985, c. C-46. The relevant sections are ss. 25-32, 494, 495.

50 This justified a rectal search in *Reynen v. Antonenko* (1975), 20 C.C.C. (2d) 342 (Alta. T.D.). The defendant may rely on this provision even if he or she made a mistake and the situation was not as the defendant believed it to be, as long as a reasonable person acting under that mistake would have believed he or she was acting lawfully: *Hucul v. Hicks* (1965), 15 D.L.R. (2d) 267 (Sask. Q.B.), with which contrast *Foley v. Shannahan* (1990), 82 Nfld. & P.E.I.R. 271 (Nfld. T.D.).

51 Hence shooting at an escaped prisoner was protected in *Priestman v. Colangelo and Smythson*, [1959] S.C.R. 615. Contrast *Lang v. Burch* (1983), 140 D.L.R. (3d) 325 (Sask. C.A.).

the mistaken party or anyone assisting him or her in the arrest in guilt; presumably this would also protect any such person from liability in tort in the event of such a mistake. Finally it should be noted that the use of excessive force will be criminal — and therefore presumably tortious as well — wherever the use of force is lawful and authorized in any of the above situations.

What has been said in the previous paragraph applies to situations involving arrest under a warrant issued by a justice of the peace or magistrate, or arrest for the commission of a breach of the peace in front of the arrester. In some circumstances, however, an arrest may lawfully take place without involving the arrester in criminal or civil liability, even in the absence of a judicially authorized and issued warrant. There is a difference between peace officers and others in respect of arrest without warrant. Subject to some exceptions (which relate to lack of belief that arrest is necessary in the public interest and that the person not arrested will fail to attend court at the appropriate time), a peace officer may arrest without warrant: (a) anyone who has committed an indictable offence;[52] (b) anyone believed on reasonable and probable grounds to have committed or be about to commit such an offence; (c) anyone found committing such an offence; (d) anyone for whose arrest he or she has reasonable and probable grounds for believing that a warrant is in force within the territorial jurisdiction in which the person in question is found. While the expression "indictable offence" does not entirely correspond to the former English category of "felonies", it does serve to differentiate more serious crimes (even though they may now be tried in some instances by magistrates, rather than by superior court judges, and possibly even without a jury) from those of a lesser nature, which are dealt with by courts of summary jurisdiction. Thus the purport of the provisions of the Code mentioned above is to permit a peace officer to undertake an arrest in serious cases without having to apply for a warrant (which would take too long and might result in the escape of the criminal) and in circumstances which might enable the officer to prevent the commission of the crime. As long as the officer is acting in accordance with and under those provisions he or she will be protected in any proceedings, including, presumably, an action for trespass, unless the victim or plaintiff alleges and establishes that the officer had undertaken the arrest without the reasonable belief as to public interest and the likelihood that the criminal will fail to attend court, that have been mentioned.

Anyone, including someone who is not a peace officer, may arrest without warrant (which would involve what is popularly called a "citizen's arrest"): (a) anyone he or she finds committing an indictable offence; (b) anyone who, on reasonable and probable grounds, he or she believes has committed a "criminal" offence, *i.e.*, not only an indictable one, "and" is escaping from and freshly pursued by persons having lawful authority to arrest the actual or supposed criminal.[53] In addition, the

---

[52] There are varying judicial opinions about the meaning of this provision. Some think it means the defendant must know the plaintiff committed the offence: others that only reasonable and probable grounds for believing the offence was committed are necessary: see, *e.g.*, *Hucul v. Hicks* (1965), 15 D.L.R. (2d) 267 (Sask. Q.B.); *Hayward v. F.W. Woolworth Co.* (1979), 8 C.C.L.T. 157 (Nfld. T.D.); *Kovacs v. Ontario Jockey Club* (1995), 126 D.L.R. (4th) 576 (Ont. Gen. Div.).

[53] See the discussion in *R. v. Biron* (1976), 59 D.L.R. (3d) 409 (S.C.C.).

owner of property, or a person lawfully in possession of property, or someone authorized by such an owner or possessor of property, may arrest without warrant anyone found committing a criminal offence, *i.e.*, not only an indictable one, on or in relation to that property. It must be noted, however, that a citizen so authorized to arrest without warrant must deliver the arrested person "forthwith" to a peace officer. Presumably the failure to do so, at least without a reasonable cause for such failure, *i.e.*, the distance to the nearest peace officer, or inclement weather making travel to such an officer impossible, will mean that the arrest will become tortious, or at the very least that the detention beyond the reasonable time required to bring the arrested person to such an officer will be wrongful and involve trespass, *i.e.*, false imprisonment.

Apart from the provisions of the *Criminal Code* outlined above, there are other federal and provincial statutes which may give protection from tortious liability.[54] However at the material time the one seeking such protection must have been acting lawfully, in accordance with the provisions of such statute.[55]

3. TRESPASS TO GOODS

The tort of trespass to goods involves a direct physical act by a wrongdoer against another's chattel. This simple definition requires elaboration in respect of: (a) the meaning of "chattel"; (b) the kind of act that will amount to a trespass; (c) the state of mind of the alleged wrongdoer; (d) the determination of who has the right to sue in regards to the alleged trespass.

The expression "chattel" has the same meaning as "goods". Both terms refer to personal property that is tangible, in contrast with real property on the one hand and, on the other, personal property that is intangible, for example, a copyright, patent, or trade mark. A wrong to realty may be trespass to land, nuisance, or something else. The improper use of another's copyright, patent or trade mark may be actionable under the provisions of a statute such as the *Trade-marks Act*.[56] Only if the wrongful act is directed against something that is considered to be "goods" can such act be a trespass to goods. Thus a cheque, a share certificate, or trading stamps given by a store, are "goods" against which trespass can be committed. So are coins which are in current use, even though such coins, as opposed to ancient coins which may be part of a special collection in a house or museum, would not be "goods" within the meaning of that term as defined in a provincial *Sale of Goods Act*.[57] A chattel that is attached to land continues to

---

54 *E.g.*, *Youth Criminal Justice Act*, S.C. 2002, c. 1; *Identification of Criminals Act*, R.S.C. 1985, c. I-1; *Liquor Licence Act*, R.S.O. 1990, c. L.19, s. 34; *Offence Act*, R.S.B.C. 1996, c. 338, s. 34.

55 *Ramia v. Burgess* (1980), 38 N.S.R. (2d) 200 (C.A.); *Griggs v. Southside Hotel Ltd.*, [1946] O.W.N. 576 (H.C.).

56 R.S.C. 1985, c. T-13, s. 7.

57 *E.g.* R.S.O. 1990, c. S.1, s. 1(1); Fridman, *Sale of Goods in Canada*, 4th ed. (Toronto: Carswell, 1995), pp. 16-23.

qualify as "goods", if the chattel in question can be considered to have become part of the land, for example, if it would not be possible to remove it with ease.[58]

Just as any improper touching of another's body is a trespass to the person, so any such touching of another's chattel will be a trespass to goods, unless justified or excused by law. There need be no actual damage to the chattel. As with trespass to the person, the mere fact of improper touching suffices for liability, although recoverable damages will depend on the actual loss suffered through the trespass. A trespass to goods can take the form of improper handling of the chattel in question, depriving the victim of possession of a chattel for some time, causing physical damage that is more than trivial to a chattel, or, in the extreme, completely destroying the goods in question. Whatever form the trespass takes, however, there must be some direct act by the wrongdoer against the chattel that is affected.

The act in question may be deliberate or negligent. If it is accidental, in the sense that expression has been explained in relation to trespass to the person,[59] it would appear that no trespass to goods will have been committed. A defendant may therefore escape liability for trespass to goods by establishing that he or she acted neither with intent to commit a trespass nor with negligence.[60] However, a plea of mistake, it seems, will not excuse someone accused of trespass to goods. A party who mistakenly, even if honestly, believes he or she is entitled to handle, possess or use the affected chattel, for example, where the wrongdoer believes the chattel to be his or hers when in fact it is not, will not escape liability. However a mistake by the wrongdoer that is induced by the alleged victim of the trespass may excuse the alleged trespasser.[61]

Trespass is a wrong to possession, not ownership. Hence all the plaintiff has to prove is that at the material time he or she was in possession of the goods;[62] ownership does not have to be established. Thus a person who is: (a) a bailee of the chattel, that is, someone to whom it has been lent, or with whom it has been deposited, either gratuitously or for reward; (b) a finder, whether or not the true owner is easily traceable; or (c) an unlawful possessor, such as a thief or a receiver of stolen goods, may bring the action for trespass unless the alleged trespasser is the true owner or someone acting under his or her authority, acting in circumstances in which it is lawful for him or her to do so. Thus a bailor of a chattel — the owner — may not retake the goods without the consent of the bailee, unless the bailment has been validly determined. If it is a bailment at will, the bailor must have determined the bailment by some appropriate act prior to the recaption of the chattel. The finder may be able to claim not only possession, where the true owner is not claiming the return of his or her goods, but also a better title than anyone else apart from the true owner. This question has arisen

---

58 *Morrison v. Thomas* (1922), 65 D.L.R. 364 (Sask. C.A.).

59 Above p. 43.

60 *384238 Ontario Ltd. v. Canada* (1983), 8 D.L.R. (4th) 676 (F.C.A.).

61 *Ibid.*

62 Or has the immediate right to possession, for example, by being a bailor who has lawfully terminated the bailment. But this does not entitle the bailor to seize bailed goods from the bailee: *Devoe v. Long & Long*, [1951] 1 D.L.R. 203.

in several cases involving actions for conversion litigated between a finder and the owner of land or premises on which the chattel was found.[63] Therefore, although the finder will have sufficient possession to support an action for trespass by him or her against some other person, more often than not the problem arises out of his or her dispossession by the owner of the premises or land, and a subsequent action for conversion brought by the finder. Similarly, a person who is in possession, even if without title, can sue in trespass and cannot be defeated by a plea that someone else, *i.e.*, not the defendant, is the true owner.

To an action for trespass to goods the defendant may plead accident, as noted above, consent on the part of the plaintiff, sometimes even necessity.[64] The common law recognizes "recaption of chattels", where someone retakes possession of goods unlawfully in the possession of another. Statutes sometimes confer a right to take possession of goods that otherwise would amount to trespass.[65] For example, under the *Criminal Code*,[66] if police have been granted a search warrant they may take and retain goods found while the warrant was exercised as long as the goods in question were specified in the warrant or were goods reasonably believed to have been used in the commission of an offence.

4. TRESPASS TO LAND

Just as trespass to the person involves a direct application of force to the victim and trespass to goods requires a similar application of force to the chattel of another, so trespass to land is committed where a person unlawfully and directly applies force to the land of another. Usually a trespass to land takes place by an invasion of the plaintiff's land by the wrongdoer personally, by someone on his or her behalf, or by some article such as machinery or a car, belonging to the alleged trespasser. This form of trespass, like trespass to goods, requires explanation of the kind of acts that constitute commission of the tort: the subject of such acts, in this instance what is understood by the expression "land": and the nature of the relationship between a person and the land on which the trespass has been committed that is necessary to entitle someone to sue.

Any invasion of another's land, however slight, is an actionable trespass if it is not justified or excused by law.[67] No actual damage need be caused, since trespass is, and always was, actionable *per se*.[68] Force need not be established,

---

63 In this regard compare an English case, *Parker v. British Airways Board*, [1982] 1 All E.R. 834 with two Canadian cases, *Kowal v. Ellis* (1977), 76 D.L.R. (3d) 546 (Man. C.A.) and *Grafstein v. Holme & Freeman* (1958), 12 D.L.R. (2d) 727 (Ont. C.A.).

64 *E.g.*, where to save passengers a ship's cargo must be jettisoned: *Mouse's Case* (1609), 12 Co. Rep. 63.

65 See, *e.g.*, *Mandziuk v. Manitoba* (1998), 124 Man. R. (2d) 199 (Q.B.).

66 R.S.C. 1985, c. C-46, s. 89.

67 *Entick v. Carrington* (1765), 19 State Tr. 1029.

68 *Cf.* the criminal liability created by statutes such as the Ontario *Trespass to Property Act*, R.S.O. 1990, c. T.21: on which see *R. v. Burko*, [1969] 1 O.R. 598 (Mag. Ct.): *R. v. Peters* (1971), 17 D.L.R. (3d) 128*n* (S.C.C.), affirming [1971] 1 O.R. 597 (C.A.). But although the hitting of golf

although a forcible entry may be a more aggravated trespass, giving rise to liability for a higher amount of damages, and some ancient English statutes, the effect of which is to be found in the *Criminal Code* in Canada, prohibited forcible entry even for the purpose of retaking one's own land as against a wrongdoer.[69] Trespass may occur when a person misuses another's land, *i.e.*, walks or rides over it without permission, or, having entered on it with permission, proceeds to act on it in a manner not within the scope of the permission. Once he or she engages in such behaviour he or she becomes a trespasser. Thus it has been held that a person who stands or walks on a highway owned by the plaintiff, for the purpose of spying on what is being done on the owner's property, commits trespass.[70] So too, picketers may commit trespass if they are acting without the authority of the law, in furtherance of some trade dispute.[71] At common law, where a person entitled by law to enter premises abuses his or her privilege and begins to perform acts which are outside the scope of his or her right to enter the land, he or she might be treated as if he or she has always been a trespasser, from the moment he or she first entered the land. He or she becomes what was called a trespasser *ab initio*. This ancient doctrine of the law may no longer be applicable.[72] However, it is still true that the moment permission to come onto land, in the form of a licence to enter, is terminated either by the wrongful act of the licensee or the revocation of the licence on the part of the landowner, the licensee becomes a trespasser. This will be so even if the latter acted improperly in revoking the licence (which may expose him or her to an action for breach of contract). It has been held, however, that where a licence is revoked, whether validly or not, the landowner must give the ex-licensee a reasonable time within which to remove himself or herself (and any property that was with him or her under the terms of the licence) before the landowner can treat the licensee as a trespasser and either sue the licensee for trespass or eject him or her by the use of reasonable force.[73]

Although, as previously noted, the tort of trespass, in all its forms, began as a tort of strict liability,[74] in more modern times courts have accepted that, in the case of trespass to the person and, possibly, trespass to chattels, the absence of any intent to trespass or of negligence will excuse a party who has in

---

balls into the plaintiff's land was a trespass in *Segal and Segal v. Derrick Golf & Winter Club*, [1977] 4 W.W.R. 101, it was held not to be actionable.

69 R.S.C. 1985, c. C-46, s. 72. But this does not prevent the owner from retaking possession, as long as he does not use force: *Hemmings v. Stoke Pages Golf Club*, [1920] 1 K.B. 720; *cf. Allan v. Kirk*, [1917] 2 W.W.R. 527.

70 *Hickman v. Maisey*, [1900] 1 Q.B. 752.

71 There are some conflicting decisions which turn on the meaning or existence of a provincial Petty Trespass Act: see *Harrison v. Carswell*, [1976] 2 S.C.R. 200; *281856 B.C. Ltd. v. Kamloops Revelstoke Okanagan Building Trades Union* (1986), 37 C.C.L.T. 262 (B.C.C.A.); *Wildwood Mall Ltd. v. Stevens*, [1980] 2 W.W.R. 638 (Sask. Q.B.).

72 *Chic Fashions Ltd. v. Jones*, [1968] 2 Q.B. 299; *Cinnamond v. British Airports Authority*, [1980] 1 W.L.R. 582.

73 *Winter Garden Theatre (London) Ltd. v. Millennium Productions Ltd.*, [1948] A.C. 173; *cf. Cottreau v. Rodgerson and Saulnier* (1965), 53 D.L.R. (2d) 549 (N.S.S.C.).

74 Above p. 40. And in the special case of "cattle trespass", below p. 120, remains a tort of strict liability.

fact, unlawfully and without permission, come upon the plaintiff's property.[75] The same has been held to apply to trespass to land.[76] If the invasion of the plaintiff's land is committed involuntarily, for example, where the alleged wrongdoer is involved in a car crash which was not his or her fault, and as a result was hurled through the air so as to land on the plaintiff's property, no trespass will have occurred.[77] Such will not be the situation, however, if the trespass is committed voluntarily but as the result of a mistake, for example, where the wrongdoer honestly and reasonably believes that the land is his or hers.[78]

There are other situations, apart from accident or the granting of a licence whereby the plaintiff consents to the defendant's entry on the land, in which what might otherwise be a trespass to land is not, because the alleged trespasser is justified in what he or she has done, or is excused from liability on other grounds.

Anyone who enters another's land for the purpose of recovering his or her own property, which is on that other's land because of the acts of that other, and possibly when it is the fault of someone else, will not be considered a trespasser, as long as he or she restricts entry to what is reasonable and necessary for the purpose of such recaption of his or her own goods. The same would be true where the alleged trespass was caused by necessity[79] including the need to defend oneself against another's wrongdoing, such as avoiding an obstruction on the highway, or where something on the victim's land is causing a nuisance to the alleged wrongdoer, who comes on to the former's land to abate the nuisance (for example, by removing something that is blocking a stream and so causing an overflow of water onto the alleged trespasser's land). Finally, some mention should be made of the possibility that the entry onto another's land may be authorized by law, even though the landowner has not given express permission to such entry.[80] Such authorization by law may occur when police officers are granted a warrant to enter and search premises under the provisions of the *Criminal Code*.[81] There is a long history attached to the question of such warrants, which are now strictly regulated by the provisions of the law (though it must be noted that in some circumstances wide powers may be given to police under the provisions dealing with writs of assistance). It should also be noted that where such officers exceed the powers given to them by a warrant or otherwise under the law, they will be guilty of trespass, either to land, or if seizure of

---

75 Above pp. 44-45, 51.

76 See *Manitoba Hydro v. Minsky* (1999), 130 Man. R. (2d) 374 (Q.B.). To the contrary, however, *Costello v. Calgary (City) (No. 2)* (1998), 53 Alta. L.R. (3d) 15 (C.A.).

77 *Smith v. Stone* (1647), Style 65.

78 *Basely v. Clarkson* (1681), 3 Lev. 37; *Turner v. Thorne* (1959), 21 D.L.R. (2d) 29 (Ont. H.C.).

79 *King's Prerogative in Saltpetre* (1606), 12 Co. Rep. 12. Expropriation of another's property is permitted and regulated by statutes, under which compensation is payable.

80 *Reference Pursuant to s. 27(1) of the Judicature Act* (1984), 35 Alta. L.R. (2d) 97 (S.C.C.).

81 Or in order to effect an arrest: *Eccles v. Borque*, [1975] 2 S.C.R. 739. Note the *Canadian Charter of Rights and Freedoms*, Part I of the *Constitution Act, 1982*, being Schedule B to the *Canada Act 1982* (U.K.), 1982, c. 11, s. 8, under which "everyone has the right to be secure against unreasonable search or seizure".

chattels is involved, to goods. And no plea of mistake or necessity may be available in cases of such excess.[82]

Once it was thought that the expression "land" included within its scope everything that was under the surface, as deep as the centre of the earth, and the air above the land to an indefinite height. This would mean that trespass could be committed by entering the land of another at some depth below the surface, for example, by digging through a mine shaft; or crossing the land of another in the air; or putting something in such a position that it overhung the land of another; or where a horse puts his head over a fence and bites the plaintiff's animal. There were some early 19th century cases involving shooting across the property of someone else, and ballooning. Later, however, the concept of ownership of land to the core of the earth and to the heavens was regarded as "somewhat fanciful". In the modern law of torts, a person who owns land, owns, in addition to the surface, the earth below to a reasonable depth (and in Canada of course, may not own the mineral rights in respect of what is underground) and the airspace above the land to a reasonable height, *i.e.*, to such depth and height as is reasonable for the purpose of enabling him or her to use and enjoy the rights to the surface.[83] This conclusion has been utilized to enable a landowner to prevent, or obtain damages in respect of, the conduct of the defendant in placing a sign over the plaintiff's land, albeit by extension from land of the defendant.[84] It may also be used in cases where the defendant has improperly dug a hole in the plaintiff's land — whether deep, *e.g.*, a mine or well, or shallow, *e.g.*, in order to make seismographic soundings or tests for the purposes of oil exploration — even though the plaintiff's rights of property may not normally extend quite so far, there can be little doubt that the law would protect the plaintiff in the event of such an invasion.[85] The same might well be true even if the invasion occurs laterally and not vertically, so that the surface of the plaintiff's land is not touched by the defendant, unless the invasion is at such a depth that it might be said to have occurred beyond the limits of the plaintiff's proprietary rights.

Not that the plaintiff need be the owner of land in order to maintain an action for trespass. Trespass is a wrong to possession. Hence, a mere possessor of land, even a wrongful possessor — such as a squatter without any title or legal claim to the land, as long as he or she claims immediate and exclusive possession — may maintain an action for trespass, unless the alleged trespasser is the true owner or one who acts in the right of, or on behalf of, the true owner. Hence, an owner who is out of possession may not bring an action for trespass unless the conduct of the wrongdoer would have the effect of destroying the plaintiff's

---

82 *Elias v. Pasmore*, [1934] 2 K.B. 164; *Chic Fashions Ltd. v. Jones*, [1968] 2 Q.B. 299. On the power of the police to make a forcible entry after notice (except in "exigent" situations, when notice is unnecessary), see *Eccles v. Borque*, [1975] 2 S.C.R. 739, which was based on the common law, not the provisions of the *Criminal Code*, R.S.C. 1985, c. C-46.

83 Contrast *Atlantic Aviation Ltd. v. Nova Scotia Light & Power Co.* (1965), 55 D.L.R. (2d) 554 with *Lacroix v. R.*, [1954] 4 D.L.R. 470 (Ex. Ct.).

84 *Kelsen v. Imperial Tobacco Co. Ltd.*, [1957] 2 Q.B. 334; *Woollerton and Wilson v. Costain*, [1970] 1 W.L.R. 411; *Didow v. Alberta Power Ltd.* [1985] 5 W.W.R. 606 (Alta. C.A.); *Lewvest Ltd. v. Scotia Towers Ltd.* (1981), 126 D.L.R. (3d) 239 (Nfld. T.D.).

85 *Wasson v. California Standard Co.* (1964), 48 W.W.R. 513 (Alta. C.A.).

claim to possession when his or her rights as owner would come back, *e.g.*, after the termination of a lease to a third party.[86] Nor can a user of land without exclusive possession, such as a lodger, maintain an action for trespass.

[86] Or the land is vacant: *Townsview Properties Ltd. v. Sun Construction & Equipment Co.* (1973), 2 O.R. (2d) 213 (H.C.), affirmed (1975), 56 D.L.R. (3d) 330 (Ont. C.A.).

Chapter 6

NUISANCE

1. NUISANCE EXPLAINED

As stated in a previous chapter, trespass to land occurs when a defendant commits some direct act against the land of another.[1] If harm to the plaintiff results indirectly from the defendant's use of the plaintiff's or someone else's land, no trespass is committed.[2] However, the conduct of the defendant might amount to an actionable nuisance. For example, to throw something onto a neighbour's land, unless with the neighbour's permission, will be trespass: to build eaves in such a way that rainwater collected therein falls onto the neighbour's land will not be trespass but could be nuisance. It is important to determine whether the wrongful act alleged against the defendant is trespass or nuisance for several reasons. First, merely to cause the plaintiff inconvenience without resulting in any damage to the land will not suffice for trespass, but could amount to nuisance. Second, any possessor of land may sue for trespass to the land: in nuisance the right to sue vests only in someone who has a legal interest in the land, not merely possession. Third, only the person who actually commits the trespass (or that person's employer, in accordance with the doctrine of vicarious liability)[3] can be guilty of trespass: someone who has not committed the act that involves the nuisance, that is to say has not "created" the nuisance will nevertheless be liable if he or she has "adopted" or "continued" the nuisance in ways that will be explained later.[4] Fourth, although nuisance, like trespass to land, is usually a matter of private law, resulting in civil liability on the part of one individual towards another, some nuisances may give rise to criminal, but not civil liability.[5]

In this regard the law distinguishes between private and public nuisances. A private nuisance is a tort committed usually by one landowner against his or her neighbouring landowner. A public nuisance is not a tort. It is a crime at common

---

1 Above p. 52.

2 *Mann v. Saulnier* (1959), 19 D.L.R. (2d) 130 (N.B.C.A.). The wrongful act may constitute both trespass to land and nuisance: *Segal & Segal v. Derrick Golf & Winter Club*, [1977] 4 W.W.R. 101 (Alta. S.C.T.D.).

3 Above p. 31.

4 Below p. 63.

5 Or may only be remediable at the suit of the federal or a provincial Attorney-General: see *Stein v. Gonzales* (1984), 14 D.L.R. (3d) 263 (B.C.S.C.); *Nova Scotia (Attorney General) v. Beaver* (1984), 66 N.S.R. (2d) 419 (T.D.), affirmed (1985), 32 C.C.L.T. 170 (N.S.C.A.).

law or under statute involving conduct that harmfully affects people generally, that is the community as a whole or some significant section of it.[6] However, in certain circumstances a public nuisance may lead to the granting of a private remedy to an individual, in which event the public nuisance can be regarded as a tort. Such will be the case when the public nuisance results in the suffering of "special" or "particular" damage on the part of an individual. For example, it may be a criminal, public nuisance to dig a hole in the highway without permission, thereby creating an obstruction that causes inconvenience to the public at large. However, if an adjoining landowner is prevented by this obstruction from free ingress to and egress from his or her property, or, in the absence of any light indicating the presence of the hole, falls into the hole on a dark night and sustains a broken leg, that landowner may have an action for damages that is quite distinct from any prosecution that might be brought against the one who made the hole and caused the obstruction.[7] The public nuisance becomes, to that extent, a private nuisance.

The tort of nuisance may be committed in one of two ways. The conduct of the defendant may lead indirectly to the causing of physical damage to the land of the plaintiff. Alternatively, the conduct of the defendant may not damage the plaintiff's land but may take the form of indirect interference that causes the plaintiff inconvenience by making it difficult, if not impossible, to enjoy the use of the land, by creating an unpleasant situation or atmosphere. This distinction between two types or varieties of nuisance was emphasized in *St. Helen's Smelting Co. v. Tipping*[8] and has been recognized and accepted in more modern times.[9] Two important differences exist between them. In the first place, there can be liability in nuisance, where physical damage is caused, even where the occurrence was singular:[10] but for liability to be incurred in a case of interference it is necessary for the plaintiff to establish that the alleged interference was a continuing state of affairs not merely something that occurred on one occasion.[11] Second, where physical damage is caused liability is "strict", and will follow unless a valid defence, such as statutory authority, can be raised: but in cases of interference various factors, some of which concern the defendant's state of mind, must be satisfied before liability can ensue.

---

6 In modern times legislation has been enacted to regulate activities that affect the environment. Such statutes create an administrative structure to deal with disputes and provide for administrative remedies rather than private law remedies where the requirements of the legislation are not met.

7 *Cf. Stephens v. MacMillan*, [1954] 2 D.L.R. 135 (Ont. H.C.). Diminution in the value of the plaintiff's property as a result of the public nuisance may also give rise to civil, tortious liability: *Culp v. Township of East York* (1956), 6 D.L.R. (2d) 417 (Ont. H.C.), affirmed (1956), 9 D.L.R. (2d) 749 (Ont. C.A.).

8 (1865), 11 H.L.C. 642.

9 *Kent v. Dominion Steel & Coal Corp.* (1965), 49 D.L.R. (2d) 241 (Nfld. S.C.).

10 *Aldridge v. Van Patter*, [1952] O.R. 595 (S.C.).

11 *Walker v. Pioneer Construction Co. (1967) Ltd.* (1975), 56 D.L.R. (3d) 677 (Ont. H.C.).

2. DAMAGE

The kind of damage that will entitle a landowner to sue for nuisance can take many forms, and can be brought about by many different activities on the part of the defendant. In most instances the damage in question will be damage to the property of the defendant, the land itself or something belonging to the plaintiff that is on the land. However if the damage is physical injury to the plaintiff, the latter may be able to claim in nuisance, rather than in trespass or negligence, if the injury was caused indirectly, by something done by the defendant on the defendant's land, and the defendant cannot be shown to have been acting negligently so as to bring about the injury. It would seem, also, that if the harm caused to the plaintiff by the defendant's conduct is not physical but mental, the defendant may still be liable in nuisance rather than for some other tort. This is suggested by the decision in *Motherwell v. Motherwell.*[12] There the nuisance alleged against the defendant was the making of many harassing telephone calls to the home of her father, who was one of the plaintiffs, and to the home of her brother, another plaintiff. These calls upset not only the defendant's father and brother but also a third plaintiff, the brother's wife, who was neither a landowner nor a lessee of her husband's house where the calls were received. The Alberta Court of Appeal held that the wife, as well as the husband, could maintain, *inter alia*, an action for nuisance in respect of the mental harm caused by the calls, although no physical damage was done to them. As will appear later,[13] this case raises a difficult problem with respect to determining who has the right to sue for nuisance, as to which the decision has been criticized and doubted in England by the House of Lords.[14] However, the right of someone to sue for nuisance when what has occurred has been mental rather than physical harm does not appear to have been repudiated.

Since liability in nuisance for damage is strict, a defendant will be liable in such situations even if he or she did not intend to cause harm and was not negligent in performing the act or acts that resulted in the damage. Hence even if it is pleaded and proved that reasonable care was taken to avoid the damage this will not excuse or relieve the defendant from liability. It is a different matter, however, where a nuisance is said to cause inconvenience and interference rather than physical or, as in *Motherwell*, mental damage.

3. INTERFERENCE

An action for nuisance may also lie where the defendant's conduct affects the plaintiff's land in such a way and to such an extent as to make it impossible or inconvenient for the plaintiff to enjoy the use of that land. Such interference can

---

12 (1977), 73 D.L.R. (3d) 62 (Alta. C.A.).

13 Below p. 63.

14 In *Hunter v. Canary Wharf Ltd.*, [1997] A.C. 655 at 690-695, 698, 707. But one member of the House, a former New Zealand judge, did not agree with this criticism: *ibid.*, at 712-719.

take many forms. What is usually involved in cases of this kind is that the defendant is carrying on some activity that results in, for example, smoke, fumes, dust, smells, excessive noise, sewage, large quantities of water, being carried from the land of the defendant on to that of the plaintiff, with the consequence that the normal and legitimate activities of the plaintiff are disrupted. There appears to be almost no limitation on the kind of "pollution" that can lead to liability for nuisance. In one, seemingly extreme instance a nuisance was committed when the defendants built, near the plaintiff's cable television operation, an installation that emitted electric power which interfered with the ability of the plaintiff to deliver cable television services to its customers.[15] However, some limitations do exist. Thus, for example, although people may not be subjected to unpleasant smells, atmosphere, noise, or other inconveniences, they are not entitled to object if they are faced with an unpleasant vista. It is not an act of nuisance for a landowner to create or permit the existence of an eyesore on land adjoining a neighbour's property.[16]

Whether the defendant's activity will be classified as a nuisance depends on a variety of factors which have to be taken into account when determining the issue of liability. These include the nature of the locality where the alleged nuisance is said to be committed;[17] whether the defendant was making a reasonable or unreasonable use of the defendant's land;[18] and the intensity and duration of the alleged nuisance. Any interference that is substantial and results in the loss of convenience on the part of the plaintiff will be wrongful, as long as the reason why the plaintiff suffers is not because he or she is abnormally sensitive and so incurs such inconvenience when the ordinary reasonable person would not. Thus if the plaintiff is unusually allergic to some smell or fumes, or is carrying on a particularly sensitive trade or occupation that is susceptible to the heat emanating from the defendant's land when a normal occupation would be unaffected, such plaintiff may not be able to claim to be the victim of an actionable nuisance.[19] The plaintiff's enjoyment of land, and life on such land, must be significantly affected by the defendant's conduct if the latter is to be characterized as a nuisance in law.[20] Anything can therefore amount to such a nuisance, whether it be building a structure close to the plaintiff's land or house so as to interrupt the free flow of air or light to the latter; burning rubbish so as to make a profuse

---

15 *Nor-Video Services Ltd. v. Ontario Hydro* (1978), 19 O.R. (2d) 107 (H.C.). This may be a questionable decision: see *St. Pierre v. Ontario (Minister of Transportation & Communications)* (1987), 40 C.C.L.T. 200 (S.C.C.); *Hunter v. Canary Wharf Ltd.*, [1997] A.C. 655.

16 *Walker v. Pioneer Construction Co. (1967) Ltd.* (1975), 56 D.L.R. (3d) 677 (Ont. H.C.).

17 *Royal Anne Hotel Co. v. Village of Ashcroft* (1979), 95 D.L.R. (3d) 756 (B.C.C.A.).

18 *Zbarsky v. Lukashuk* (1991), 61 B.C.L.R. (2d) 349 (C.A.). Hence a landowner who, negligently, neglects a natural hazard that threatens and ultimately interferes with a neighbour's property may be guilty of an unreasonable use of land: *Leakey v. National Trust for Places of Historical Interest or Natural Beauty*, [1980] 1 All E.R. 17; *PPG Canada Inc. v. R.B. Collier Ltd.* (1991), 7 C.C.L.T. (2d) 31 (N.S.T.D.); *Hayes v. Davis* (1991), 54 B.C.L.R. (2d) 350 (C.A.); *Doucette v. Parent* (1996), 31 C.C.L.T. (2d) 190 (Ont. Gen. Div.).

19 *Robinson v. Kilvert* (1889), 41 Ch. D. 58 (C.A.); contrast *McKinnon Industries Ltd. v. Walker*, [1951] 3 D.L.R. 577 (P.C.).

20 *Muirhead v. Timber Brothers Sand & Gravel Ltd.* (1977), 3 C.C.L.T. 1 (Ont. H.C.).

cloud of smoke that makes the plaintiff's eyes smart or prevents the plaintiff from seeing; or preventing the plaintiff from making use of a path which he or she is entitled to use (by way of easement) in order to get to the highway.

In this respect it should be mentioned that the law of nuisance is closely involved with the law relating to easements, profits *à prendre*, and licences, that is those rights which one person can give over land to another person. A wrongful interference with the enjoyment of such rights may amount to a nuisance, whether the interference is on the part of the grantor of the right or a third person.

In contrast with cases of damage to property resulting from a nuisance, the attitude of the law in cases now under discussion is less absolute, more relative. Thus it may be important to determine, for example, whether the defendant has exceeded the bounds of reasonable conduct in relation to the place where the nuisance occurred, the nature of what was being done, the steps taken to ensure that no harm would result to others. A nuisance of this kind only occurs where the defendant has been guilty of unreasonable use of land or unreasonable conduct.[21] The common law recognizes a doctrine of "give and take", "live and let live". People must accept the normal condition of the area in which they live or work. This does not mean, however, that a person who comes to a place and so suffers inconvenience which would have been avoided if that person had stayed away will be unable to claim that the conduct of the defendant is a nuisance.[22] Something which has not affected anyone prior to the advent of the plaintiff will become a nuisance once it affects the plaintiff. The defendant cannot claim to have acquired the right to commit a nuisance by the passage of time, except where such a claim is made against a plaintiff who has suffered the nuisance without complaint for the necessary length of time, *viz.* 20 years, to create a prescriptive right in the defendant as against the plaintiff in question.[23] But such a prescriptive right applies only to the specific property. It will not validate the nuisance against the whole world.[24]

The defendant's frame of mind is also relevant. Where it is claimed that all the defendant is doing is making a reasonable use of land, the defendant's motives or negligence will be a factor in determining whether or not the conduct in question amounts to an actionable nuisance. Despite the decision of the House of Lords at the end of the 19th century, to the effect that a bad motive could not turn a lawful act into an unlawful, tortious one[25] there have been decisions since then clearly indicating that if the purpose for the commission of the act which damaged the plaintiff was not the legitimate use of land by the defendant but the desire to injure the plaintiff — there being no valid, lawful reason to support the

---

21 *Kent v. Dominion Steel & Coal Corp.* (1964), 49 D.L.R. (2d) 241 (Nfld. S.C.); *Russell Transport Ltd. v. Ontario Malleable Iron Co.*, [1952] 4 D.L.R. 719 (Ont. H.C.). But the natural growth of tree roots may involve a nuisance: *Mendez v. Palazzi* (1976), 68 D.L.R. (3d) 582 (Ont. Co. Ct.).

22 *Morley v. Dubinsky* (1966), 59 D.L.R. (2d) 217 (N.S.S.C.); *Miller v. Jackson*, [1977] 3 All E.R. 338.

23 *Sturges v. Bridgeman* (1879), 11 Ch. D. 852.

24 Note also the effect of statutes such as the *Easements Act*, R.S.N.B. 1973, c. E-1, s. 1.

25 *Bradford Corp. v. Pickles*, [1895] A.C. 587.

infliction of such injury — then the defendant will be guilty of nuisance. For example, it has been held that shooting guns, which frightened the plaintiff's animals, or banging on walls, which prevented the plaintiff from exercising her profession of music teacher, involved liability for nuisance when in each instance the aim of the defendant was simply to annoy, harm, or avenge himself upon the plaintiff.[26] Promoting one's legitimate economic or similar interests at the expense of someone else is one thing; deliberately and maliciously going out of one's way to harm another person is quite different.

Even if the defendant does not intend or desire to commit a nuisance, liability will ensue if the defendant's foresight of potential harm from a legitimate activity or use of land in question and neglect of reasonable steps to preclude such harm result in the interference or inconvenience of which the plaintiff complains.[27] Indeed, if what the defendant wishes to do on the land cannot be done without causing the nuisance, no matter how much care and skill were to be employed by the defendant, the fact that the defendant carried on with the activity and the nuisance followed will suffice for liability.[28]

4. THE RANGE OF LIABILITY

Usually the one who creates a nuisance is the occupier of the land or premises from which the nuisance emanates,[29] even if the nuisance is the result of the actions of the occupier's independent contractor (not agent or servant — for whose acts alone an employer will usually be responsible).[30] By "occupier" here is meant one who is the owner, lessee or licensee of the land or premises. However one who creates on land or premises occupied by someone else the situation from which a nuisance emerges will be liable as the creator of the nuisance. If the occupier is ignorant that the land or premises are in such a state that a nuisance is being, or can be committed against another person or another's property, liability will not ensue, where the acts of an independent contractor of the

---

26 *Hollywood Silver Fox Farm Ltd. v. Emmett*, [1936] 2 K.B. 468; *Christie v. Davey*, [1893] 1 Ch. 316; *cf. MacGibbon v. Robinson*, [1952] 4 D.L.R. 142 (B.C.S.C.), affirmed [1953] 2 D.L.R. 689 (B.C.C.A.).

27 *Cf. Cowan v. Harrington*, [1938] 3 D.L.R. 271 with *Nikka Overseas Agency v. Canada Trust Co.* (1961), 31 D.L.R. (2d) 368. See also *Zbarsky v. Lukashuk* (1991), 61 B.C.L.R. (2d) 349 (C.A.). *Leakey v. National Trust for Places of Historical Interest or Natural Beauty*, [1980] 1 All E.R. 17; *PPG Canada Inc. v. R.B. Collier Ltd.* (1991), 7 C.C.L.T. (2d) 31 (N.S.T.D.); *Hayes v. Davis* (1991), 54 B.C.L.R. (2d) 350 (C.A.); *Doucette v. Parent* (1996), 31 C.C.L.T. (2d) 190 (Ont. Gen. Div.).

28 *B.C. Pea Growers v. Portage la Prairie* (1964), 49 D.L.R. (2d) 91 (Man. C.A.).

29 An owner of land out of possession, because the owner has granted another person a lease or license to occupy the land, has sometimes been held liable in nuisance even though not personally guilty of creating the offending situation: see, for example, *Aldridge v. Van Patter*, [1952] O.R. 595 (S.C.); *Banfai v. Formula Fun Centre Inc.* (1985), 51 O.R. (2d) 361 (H.C.). These, it is suggested, are anomalous cases based on the owner's foresight of possible harm arising from the activity of the lessee or licensee.

30 Above p. 36.

occupier are not in issue, except in two circumstances, both of which involve the factor of negligence.[31]

One is where someone who is not the creator of the nuisance "continues" the nuisance. This will occur when the occupier, who knows or has reasonable means of knowledge of the existence of the nuisance, fails within a reasonable time to take steps to terminate the situation that leads to the nuisance. The other is where the occupier "adopts" the nuisance. This occurs when the nuisance has been created, or permitted to develop, by a previous occupier, the current occupier knows or ought to have known of its existence, and fails to do anything to prevent the occurrence of the nuisance. In both instances the occupier has made the nuisance his or her own. Such liability for a nuisance not originally created by the occupier stem from the fact that nuisance, unlike trespass, does not necessarily consist of one single act that causes damage. It involves a continuing state of affairs. Nuisance flows from the creation or continuance of a situation as a result of which there is damage to the property of the victim, personal injury to such victim, or serious inconvenience. Such a situation may result in the harm in question only once. That will suffice, as already noted, if proprietary or personal damage is the consequence. If inconvenience is alleged, perhaps something more than one isolated occasion may be essential before liability can follow, although it has been said that the loss of a night's sleep by itself is enough to found an action.[32] Whichever is the case, the foundation of liability is the fact that originally or subsequently the defendant permitted the existence of a state of affairs that was capable of producing, and did produce, harm to the plaintiff. In situations in which the wrongdoer did not personally create the relevant situation, it having been created or caused by some other person outside the defendant's control, or an act of nature (*e.g.*, lightning setting alight a tree), the defendant will nonetheless be liable if it can be shown that he or she was negligent in not putting an end to the dangerous or potentially dangerous situation once there was knowledge or the means of such knowledge of its existence.[33]

5. WHO MAY SUE

Whereas liability for nuisance, as seen above, may be spread widely, and encompass not only the creator of the nuisance but others, the right to sue in nuisance is, or, until a recent decision in Canada, was confined to those who owned or had some other legal or equitable interest in the land on which the effect of the nuisance, whether damage to person or property or inconvenience, was felt. Leading cases in England held that if the wife or friend of an occupier of land or premises were injured as a consequence of a nuisance committed by the defendant, no action in nuisance could be brought by such person, although, in appropriate circumstances, an alternative action, such as negligence, might be

---

31 *Sedleigh-Denfield v. O'Callaghan*, [1940] A.C. 880.

32 *Andreae v. Selfridge & Co.*, [1938] Ch. 1 at 8 *per* Greene M.R.

33 *Goldman v. Hargrave*, [1967] 1 A.C. 645. See also the judgment of Matas J.A. in *Penno v. Government of Manitoba* (1976), 64 D.L.R. (3d) 256 at 269-278 (Man. C.A.).

brought.[34] This doctrine was called in question and rejected by the Alberta Court of Appeal in *Motherwell v. Motherwell*,[35] to which reference was made earlier.[36] There it was held, despite the earlier English decisions, that the wife of the occupier of the land could sue for a nuisance which took the form of an invasion of privacy or harassment. Some subsequent English cases appear to have approved and followed this Canadian one. However, as noted earlier, in *Hunter v. Canary Wharf Ltd.*[37] certain members of the House of Lords regarded *Motherwell* as incorrect. Perhaps the Canadian decision can be treated as valid in the special circumstances of the case, and not as invalidating completely the principle that one who has no interest in the land where the nuisance is suffered, for example, a lawful visitor or a trespasser (but not, perhaps, a squatter who is in the process of acquiring title by prescription or the limitation of actions), does not come within the ambit and protection of the law of nuisance.

6. EXCLUSION OF LIABILITY

The possibility that a right to commit what otherwise would be a nuisance by prescription has previously been mentioned. Such a right may be acquired by 20 years uninterrupted use of land by the defendant that causes the nuisance. Such use must be open, without involving violence and not by virtue of any agreement between the defendant and the victim of the nuisance. Once the 20 years have passed no action for nuisance will lie as between the one who suffered the nuisance for that time and the one responsible for it. But a successor in title to the former will not be precluded from claiming in nuisance, unless the effect of the expiration of the 20-year period has been to create an easement in favour of the one guilty of the nuisance. An easement attaches to the "dominant" tenement, the land on which the nuisance is created, and operates against the "servient" tenement, the land on which the nuisance is suffered. However the common law of prescription has been affected by various provincial statutes, the contents and effect of which differ.

That the plaintiff came to the nuisance, rather than the nuisance coming to the plaintiff, will not be a defence. However there may be circumstances in which the consent of the plaintiff to the activity being carried on by the defendant will exclude any liability of the latter for nuisance.

The most important limitation upon possible liability for nuisance, however, is the defence of statutory authority. A statute may provide for some immunity, either absolute or qualified, in respect of doing acts which would otherwise entail liability for nuisance. By and large it would be true to say that such statutory protection is given to governmental authorities, federal, provincial or municipal, rather than to private persons, though it would be possible and entirely lawful for a legislature to confer similar immunity or privilege from liability upon a

---

34 *Malone v. Laskey*, [1907] 2 K.B. 141; *Cunard v. Antifyre Ltd.*, [1933] 1 K.B. 551.

35 (1977), 73 D.L.R. (3d) 62 (Alta. C.A.).

36 Above p. 59.

37 [1997] A.C. 655.

private individual. Indeed, insofar as such privileges have been confered upon certain types of corporations of a *quasi*-governmental or public nature, albeit that they are not instruments or organs of any type of government, legislatures have invested "private" persons with such authority to act without necessarily involving themselves in liability in tort. This will often be found to be the situation with respect to certain kinds of activity which, though "private" in one sense, as contrasted with governmental, are yet "public" in another, in that they provide services of a more general type, such as hospitals, sewage disposal, gas and electricity production and distribution.

Much depends, of course, upon the scope and language of the particular statute that is involved. What must be determined, first of all, is whether the statute concerned applies to the defendant whose conduct is in issue. Given that it does, the next question is whether the conduct in issue is within the scope of the statutory provisions. This involves deciding whether the statute confers powers or imposes duties upon the body in question, and construing the nature, meaning and extent of such powers or duties. This is a matter of statutory construction, necessitating the application of well-settled principles.[38] Thus, for example, courts will look very carefully at any suggestion that a statutory provision removes, or reduces, liability that would otherwise exist under the law of tort. There is a presumption that a legislature does not intend to interfere with private rights.[39] Second, it will be essential to decide whether the statute provides protection from liability in any event or only if the powers or duties concerned have been performed without negligence. If negligence is relevant, then it may be that the defendant has the burden of establishing that the power or duty in question was performed with the appropriate degree of care that was due in the circumstances.[40]

Under such statutes, the body concerned, *e.g.*, a municipal government, or utilities corporation, is empowered, even obliged, to carry on an undertaking, such as sewage disposal, or manufacture of gas or electricity, which will almost inevitably result in some dislocation of the environment, and interference with the condition of the land in question carrying with it some increased danger of interference with, and danger to the land of adjoining occupiers. If this were being done by a private individual or corporation, the consequences might give rise to liability in tort if damage or interference resulted. The mere fact that the activity in question might be considered for the public benefit would not at common law entitle the tortfeasor to escape liability. The existence of some statutory authorization for the carrying on of the undertaking may create a difference.

Exactly what difference will depend upon whether there are several ways in which the undertaking can be performed. If it can be done without causing harm

---

[38] These are discussed at length in *Tock v. St. John's Metropolitan Area Board* (1989), 64 D.L.R. (4th) 620 (S.C.C.).

[39] Private rights are guarded very jealously, so that the defence of statutory authority is not overly favoured by the courts: *Ryan v. Victoria (City)* (1999), 44 C.C.L.T. (2d) 1 (B.C.C.A.).

[40] See *Ryan v. Victoria (City)* (1999), 44 C.C.L.T. (2d) 1 (B.C.C.A.); *Rideau Falls Generative Partnership v. Ottawa (City)* (1999), 174 D.L.R. (4th) 160 (Ont. S.C.J.).

to others, such as adjoining occupiers, the statutory power or duty may be construed by a court as being one which only authorizes the body concerned to carry on the undertaking, not to do so without the possibility of liability in the event that damage or harm follows. The fact that it does follow may indicate that the body concerned had not used reasonable care or behaved in a reasonable way in performing the undertaking. If, on the other hand, the duty or power is absolute, or the undertaking can only be performed in one way, which can or might inevitably result in the interference, damage or harm concerned, then there will be no liability for nuisance.[41]

7. REMEDIES FOR NUISANCE

Usually, as with most, if not all torts, the appropriate common law remedy for a nuisance is an award of damages, especially where the nuisance has caused physical damage to the plaintiff or to property. In such an action damages may also be awarded for any consequential loss occurring because of the damage, such as loss of rent or dimunition in the value of a building.[42]

In cases of nuisance, however, an award of damages may not be satisfactory for the future protection of the plaintiff. Hence it may be possible for the plaintiff to obtain an injunction. Such remedy was equitable, not common law, in origin but, since courts can now award either kind of remedy, may be granted, in place of or in addition to damages, where damages would not adequately take care of the problem.[43] However, the granting of an injunction is a matter of discretion for the court, and will depend on numerous factors. Injunctions, if granted, may be permanent or temporary as far as their duration is concerned. They may also be mandatory — ordering the defendant to do something positive, such as pull down a wall — or prohibitive — ordering the defendant to stop doing something, such as emitting smoke from a factory. An injunction may also be awarded "before" the defendant has actually caused a nuisance, if the defendant is threatening or proposing to undertake an activity which will inevitably create a nuisance. Such *quia timet* injunctions can be granted to prohibit such activity in advance. A curious consequence of this is that, since a court can refuse an injunction but award damages, it may be possible for damages to be awarded to a plaintiff before the plaintiff has incurred damage or loss[44] (which is the antithesis of the way the common law operates).

A third possible remedy for a plaintiff injuriously affected by a nuisance is that of abatement, which occurs when the plaintiff takes steps to terminate the continuation of the nuisance. Such self-help, although recognized as possible in some circumstances, is not favoured by the law, because it may lead to distur-

---

41 *Metropolitan Asylum District v. Hill* (1881), 6 App. Cas. 193; *Manchester Corp. v. Farnworth*, [1930] A.C. 171; *Dunne v. North Western Gas Board*, [1964] 2 Q.B. 806 (C.A.).

42 *340909 Ontario Ltd. v. Huron Steel Products (Windsor) Ltd.* (1990), 73 O.R. (2d) 641 (H.C.), affirmed (1992), 9 O.R. (3d) 305*n* (C.A.).

43 *Shelfer v. London Electric Lighting Co.*, [1895] 1 Ch. 287.

44 *Leeds Industrial Co-operative Society v. Slack*, [1924] A.C. 851.

bance of the peace and, perhaps, other damage. Nonetheless, in appropriate situations, as long as it is carried out in a manner that does not cause damage to the land from which the nuisance emanates[45] or is otherwise not offensive,[46] abatement may be possible.

[45] *Richardson v. Thorkelson* (1995), 99 Man. R. (2d) 47 (Q.B.).
[46] *Stewart v. Gustafson* (1998), 171 Sask. R. 27 (Q.B.).

Chapter 7

THE TORT OF NEGLIGENCE

1. DUTIES OF CARE

Until almost the middle of the 20th century there was no unifying principle underlying the various situations in which liability could arise because of negligent, that is to say careless, behaviour. It was accepted that certain people who occupied certain positions, performed certain functions, or dealt with certain kinds of property, might be responsible if, through their failure to observe appropriate standards, harm was caused to others. The determination of those who bore such responsibility, those to whom that responsibility was owed, when that responsibility arose, and how it was to be analyzed and expressed in legal terms, were answered in piece-meal fashion. Negligence might lead to tortious liability on the part of, for example, an occupier of premises towards certain categories of visitors: one who transferred a dangerous chattel or a chattel known to be defective towards anyone who, eventually, used such chattel and was injured: an employer towards an employee. The state of the law was transformed by the decision of the House of Lords in *Donoghue v. Stevenson*[1] which effectively created a tort of negligence where, before, there were merely isolated instances of liability for negligence, by holding that the tort of negligence was committed whenever a person who was under a duty of care to another breached that duty and caused harm. Everything turned on whether such a duty was owed.

In this respect of particular importance was the language of Lord Atkin, who gave utterance to his now-famous "neighbour" principle of negligence liability. What he said was:

> . . . in English law there must be and is some general conception of relations giving rise to a duty of care, of which the particular cases found in the books are but instances. The liability for negligence . . . is no doubt based upon a general public sentiment of moral wrongdoing for which the offender must pay. But acts or omissions which any moral code would censure cannot in a practical world be treated so as to give a right to every person injured by them to demand relief. The rule that you are to love your neighbour becomes in law: You must not injure your neighbour, and the lawyer's question: Who is my neighbour? receives a restricted reply. You must take reasonable care to avoid acts or omissions which you can reasonably foresee would be likely to injure your neighbour. Who then, in law, is my

---

1 [1932] A.C. 562.

> neighbour? The answer seems to be persons who are so closely and directly affected by my act that I ought reasonably to have them in contemplation as being so affected when I am directing my mind to the acts of omissions which are called in question.[2]

To the elements of foresight, likelihood of injury, reasonable care, Lord Atkin added another notion, that of "proximity", as being material to determine whether a duty of care existed so as to involve liability for an act or omission that caused harm. A person owes a duty of care, therefore, to anyone whom he or she ought reasonably to have contemplated would be likely to be injured, as a proximate result of such act or omission, so that his or her failure to observe such duty, by acting or omitting to act in a manner that was careless, would result in his or her liability in negligence for such damage as resulted. One purpose of the "neighbour" principle of Lord Atkin was to justify the extension of the law that governed previous instances of liability for negligence to the case before the House of Lords. This involved personal injury caused by a defective product, ginger beer, which was in a bottle in which there was, or was alleged to be a decomposed or decomposing snail. The injury was suffered by someone who had not purchased the ginger beer. The decision in this case made it clear that the contractual doctrine of privity of contract, by virtue of which the injured party would not have had a remedy because she was not a party to the contract under which the ginger beer bottle was sold, did not preclude recovery. The injured party was not suing, and did not have a remedy against the retail supplier of the bottle of ginger beer. She was suing the manufacturer of the ginger beer. Hence, transcending the contract of sale and the duties which arose thereunder as between seller and buyer, there was another duty, owed by a different party, not the seller, and not arising out of contract, that was owed to persons other than the party to the contract of sale. It was a tortious not a contractual duty. And, as Lord Atkin explained, it was not a specific duty restricted in application to one specific fact-situation, but a general duty capable of applying to many different fact-situations.

What emerged from *Donoghue v. Stevenson* was the idea that there could be jural relationships based upon a nexus other than contract, even where there was no other connecting factor such as fraud, ownership of property, occupation of land or premises, or the intent to cause injury. For there to be liability for harm caused by one person to another a "duty of care" had to be owed by the former to the latter. The existence of such a duty was not enough by itself. But such a duty was a *sine qua non* of liability, an essential condition. As Lord Macmillan pointed out in *Donoghue v. Stevenson*: "The law takes no cognizance of carelessness in the abstract. It concerns itself with carelessness only where there is a duty to take care and where failure in that duty has caused damage".[3] Whether such a duty was owed was, to a large extent, dependent upon the notion of "risk". *Negligence* is based upon the risk of injury to another. Carelessness may exist without risk: negligence refers and relates to the risk of injury. Risk, in

---

2 *Ibid.*, at 580.

3 *Ibid.*, at 618.

turn, depends upon what is foreseeable by the reasonable man. In this way the law imposes obligations upon people in circumstances in which: (a) it is desirable; and (b) it is practicable to make them behave in a certain way, or make amends in the form of paying damages if they do not.

The problem, however, has been to express the scope of the tort of negligence in language that gives sufficient flexibility to enable courts to apply the notion of duty of care, and therefore the tort of negligence, in appropriate circumstances without being so broad and general as to be too expansive. Forty years after Lord Atkin's promulgation of the "neighbour" principle, in *Anns v. Merton London Borough Council*, Lord Wilberforce attempted to explain how that principle could be applied.

> . . . in order to establish that a duty of care arises in a particular situation, it is not necessary to bring the facts of that situation within those of previous situations in which a duty of care has been held to exist. Rather the question has to be approached in two stages. First one has to ask whether, as between the alleged wrongdoer and the person who has suffered damage there is a sufficient relationship of proximity or neighbourhood such that, in the reasonable contemplation of the former, carelessness on his part may be likely to cause damage to the latter — in which case a prima facie duty of care arises. Secondly, if the first question is answered affirmatively, it is necessary to consider whether there are any considerations which ought to negative, or to reduce or limit the scope of the duty or the class of person to whom it is owed or the damages to which a breach of duty may give rise. . . .[4]

This formulation of a two-stage or two-step process, entailing first the question of foresight and/or proximity and second the question of policy, was accepted by the Supreme Court of Canada[5] and, thereafter, frequently elaborated and applied by that and other courts.[6] However it was later rejected by the House of Lords[7] in favour of a three-stage test of forseeability, proximity, justice, and reasonableness. It was also originally rejected by the High Court of Australia in favour of an "incremental" approach.[8] The latter court now appears to have changed its mind and abandoned both the three-stage test of the post-*Anns* House of Lords and its own incremental approach in favour of a multi-factoral approach seeking to find salient features that point to a duty of care: which may entail looking at, and following previous authoritative decisions.[9]

Recently, while continuing to endorse the *Anns* approach, the Supreme Court of Canada may have changed the meaning, content and application of

---

4 [1978] A.C. 728 at 751.

5 In *Nielsen v. Kamloops (City)* (1984), 10 D.L.R. (4th) 641 (S.C.C.).

6 See *e.g.*, *Ryan v. Victoria (City)* (1999), 168 D.L.R. (4th) 513 (S.C.C.); *Ingles v. Tutkaluk Construction Ltd.* (2000), 183 D.L.R. (4th) 193 (S.C.C.).

7 In *Murphy v. Brentwood District Council*, [1991] 1 A.C. 398: *Caparo Industries plc v. Dickman*, [1990] 2 A.C. 605.

8 *Sutherland Shire Council v. Heyman* (1985), 157 C.L.R. 424.

9 *Sullivan v. Moody* (2001), 183 A.L.R. 404.

that approach by the way in which the court explained how the concepts of reasonable foresight, proximity and policy were to be understood and applied.[10] Proximity, in particular, was said to be explicable and was to be established by reference to analogous categories of cases in which proximity has been recognized. This suggests that, like the Australian court, the Canadian court has taken a less expansive view of the scope of the tort of negligence, even though, as was said in *Donoghue v. Stevenson*, there was no limit to the creation of "new" instances of a duty of care since "the categories of negligence are never closed".[11]

2. FORESIGHT, PROXIMITY, AND POLICY

These three ingredients, or necessary elements, of a duty of care are closely intertwined. Foresight of potential harm entails the existence of a sufficient proximity of relationship between the defendant and the potential victim, a proximity that is not necessarily, though it possibly may be, physical.[12] Proximity requires an examination of the expectations, representations, reliance, and property interests involved in any given situation.[13] But a conclusion about proximity for the purpose of deciding whether a duty of care was owed also involves broad questions of policy.[14] These are not the same questions as are raised under the second stage of the *Anns* approach. Policy in relation to proximity is a matter of determining whether, given the relationship between the parties, it is just and fair to impose a legal duty of care on the defendant. The issues of policy that are raised under the second stage of *Anns* concern the effect of recognizing a duty of care on other legal obligations, the legal system and society generally.[15] It must be asked whether the law already provides a remedy (as it did in the

---

10 *Cooper v. Hobart* (2002), 206 D.L.R. (4th) 193 (S.C.C.). See also *Edwards v. Law Society of Upper Canada* (2002), 206 D.L.R. (4th) 211 (S.C.C.).

11 [1932] A.C. 562 at 619 *per* Lord Macmillan.

12 For example, where the parties are both road users and negligence by one results in a collision.

13 *Hercules Managements Ltd. v. Ernst & Young* (1997), 146 D.L.R. (4th) 577 (S.C.C.); *Canadian National Railway v. Norsk Pacific Steamship Co.* (1992), 91 D.L.R. (4th) 289 (F.C.T.D.); *Cooper v. Hobart*, (2002), 206 D.L.R. (4th) 193 (S.C.C.).

14 *Cooper v. Hobart* (2002), 206 D.L.R. (4th) 193 (S.C.C.).

15 In this respect courts in Canada have been required to consider whether, when a public authority is alleged to have acted negligently, the alleged negligence was in the making of a "policy" decision (in respect of which there would be no liability in the absence of proof that the authority acted maliciously, with intent to cause harm): *Welbridge Holdings Ltd. v. Greater Winnipeg (Municipality)* (1970), 22 D.L.R. (3d) 470 (S.C.C.); or occurred in the carrying out, the "operation", of the policy (in respect of which liability for such negligence is possible): *Just v. British Columbia* (1989), 64 D.L.R. (4th) 689 (B.C.S.C.); *Brown v. British Columbia (Minister of Transportation & Highways)* (1994), 112 D.L.R. (4th) 1 (S.C.C.); *Swinamer v. Nova Scotia (Attorney-General)* (1994), 112 D.L.R. (4th) 18 (S.C.C.); *Ingles v. Tutkaluk Construction Ltd.* (2000), 183 D.L.R. (4th) 19 (S.C.C.). This distinction has been criticized in England, where the test of liability is whether the statute creates a common law duty of care: *Stovin v. Wise*, [1996] A.C. 923.

Cooper and *Edwards* cases).[16] The Court should consider whether recognizing a duty of care would create the spectre of unlimited liability to an unlimited class (which was the problem that exercised courts when the question of imposing liability for negligent misrepresentations came before them).[17] It was also to be taken into account whether there were other reasons of broad policy standing in the way of recognizing a duty of care in the particular circumstances. What is involved in this last factor can be illustrated by comparing an English case[18] which held that police were not under a duty of care towards the public in respect of the manner in which they dealt with someone later found to be the "Yorkshire Ripper" with a Canadian case[19] in which police were held to have been guilty of a breach of a duty of care to certain members of the public, women living in a particular area, in not giving them information about a rapist that might have prevented the attack that occurred on the plaintiff.

Foresight and proximity, though distinct, are connected in meaning and application. Policy, although to some extent an aspect of proximity, is a distinct factor that can come into play once a court has determined, by the application of the concepts of foresight and proximity to the facts of a case, that *prima facie* a duty of care arose in the circumstances. Without in any way minimizing the relevance and importance of proximity and policy, it is suggested that the first, and most vital issue before a court in this context is the issue of foresight of harm. Should it not be incumbent on a defendant to foresee the "probability" of harm (a mere possibility will not suffice),[20] no duty of care will be owed; and, consequently, such defendant cannot be liable for negligence.

3. FORESIGHT IN RELATION TO DUTY

Whether a duty of care was owed in the particular circumstances of an individual case is in the first instance a matter of determining whether, given the circumstances in question, the defendant should have foreseen the possibility of harm to the victim. The answer to this inquiry involves consideration of the notion of *risk*. In all instances the issue is whether the risk of what happened was within the contemplation not of the particular defendant accused of negligence but of the reasonable person in the position of that defendant, the alleged

---

16 *Cooper v. Hobart* (2002), 206 D.L.R. (4th) 193 (S.C.C.); *Edwards v. Law Society of Upper Canada* (2002), 206 D.L.R. (4th) 211 (S.C.C.) These cases involved provincial legislation which governed the activities of the defendants and was couched in such terms that anyone injuriously affected by a breach of the legislation was not permitted any personal, private law remedy. See further below p. 108, on the subject of liablity for breach of a statutory duty. *Cf.* what is said above at note 15 on the "policy/operation" dichotomy.

17 Below pp. 102-105.

18 *Hill v. Chief Constable of West Yorkshire*, [1989] 2 All E.R. 238.

19 *Jane Doe v. Metropolitan Toronto (Municipality) Commissioners of Police* (1989), 58 D.L.R. (4th) 396 (Ont. H.C.), affirmed (1990), 74 O.R. (2d) 225 (Div. Ct.), leave to appeal refused (1991), 1 O.R. (3d) 416*n* (C.A.); (1998), 39 O.R. (3d) 487 (Gen. Div.).

20 *Engele v. Poss* (1959), 16 D.L.R. (2d) 430 (Sask. C.A.); *Oke v. Weide Transport Ltd.* (1964), 41 D.L.R. (2d) 53 (Man. C.A.); *Sturdy v. The Queen* (1974), 47 D.L.R. (3d) 71 (F.C.T.D.).

wrongdoer, such that the latter ought to have acted with reasonable care and skill to avoid what happened.

This notion of risk is compounded of many elements. In the first place it is necessary to bear in mind the degree of danger that was to be expected from the particular activity involved. This may also involve a consideration of the extent of the danger to particular individuals. Thus if a certain activity is more dangerous to some persons (whose existence is known to the actor) than it would be to others, there is a risk inherent in this activity even though, usually, there would be none. As was held in a leading English case,[21] it is not only the greater risk of injury that is relevant, it is also the risk of greater injury. Thus the existence of a duty of care will depend to some extent upon the possibility and scope of danger from what the person whose conduct is in question is engaged upon doing. Second, the difficulty and expense of preventing harm from what is being done are also material. If it would be possible, but prohibitive or unreasonable, to act in a way which would preclude any danger, *e.g.*, by refraining from the activity in question, or taking such precautions as would render the enterprise useless or unprofitable, then in some situations, there may be no obligation to exercise care. The real issue is whether the comparison between possible danger and what is required to prevent or avoid it produces the conclusion that it is reasonable or unreasonable in the circumstances to expect the person in question to take steps which would avoid any harm to others.[22] A third element to be considered is whether what is being done by the person whose conduct is in question is so important, in comparison with possible harmful consequences, as to justify the action in question even though there may be danger to others as a result.[23] The achievement of some generally worthwhile purpose may permit someone to act without being subject to any duty of care to others, despite potential danger. Of course, for the law to allow someone to escape from any obligation to use care when he or she is doing something inherently dangerous, will only take place very infrequently, in the same way that the idea of necessity will excuse someone from culpability only rarely. Yet it must be mentioned that the question of risk is, in some degree, affected by the nature of what is being perpetrated by the person said to be under a duty of care. In this respect, also, the issue is the reasonableness or unreasonableness of what is being done.

The question is ultimately whether a reasonable person,[24] in the position of the alleged wrongdoer, would have foreseen, in the ordinary course of things, that his or her acts or omissions might probably cause harm in such a way and to

---

21 *Paris v. Stepney Borough Council*, [1951] A.C. 367; as to abnormally sensitive persons, outside the scope of foreseeable injury, see *Munshaw Colour Service Ltd. v. City of Vancouver*, [1962] S.C.R. 433.

22 *Latimer v. A.E.C. Ltd.*, [1953] A.C. 643: *Morris v. West Hartlepool Steam Navigation Co. Ltd.*, [1956] A.C. 522; *Goldman v. Hargrave*, [1967] 1 A.C. 645 (C.A.). See also below pp. 87-90, in relation to standards of care.

23 *Schacht v. R.*, [1973] 1 O.R. 221 (C.A.), varied (1974), 55 D.L.R. (3d) 96 (S.C.C.); *Millette v. Cote*, [1971] 2 O.R. 155 (H.C.), affirmed [1972] 3 O.R. 224 (C.A.), affirmed [1976] 1 S.C.R. 595; *Vallery v. Po* (1971), 23 D.L.R. (3d) 92 (B.C.S.C.); *Priestman v. Colangelo*, [1959] S.C.R. 615; *Beim v. Cooper*, [1965] S.C.R. 638.

24 Children and mentally handicapped persons can be regarded differently; *cf.* Chapter 3 at p. 27.

such an extent that harm could reasonably have been, and ought to have been prevented. The reasonable man or woman is not expected to foresee or take steps to guard against something which is totally out of the ordinary, and therefore not capable of being avoided by ordinary reasonable care, and is not expected to take steps to avoid something which is comparatively trivial in nature, nor to go to extreme and unreasonable lengths, in terms of cost, difficulty, and trouble, nor obliged to use care when the circumstances make it unreasonable to do so in order to achieve an ultimate object, which is more important even than the prevention of harm to others. He or she is expected, however, to attempt to prevent a danger that is foreseeable; one that is likely to cause serious harm to another; one that is within his or her physical and financial resources to prevent, at least insofar as reasonable precautions may do so; and one that outweighs the possible value of what he or she is doing.

Many examples can be culled from the decided cases to illustrate when something was foreseeable, so as to oblige a defendant to exercise reasonable care,[25] and when what happened was not foreseeable, so that the defendant owed no duty of care to the plaintiff.[26] The novelty of the situation will not by itself mean that no duty of care was owed, as long as the situation satisfied the criteria for such a duty referred to above.[27] Thus, in recent years, courts have held tavern owners to be under a duty of care to take reasonable steps to protect patrons from causing harm to themselves once they have left the tavern's premises because they have become intoxicated;[28] and, as held in *Stewart v. Pettie*,[29] under a duty of care to third parties who might be expected to be harmed by the conduct of a tavern's patron, for example, one who, though intoxicated, drives a vehicle that causes injury to another person. Doctors have been held to be under a duty of care to their patients not only to operate upon them with reasonable care and skill but also to provide warning of the risks inherent in any medical procedure so that the patient can make an informed choice whether to submit to such procedure.[30] Public authorities have been held to owe a duty of care to those who could be injured if the authority failed to carry out with reasonable care and skill some power entrusted to the authority, not only when the activity in question related to the condition of public highways,[31] but also when it was concerned with the standards to be observed in the construction of a house.[32]

There are two other important aspects of the problem of risk. Since there is no such thing as negligence in the abstract, it must always be asked whether the

---

[25] See *e.g.*, *Bain v. Calgary Board of Education* (1993), 14 Alta. L.R. (3d) 319 (Q.B.), teacher towards adult student climbing a mountain.

[26] *Nespolon v. Alford* (1998), 40 O.R. (3d) 355 (C.A.), friends allowing intoxicated friend to leave car.

[27] *Crocker v. Sundance Northwest Resorts Ltd.*, [1988] 1 S.C.R. 1186.

[28] *Jordan House Ltd. v. Menow* (1973), 38 D.L.R. (3d) 105 (S.C.C.).

[29] (1995), 25 Alta. L.R. (3d) 297 (S.C.C.).

[30] *Reibl v. Hughes* (1980), 114 D.L.R. (3d) 1 (S.C.C.).

[31] See *e.g.*, *Just v. British Columbia* (1989), 64 D.L.R. (4th) 689 (B.C.S.C.).

[32] *Kamloops (City) v. Nielsen* (1984), 10 D.L.R. (4th) 641 (S.C.C.); *Rothfield v. Manolakos* (1989), 63 D.L.R. (4th) 449 (S.C.C.); *Ingles v. Tutkaluk Construction Ltd.* (2000), 183 D.L.R. (4th) 193 (S.C.C.).

victim, who actually suffered injury as a result of the defendant's actions, was within the scope of the defendant's contemplation before the defendant acted. Was the plaintiff foreseeable as a possible victim of the defendant's acts or omissions? Furthermore, was the harm suffered by the victim within the contemplation of the defendant? In other words, for there to be a duty of care owed by the defendant, there must be a foreseeable plaintiff who suffers foreseeable harm or damage. If the victim is not one who ought to have been contemplated by the defendant as being affected by the latter's acts or omissions, or the harm the victim incurred was outside the scope of reasonable contemplation, having regard to the situation and knowledge of the defendant, then there was no risk of injury or damage against which the defendant ought to have guarded. No duty of care will have been owed to the victim.

4. FORESEEABLE PLAINTIFFS

(a) Normal and Abnormal Victims

A person is only obliged to exercise care in respect of those whom he or she can foresee may be injuriously affected by his or her acts or omissions. This means that, normally, everyone should be aware of what is likely to occur to the ordinary reasonable person, as a consequence of what is done or not done. One does not have to look out for abnormal people, those suffering from some physical or other peculiarity which makes them more susceptible to injury, or susceptible when others would not be.[33]

Knowledge of the peculiarity of someone likely to be affected by one's acts will suffice to oblige the person so knowing to take care with respect to *that* individual and that individual's peculiar susceptibility. In the same way, if the likelihood of such "abnormal" persons being affected is not out of the ordinary, because there are sufficient of such persons who might be affected by the defendant's conduct, the latter will be obliged to exercise care with respect to such persons, not merely normal ones, even if this involves taking extra precautions that are not necessary to prevent injury to normal persons. This was stated by the House of Lords, in *Haley v. London Electricity Board*,[34] in which the House was concerned with the existence of a duty of care towards blind people, there being a significant minority of blind people in England generally, and therefore in the locality in which the defendants' actions were taking place. What the House did was to take the statistics for blind persons in the United Kingdom, and extrapolate from them the conclusion that the presence of blind persons was something which the defendants should have expected so as to involve them in taking steps to prevent injury from an obstruction in the street.

The principle is clear. To establish that a duty of care is owed by the defendant, the victim must belong to a class of persons who existence and likelihood

---

[33] *Cf. Nova Mink v. Trans-Canada Airlines*, [1951] 2 D.L.R. 241 (N.S.S.C.), damage to extra-sensitive minks.

[34] [1965] A.C. 778.

of being injured was reasonably capable of being contemplated and foreseen by the defendant, or must establish that the victim's peculiar likelihood of being injured was actually known by the defendant, who was aware of the victim's existence and proximity to the defendant and to what the defendant was doing.

(b) Victims of Emotional or Nervous Shock

The common law was originally concerned only with purely physical injuries. In the 19th century a decision of the Privy Council on appeal from Australia[35] held that a plaintiff could not recover damages in respect of alleged shock caused by the defendant's negligence. Their Lordships took the view that such shock was not easily attributable to the defendant's conduct. However some years later an English court decided that, if the shock could be traced to the defendant's negligence it was a kind of injury in respect of which a claim would lie.[36] Since that date courts have been prepared to award damages for nervous shock caused by a defendant's wrongful acts. By "shock" here is meant not simply grief or emotional distress but some recognizable and severe physical damage resulting from the effect on the senses of the victim of some external events.[37] The issue that has arisen in such cases is whether the nervous shock incurred by the plaintiff ought to have been foreseen by the defendant. The decided cases concern what the House of Lords more recently termed both "primary" and "secondary" victims of such shock.[38]

Primary victims are those who incurred the shock through fear of physical injury to themselves because, in the circumstances, such victim was within the contemplation of the defendant as being likely to be affected *physically* by the defendant's negligence. In such instances the question is not whether damage to the victim was foreseeable but whether damage in the form of nervous shock was foreseeable. In all such cases, therefore, no question as to duty of care arises.[39] Secondary victims are those who suffer nervous shock although such a victim was not in immediate danger of physical injury, but was shocked by reason of what the secondary victim saw or heard from other people. In such instances the victim who suffers shock is someone other than a person in respect of whom the defendant ought to have foreseen some injury, for example, where the defendant injures X by the defendant's negligence and Y suffers shock by seeing the accident or by being told about it later. The issue in such cases is whether the defendant owed a duty of care to Y to avoid causing Y injury in the form of nervous shock. In other words, it has to be determined whether Y was a foreseeable plaintiff.

To begin with, prior to the exposition of the tort of negligence in *Donoghue v. Stevenson*,[40] courts treated this question as one of causation, inquiring whether

---

35 *Victorian Railways Commissioners v. Coultas* (1888), 13 App. Cas. 222.
36 *Dulieu v. White & Sons*, [1901] 2 K.B. 669.
37 *MacLaughlin v. O'Brian*, [1982] 2 All E.R. 298 at 301 *per* Lord Wilberforce.
38 *Page v. Smith*, [1996] 1 A. C. 155.
39 The issue became one of remoteness of damage: *cf.* below pp. 82-85.
40 [1932] A.C. 562.

the shock to Y was a direct result of the defendant's negligence towards X.[41] In more recent times, because of the way in which the law relating to liability for negligence has evolved, courts have approached these situations by asking whether the defendant ought reasonably to have foreseen that by endangering X the defendant would be likely to cause shock to Y. In *McLaughlin v. O'Brian*[42] the House of Lords held that in such cases "reasonable foreseeability" was to be interpreted by reference to whether there was a close family relationship between X and Y; the proximity of Y to the accident after, if not at the time of its occurrence; and whether Y actually saw the accident or heard about it almost immediately. Courts in Canada, before[43] and after[44] the decision in *McLaughlin*, have also applied the idea of reasonable foresight that nervous shock would be caused to the plaintiff, Y. However the test of what is reasonably foreseeable and when something should be reasonably foreseeable for this purpose does not appear to have been formulated with any degree of certainty.[45]

(c) Unborn Children

As noted earlier, a person who is negligent may be liable if the victim suffers from some abnormality or defect that may make such victim more vulnerable, if the abnormality or defect is one that affects a sufficiently large section of the public that a reasonable person in the situation of the defendant ought to have contemplated the likelihood that his or her victim might belong to the class of persons with such abnormality or defect.[46] Hence a defendant will not be liable for causing nervous shock, despite what was said in the previous section, where the one suffering such shock does so only because that person is abnormally sensitive and suffers when someone not abnormally susceptible to shock would not. By way of contrast, a defendant can expect that someone who will be affected injuriously by his or her careless acts or omissions may be pregnant at the material time. Pregnancy is not such an abnormal condition or defect that it is not foreseeable by a defendant. The question is, however, whether one who negligently harms a pregnant woman, for which there is liability, can also be made liable for injury to the fetus carried by the woman when the unborn child is born and is discovered to have been harmed in some material way as a consequence of the defendant's negligent behaviour with respect to the mother.

41 *Hambrook v. Stokes Brothers*, [1925] 1 K.B. 141.

42 [1982] 2 All E.R. 298.

43 *Abramzik v. Brenner* (1966), 54 D.L.R. (2d) 639 (Sask. Q.B.), reversed (1967), 65 D.L.R. (2d) 651 (Sask. C.A.).

44 *Beecham v. Hughes* (1988), 52 D.L.R. (4th) 625 (B.C.C.A.); *Rhodes v. Canadian National Railway* (1990), 75 D.L.R. (4th) 248 (B.C.C.A.), leave to appeal refused (1991), 79 D.L.R. (4th) vii (S.C.C.).

45 See *e.g.*, *Devji v. Burnaby (District)* (1998), 158 D.L.R. (4th) 747 (B.C.S.C.), affirmed (1999), 47 C.C.L.T. (2d) 111 (B.C.C.A.), leave to appeal refused (2000), 260 N.R. 393*n*; *Vanek v. Great Atlantic & Pacific Co. of Canada* (1999), 48 O.R. (3d) 228 (C.A.), leave to appeal refused (2000), 264 N.R. 191*n* (S.C.C.).

46 Above p. 76.

Formerly it was held that whatever duty of care was owed to the mother, none was owed to the fetus.[47] A different view was taken in 1933 by the Supreme Court of Canada.[48] That decision was in accordance with the civil law of Quebec where the cause of action originated. However it was subsequently held in Ontario that at common law a duty of care was owed to a fetus, since it was foreseeable by a motorist that another user of the highway, whether another motorist, passenger or pedestrian, who might be injured by negligence might be pregnant, so that the child in the womb could also be affected.[49] Hence whenever there is a likelihood that an unborn child might be affected by an act of negligence, a duty of care to avoid such negligence will exist. To this, however, a qualification was recently added in *Dobson (Litigation Guardian of) v. Dobson*.[50] If the negligent person whose conduct caused, or helped to cause, injury to the unborn child is that child's mother, the mother cannot be made liable to the child. The justification of this decision was not that the child was an unforeseeable plaintiff, but a combination of the privacy rights of the mother and the difficulty of establishing a standard of conduct for pregnant women.

(d) Rescuers

The common law has also had to contend with the problem of determining the legal situation of the victim who brings about his or her own injury by intervening in a dangerous situation in order to save, or attempt to save, another person who has been endangered by the negligence of the defendant. In such circumstances the defendant has been guilty of a breach of a duty of care owed to the endangered party, and the issue is whether the defendant is also liable to the rescuer or would-be rescuer. One important issue raised by such cases is whether it is possible to conclude that the defendant also owed a duty of care to the rescuer or would-be rescuer.[51]

The approach of the courts has been along the lines of whether the defendant ought to have foreseen, in all the circumstances, that someone would be likely to attempt a rescue, and whether the nature of the attempt was reasonable in the sense that the intervention of the victim was foreseeable and in a foreseeable form.[52] Hence if the defendant by his or her negligence endangered people in a public street, on a railway train, on a ship, or in a well, and the rescuer or would-be rescuer did, or was trying to do what any reasonable person, similarly placed, would have been expected or foreseen to do, it has been held that the defendant owed a duty of care not only to the originally harmed or endangered victim, but also, and quite separately and distinctly, to the person who rescued or attempted

---

47 *Walker v. Great Northern Railway Co. of Ireland* (1891), 28 L.R. Ir. 69.

48 *Montreal Tramways Co. v. Leveille*, [1933] S.C.R. 456.

49 *Duval v. Seguin* (1972), 26 D.L.R. (3d) 418 (Ont. H.C.), affirmed (1974), 40 D.L.R. (3d) 666 (Ont. C.A.).

50 (1999), 174 D.L.R. (4th) 1 (S.C.C.).

51 Other issues raised in these cases have been whether the rescuer can be defeated by the defences of consent or contributory negligence: below pp. 90, 94.

52 *Dupuis v. New Regina Trading Co.*, [1943] 4 D.L.R. 275 (Sask. C.A.).

to rescue the other victim.[53] This has been the case where the rescuer suffered nervous shock as a result of what he saw while attempting a rescue,[54] and where the rescuer was endeavouring to rescue property, rather than a person, which had been endangered by the defendant's negligence.[55]

What has happened has been that the ambit of duties of care has been extended so as to afford protection and the privilege of the recovery of damages to a class of persons who might otherwise not be within the scope of the law. This has been done on the grounds that the policy of the law is to encourage and promote such desirable behaviour. As Cardozo J. said in a famous American case: "Danger invites rescue".[56] Hence it is not unreasonable to expect that the creation of a dangerous situation may lead to injury to others who come forward to help, and should be regarded and treated as being within the area of foreseeable risk and harm. Only if the conduct of the rescuer is ridiculous, unnecessary, or absurd, or involves the taking of risks which are irrelevant and excessive having regard to what is at stake, will the rescuer be outside the ambit of protection of a duty of care.[57] Of course, it must always be remembered that before a rescuer can claim to be within the scope of a duty of care: (a) a duty must have been owed to the party who was being rescued, and (b) that duty must have been broken. In other words, if the defendant would not have been liable to the party being rescued it is unlikely he or she would be liable to the rescuer.

(e) Other Consequential Victims

"Secondary" victims who suffer nervous shock[58] and rescuers or would-be rescuers who are injured are consequential victims of a breach of duty owed by the defendant to a third person. For reasons of policy, if not of logic, the law has stretched the requirement of a "foreseeable plaintiff" to accommodate such people who have suffered physical harm as a result of negligent behaviour towards someone else. Until recent times, however, the law did not generally accept that those who suffered *economic* harm as a consequence of negligent behaviour towards a third party should be considered as being foreseeable plaintiffs to whom a duty of care was owed such that they could claim against the negligent defendant.[59] Certain relationships did give rise to a claim, at common law or under statute, on the part of those affected economically by physical harm caused by negligence to someone else. The relationships which supported an action at common law were: (a) that between spouses (the action for loss of *con-*

53 *Horsley v. MacLaren* (1972), 22 D.L.R. (3d) 545; *Corothers v. Slobodian* (1973), 51 D.L.R. (3d) 1 (S.C.C.).

54 *Chadwick v. British Transport Commission*, [1967] 2 All E.R. 945.

55 *Hutterley v. Imperial Oil Co. & Calder* (1956), 3 D.L.R. (2d) 719 (Ont. H.C.); *Toy v. Argenti*, [1980] 3 W.W.R. 276 (B.C.S.C.).

56 *Wagner v. International Rly. Co.*, 232 N.Y. Supp. 17 (1921); *Moddejonge v. Huron County Board of Education*, [1972] 2 O.R. 437 (H.C.).

57 *Meyer v. Parker* (1995), 7 B.C.L.R. (3d) 13 (S.C.), affirmed (1996), 21 B.C.L.R. (3d) 33 (C.A.).

58 Above p. 77.

59 *Cattle v. Stockton Waterworks Co.* (1875), L.R. 10 Q.B. 453.

sortium, now defunct),[60] and (b) that between employer and employee (the action for loss of services, *per quod servitium amisit*, which, to some extent, can still be maintained).[61] Under Fatal Accidents Acts, which, following the original English statute, are to be found in every province, certain family members were given a right of action in respect of their financial loss (and in the case of Ontario non-financial loss) as a result of the death (or in Ontario the death or injury) of certain other family members.[62] In addition, in a few instances, the consequential victim was held able to claim for economic loss incurred through damage to such victim's property as a result of the defendant's breach of duty towards someone else.[63] But for what is now termed "pure" economic loss on the part of such consequential victim no claim was allowed.

To some extent this was because the common law did not recognize that such pure economic loss, that was not the product or result of physical injury to a person or property, was remediable in an action for negligence. The common law recognized an action for damages for such loss where the defendant's conduct was intentional, for example where the defendant was guilty of fraud or deceit, or committed one of what are generally referred to as "economic torts".[64] Mere negligence, however, did not have the same effect, until the decision in *Hedley Byrne v. Heller & Partners*[65] in 1963. The original effect of that decision was to permit an action in tort for negligent misrepresentation.[66] Its collateral consequence was to provide support for the argument that pure economic loss suffered by a consequential victim could be remedied by an action for negligence.

In several cases Canadian courts allowed such an action where the defendant had been guilty of a duty to warn of danger that ultimately led to the loss in question caused to a stranger to the primary relationship between the defendant and another party. Such a relationship existed between the manufacturer of what proved to be a defective crane and the purchaser of the crane from whom it was subsequently hired by the plaintiff who incurred economic loss when the crane became unusable during the period it went for repair because of its defects.[67] The true turning point in the development of this instance of liability came with the majority decision of the Supreme Court of Canada in *Canadian National Railway v. Norsk Pacific Steamship Co.*[68] The defendant's tug was handled negligently which resulted in damage to a bridge owned by the federal government over which, under contract with the government, the plaintiff's railway travelled.

---

60 Not in Alberta: R.S.A. 2000, c. D-14, s. 46.

61 Below p. 107.

62 Below pp. 222-223.

63 *Morrison Steamship Co. Ltd. v. Greystoke Castle (Cargo Owners)*, [1947] A.C. 265; *Seaway Hotels Ltd. v. Cragg (Canada) Ltd. & Consumers' Gas Co.*, [1959] O.R. 177 (H.C.), affirmed [1959] O.R. 581 (C.A.); *Courtenay v. Knutson* (1961), 26 D.L.R. (2d) 768 (B.C.S.C.).

64 Below p. 165 *et seq.*

65 [1964] A.C. 465.

66 Below p. 102.

67 *Rivtow Marine Ltd. v. Washington Iron Works* (1973), 40 D.L.R. (3d) 530 (S.C.C.); see also *Nielsen v. Kamloops (City)* (1984), 10 D.L.R. (4th) 641 (S.C.C.).

68 (1992), 91 D.L.R. (4th) 289 (F.C.T.D.).

Because the bridge was out of action while being repaired the railway was forced to divert its trains resulting in substantial costs being incurred. These were held to be recoverable from the defendant. Some members of the majority dealt with the question whether the defendant owed the railway a duty of care in terms of "proximity" or closeness. One of the majority took a different approach, namely that in this instance the defendant knew or ought to have known that the railway would be likely to suffer from such negligence as occurred. The dissenting members of the Court, however, considered that the case was one of "relational economic loss" to which the general exclusionary rule applied unless there were good reasons, which did not exist in this instance, for making an exception to that rule. In other words, rather than rely on the nebulous concept of "proximity", the Court should approach each instance category by category to determine whether a particular consequential victim should be treated as a foreseeable plaintiff.

In several subsequent cases, however,[69] the Supreme Court seems to have favoured the category, not proximity, approach where relational economic loss is concerned. Other decisions, in lower courts, also appear to adopt this kind of approach, with the result that, while recovery by such consequential victims is possible, it will only be possible in select situations, whenever a court can find factors that make it reasonable and justifiable to do so.[70]

5. FORESEEABLE DAMAGE

Once it has been determined, whether on the basis of "proximity" or legal policy, that the victim was a foreseeable plaintiff, that is one who was or should have been within the contemplation of the defendant as being likely to be affected by the defendant's act or omissions, the question can then arise whether what occurred to the victim should be regarded as within the scope of the risk to the victim created by the defendant's conduct. If it is, then the defendant's duty

---

69 *Winnipeg Condominium Corp. No. 36 v. Bird Construction Co.*, [1995] 1 S.C.R. 85; *D'Amato v. Badger* (1996), 137 D.L.R. (4th) 129 (S.C.C.); *Bow Valley Husky (Bermuda) Ltd. v. Saint John Shipbuilding Ltd.* (1997), 153 D.L.R. (4th) 385 (S.C.C.).

70 See *e.g.*, *Standard Trust Co. (Liquidator of) v. Catanach* (1995), 24 O.R. (3d) 492 (Gen. Div.); *British Columbia Ferry Corp. v. T. & N. plc* (1994), 95 B.C.L.R. (2d) 87 (S.C.), affirmed (1995), 16 B.C.L.R. (3d) 385 (C.A.); *Blacklaws v. 470433 Alberta Ltd.* (2000), 187 D.L.R. (4th) 614 (Alta.C.A.), leave to appeal refused (2001), 270 N.R. 197*n* (S.C.C.). Contrast *B.C. Hydro & Power Authority v. N.D. Lea Associates Ltd.* (1992), 92 D.L.R. (4th) 403 (B.C.S.C.), affirmed (1997), 154 D.L.R. (4th) 114 (B.C.C.A.), leave to appeal refused (2001), 270 N.R. 197*n* (S.C.C.).

Note also the situation of those who would have been beneficiaries under a will had it not been for the negligence of the testator's solicitor rendering the will invalid: *Whittingham v. Crease & Co.* (1978), 88 D.L.R. (3d) 353 (B.C.S.C.); *Earl v. Wilhelm* (2000), 183 D.L.R. (4th) 45 (Sask. C.A.), leave to appeal refused (2000), 266 N.R. 394*n* (S.C.C.). Liability to the foiled beneficiary has also been recognized in England, Australia and New Zealand: *White v. Jones*, [1995] 1 All E.R. 691; *Hill v. Van Erp* (1997), 142 A.L.R. 687; *Brownie Wills v. Shrimpton*, [1998] 2 N.Z.L.R. 320.

comprehended or extended as far as such risk. If it did not, then even though the plaintiff actually suffered the loss or damage in question, the defendant will not be held responsible, on the ground that the loss or damage incurred by the plaintiff was too remote a consequence of the defendant's act or omission. A negligent defendant is not liable for consequences that are considered "remote". However, what is and is not "remote" is a question of law of some complexity.

Before the crucial date of 1932, the English courts decided in *Re Polemis*[71] that once a party was guilty of negligence, in the form of the breach of a duty of care that was owed to the victim in the circumstances, that party was responsible for all the direct consequences of such negligence. Negligence involved guilt of all the "natural and probable" consequences of the defendant's conduct, whether such consequences were foreseeable or not, as long as they followed as a natural and direct result of such conduct. In arriving at this version of the scope of negligence, the English Court of Appeal adopted and followed the view expressed in an earlier case,[72] that what the defendant was expected to foresee as a reasonable person went to the question of culpability, *i.e.*, guilt of negligence, and did not affect the issue of compensation, *i.e.*, the extent of responsibility for such guilt.

As a result of the exposition of the law of negligence in *Donoghue v. Stevenson*, and the way it was interpreted and applied in subsequent cases, a different trend became recognizable in the decisions. This was the attitude that in considering whether a duty of care was owed by the defendant to the victim, it was impossible to exclude from consideration the question of the nature or extent of damage which was suffered by the victim. Whether such damage was foreseeable by a reasonable person as a likely consequence of his or her acts or omissions was an intrinsic part of the issue of whether the defendant ought to have exercised care towards the victim. Not only was a duty owed to a particular individual (or class of persons of whom the victim was one): a duty was only owed in respect of damage which was foreseeable as a result of any failure by the defendant to act reasonably. This culminated in the decision of the Judicial Committee of the Privy Council in *The Wagon Mound (No. 1)*.[73] There it was decided that to hold a wrongdoer liable for all the direct consequences of his or her initial act of negligence was both harsh and unreasonable. It did not serve the purpose of the law, since it made a person responsible for what could not be foreseen and so could not be prevented. Hence to hold the defendant liable for such consequences would be to impose liability beyond what was socially or morally desirable. For such reasons, and on the logical or more technical ground that negligence could only occur in relation to foreseeable consequences, the Privy Council held that a negligent tortfeasor was only liable in respect of those consequences of negligent conduct that could and ought to have been foreseen as being likely to result from negligence.

---

71 [1921] 3 K.B. 560 (C.A.).

72 *Weld-Blundell v. Stephens*, [1920] A.C. 956 at 984 *per* Lord Sumner.

73 [1961] A.C. 388 (P.C.).

It would seem that Canadian courts have accepted the general approach stated and favoured in *The Wagon Mound (No. 1)*.[74] Although no one decision has firmly and decisively expressed the law in such terms, the tenor of such decisions as have occurred since 1961 is to the effect that "reasonable foresight" of consequences is the basic test of whether damage is or is not too remote. However, the apparent simplicity and straightforwardness which the Privy Council endeavoured to achieve in that case has been affected by later decisions. It may be that as a result of such decisions, the notion of reasonable foresight must be redefined. *The Wagon Mound (No. 1)* indicated that a tortfeasor, to be liable for certain consequences or events, must have had them in contemplation actually or notionally. In *Hughes v. Lord Advocate*[75] the House of Lords appears to have held that it suffices if the tortfeasor ought to have foreseen that injury of the general kind suffered by the plaintiff, and more or less in the way it was suffered, might be sustained by the plaintiff as a result of the tortfeasor's negligence. Other cases seem to waver between the two views, sometimes insisting upon more specific foresight of the damage and the way it was incurred, at others requiring only a general kind of foresight.[76]

There is one class of cases, however, in which foresight is clearly inapplicable, and directness in the older sense is the test. These are cases in which the victim suffers more extensive damage than might have been foreseen by the reasonable person, by reason of the victim's peculiar physical state at the time of the accident, unknown though that state may have been on the part of the defendant. In these so-called "egg-shell skull" cases, referred to in that way because they are based on the idea that if the victim has an egg-shell skull and so dies because of his or her injuries, when a "normal" person might have lived, despite the fact that he or she suffered at the hands of the negligent defendant, the latter will be held responsible for such death: the rule applied is that of *talem qualem*. The defendant takes his victim as he finds him, and cannot raise a plea of unforeseeable damage.[77] These are exceptional cases. However, it may be that by the application of this doctrine, and the way the "reasonable foresight" notion has been interpreted in some instances and by some courts, the doctrine of *The Wagon Mound (No. 1)* is gradually being whittled away, until it is more theoretical in nature than practical. Thus, while in theory a defendant cannot be neg-

---

74 See, for example, *Abbott v. Kasza*, [1975] 3 W.W.R. 163 (Alta. S.C.T.D.), varied [1976] 4 W.W.R. 20 (Alta. C.A.); *Price v. Milawski* (1977), 82 D.L.R. (3d) 130 (Ont. C.A.). Contrast *Shulhan v. Peterson, Howell & Heather (Canada) Ltd.* (1966), 57 D.L.R. (2d) 491 (Sask. Q.B.).

75 [1963] A.C. 837.

76 See, for example, *Lauritzen v. Barstead* (1965), 53 D.L.R. (2d) 267 (Alta. S.C.); *School Division of Assiniboine South No. 3 v. Hoffer*, [1973] 6 W.W.R. 765 (S.C.C.); *Bradford v. Kannelos* (1974), 40 D.L.R. (3d) 578 (S.C.C.).

77 *Smith v. Leech Brain & Co. Ltd.*, [1962] 2 Q.B. 405; *Winteringham v. Rae*, [1966] 1 O.R. 727 (H.C.); *Windrim v. Wood* (1974), 54 D.L.R. (3d) 667 (Ont. H.C.); *Costello v. Blakeson* (1992), 74 B.C.L.R. (2d) 3 (S.C.). But an egg-shell or thin skull must be distinguished from a "crumbling" skull, where the victim is already deteriorating at the time of the act of the defendant, the result of which is to accelerate the deterioration. For that the defendant will not be liable: *Paine v. Donovan* (1994), 118 Nfld. & P.E.I.R. 91 (P.E.I. T.D.); *Taylor v. Nice* (1999), 212 N.B.R. (2d) 1 (Q.B.), affirmed (2000), 230 N.B.R. (2d) 106 (C.A.).

ligent except in respect of those consequences which ought to have been foreseen might be likely or probable should there occur deviation from the standards of the reasonable person, any more than one can be negligent save in relation to a person who was foreseeably likely to be affected by one's negligence, it may nonetheless be true that once the defendant has been negligent with respect to a foreseeable plaintiff, the courts will endeavour to impose liability for the consequences which actually ensue, even though they might not have been strictly foreseen, or foreseeable. The whole area of the law of torts remains one of great difficulty and cannot be regarded as finally settled or resolved.

6. CAUSATION

The plaintiff must establish that the defendant's act or omission caused the loss or damage of which the plaintiff complains. This means that the negligence of the defendant was either "the" cause of that loss or damage, in other words the sole factor that was responsible for what happened, or "a" cause of such loss or damage, in other words one of several factors that were responsible.[78] There are two aspects of this. One is in reality or effect the question of remoteness of damage looked at from the perspective of causation instead of, as was considered in the previous section of this chapter, from that of duty, *i.e.*, of risk. This aspect of causation arises when, although the defendant was negligent, that negligence alone might not have resulted in the harm of which the plaintiff complains, but did so because of some natural or otherwise non-human activity or an act or omission on the part of a third party, or possibly the plaintiff, subsequent upon or in combination with the conduct of the defendant. The other is more clearly a question of physical causation, establishing whether there was a sufficient causal nexus between the defendant's conduct and the loss or damage suffered by the plaintiff.

Where an intervening or subsequent act or event has played a part in the eventual loss or damage being caused to the plaintiff, the issue that arises is whether such act or event should be regarded as a *novus actus interveniens* that severs what otherwise would be the necessary causal nexus between the defendant's negligent act or omission and the ultimate harm suffered by the plaintiff. If that is the case, then the defendant will not be liable for such harm. For example, suppose defendant A negligently runs down the plaintiff who has to go to hospital for treatment such as the amputation of a leg. If doctor B negligently amputates not only the damaged leg but also the plaintiff's other undamaged leg the question arises whether defendant A is to be held liable for the plaintiff's

[78] See, *e.g.*, *Walker Estate v. York Finch General Hospital* (2001), 198 D.L.R. (4th) 193 (S.C.C.); *Cherry (Guardian ad litem of) v. Borsman* (1990), 75 D.L.R. (4th) 668 at 720 (B.C.S.C.), varied (1992), 94 D.L.R. (4th) 487 (B.C.C.A.), leave to appeal refused (1993), 99 D.L.R. (4th) *vii*. Contrast, *e.g.*, *Wong v. 407527 Ontario Ltd.* (1999), 179 D.L.R. (4th) 38 (Ont. C.A.); *Ratt v. Wolfe* (1994), 126 Sask. R. 195 (Q.B.), affirmed (1996), 144 Sask. R. 1 (C.A.). The defendant's negligence must have materially contributed to the injury of the plaintiff: *Athey v. Leonati* (1996), 140 D.L.R. (4th) 235 (S.C.C.).

loss of *both* legs or only the one originally damaged by defendant A. That question has to be answered by determining whether the negligence of doctor B was reasonably foreseeable by defendant A as a likely, that is probable, consequence of the plaintiff's having to go to hospital for treatment as a result of the original act or negligence by defendant A. Decided cases have sometimes held that it is and that it is not.[79]

Reasonable foresight on the part of a negligent defendant of the intentional or negligent acts of others such that their combined acts cause harm to the plaintiff is also relevant when such a situation is involved. A typical situation is one in which a defendant is careless in leaving an automobile unguarded with the key in the ignition so that it is stolen by a thief who then, by negligent driving, injures the plaintiff.[80] However there are many other examples of such a combination of human acts which ultimately lead to harm to a third party. In every such instance whether the originally negligent defendant is liable for what occurred will turn on whether the other guilty party's act was foreseeable as a consequence of the original negligence.[81] The same test is applicable where what happens after the defendant's original negligence is some natural event or the act of an animal.[82] Or, it may be added, takes the form of some act of the plaintiff himself or herself, as is the case where the plaintiff intervenes to rescue someone when, if the plaintiff had not intervened, he or she would not have been within the range of foreseeable injury as a consequence of the defendant's negligence.[83] In such instances, and in others where no rescue was involved,[84] the courts have asked whether the action taken by the plaintiff which, in some measure brought about the plaintiff's injury, was reasonable. If it was, then it was foreseeable by the defendant who will be liable despite the causative nature of the plaintiff's conduct. If it was not, then it will not be considered to have been foreseeable, and the plaintiff's act will be a *novus actus interveniens*.[85]

If no intervening act or event is involved in the circumstances which led to the occurrence of harm on the part of the plaintiff, the facts may nevertheless raise a question of causation. For it may not be obvious that what the defendant did or failed to do caused what happened. The most famous instance of this is

---

79 *Powell v. Guttman*, [1978] 5 W.W.R. 228 (Man. C.A.); *Thompson v. Toorenburgh* (1973), 29 D.L.R. (3d) 608 (B.C.S.C.), affirmed (1975), 50 D.L.R. (3d) 717 (B.C.C.A.); *David v. Toronto Transit Commission* (1976), 16 O.R. (2d) 248 (H.C.).

80 *Walker v. de Luxe Cab Ltd.*, [1944] 3 D.L.R. 175 (Ont. H.C.).

81 See, *e.g.*, *Smith v. Littlewoods Organisation Ltd.*, [1987] A.C. 241; *Wince (Guardian ad litem of) v. Ball* (1996), 40 Alta. L.R. (3d) 66 (Q.B.).

82 *Sgro v. Verbeek* (1980), 111 D.L.R. (3d) 479 (Ont. H.C.); *C.P.R. v. City of Calgary*, [1971] 4 W.W.R. 241 (Alta. C.A.).

83 Above p. 79.

84 *Urbanski v. Patel* (1978), 84 D.L.R. (3d) 650 (Man. Q.B.); *Holomis v. Dubuc* (1975), 56 D.L.R. (3d) 351 (B.C.S.C.); *Janiak v. Ippolito* (1985), 16 D.L.R. (4th) 1 (S.C.C.); *Arndt v. Smith* (1997), 148 D.L.R. (4th) 48 (S.C.C.).

85 See also the "suicide" cases: *e.g.*, *Swami v. Lo* (1980), 105 D.L.R. (3d) 451 (B.C.S.C.); *Wright Estate v. Davidson* (1992), 88 D.L.R. (4th) 698 (B.C.C.A.); *Funk v. Clapp* (1986), 35 B.C.L.R. (2d) 222 (C.A.).

the case of *Cook v. Lewis*.[86] Several people were hunting. Two of them fired at the same time. The plaintiff was shot. But it was not clear which of the two hunters had fired the shot that struck the plaintiff. The Supreme Court of Canada held both hunters liable, on the ground that in the circumstances it was not possible to prove conclusively which hunter was the guilty party, and it would have been unreasonable to deny the plaintiff a remedy.

This case may be regarded as exceptional, since there was no doubt that *someone*, namely, one of the two hunters who were the defendants, had injured the plaintiff by committing a tort. But in other instances it has not been so clear whether what the negligent defendant was accused of doing had, as a matter of *fact*, not as in the cases discussed above where foresight was involved, as a matter of *law*, caused the injury of which the plaintiff complained. There are several conflicting decisions of the House of Lords on the subject of burden of proof, which leave it open to question whether the plaintiff must always prove the required causal nexus or can rely on a (rebuttable) presumption of such nexus, leaving it to the defendant to establish conclusively that no causal connection actually occurred.[87] In *Snell v. Farrell*,[88] a medical negligence case, like those in England in which this issue was discussed, the Supreme Court of Canada took the view that, at least in such cases, where the facts were within the knowledge and expertise of the defendant, the doctor, the court could draw the necessary and reasonable inference, as to causation, unless some contradictory evidence were produced by the defendant. As other courts have stated from time to time, as far as the law was concerned, causation, at least in cases like *Snell*, is a matter of common sense.

7. THE STANDARD OF CARE

For the tort of negligence to be committed it is not sufficient that the defendant owed the plaintiff a duty of care. It must then be established that the defendant's action or inaction constituted a breach of that duty. To do this the plaintiff must prove that the defendant failed to observe the standard of care that was applicable in the circumstances.[89] This means that, in light of what the defendant knew or ought to have known, the defendant did not act as a reasonable person, with such knowledge and in all the circumstances, would have acted so as to avoid causing foreseeable harm. Only when this is the situation can it be said that the defendant has been "negligent", and has committed the tort of negligence.

If a duty of care is breached as a result of an accident which causes unforeseeable harm, this will not be considered to be negligence. When this happens the occurrence is unusually described as an "inevitable accident". If a defendant

---

86 [1951] S.C.R. 830.

87 *McGhee v. National Coal Board*, [1972] 3 All E.R. 1008; *Kay v. Ayrshire & Arran Health Board*, [1987] 2 All E.R. 417; *Hotson v. East Berkshire Area Health Authority*, [1987] 2 All E.R. 909; *Fairchild v. Glenhaven Funeral Services Ltd.*, [2002] 1 A.C. 32.

88 (1990), 72 D.L.R. (4th) 289 (S.C.C.).

89 *Galaske v. O'Donnell* (1994), 89 B.C.L.R. (2d) 273 (B.C.C.A.).

is forced to act in a certain manner by what has been termed "the agony of the moment", for example, a driver forced to take steps to avoid a large animal on the highway which results in knocking down and injuring the plaintiff, such a driver cannot be said to have acted negligently.[90] Nor should negligence, which, as stated above, is defined as the failure to observe an applicable standard of care, be equated with an error in judgment on the part of the defendant, such as may occur in the course of performing a medical procedure.[91] But a defendant will be held to have been negligent if precautions that would have been taken by a reasonable person in the circumstances, such as the giving of a warning, were not taken.[92]

The standard of care to be observed by a defendant under a duty of care is frequently stated to be an objective, not a subjective one. It avoids the personal equation and is independent of the idiosyncracies of the particular person whose conduct is in question. It is the standard of the reasonable person.[93] The reasonable person is not perfect, nor someone with unusual qualities of prescience, courage, or sagacity. The reasonable person is expected to behave in the way an ordinary prudent person would act in the circumstances. And only in respect of what a reasonable person would have anticipated as being likely to occur.[94] For example, in one instance, it was not to be anticipated that a child in foster-care would be sexually assaulted by the foster-father; therefore, the Crown was not guilty of negligence in placing the child with that foster-parent.[95]

However the application of an objective standard of care may be departed from in certain situations. Thus the higher the risk of injury involved in what the defendant is doing, the higher the degree of care that must be taken. If the defendant is performing some activity that calls for the exercise of special expertise, such as the practice of law or medicine, the standard of care to be observed is that of the reasonably skillful practitioner of such expertise. In other words some people can be held to a higher standard of care than others because of the nature of what they are doing. By way of contrast, there are some who may not be held to the standard of the reasonable person, since, by reason of their age or mental incapacity, they are not to be considered to belong in the category of "reasonable" people. A child may only be held obliged to observe the standard of care to be expected of a child of similar age and experience.[96] Someone whose mental capacity is limited by illness or otherwise may not appreciate that he or

---

90 *Hogan v. McEwan* (1975), 64 D.L.R. (3d) 37 (Ont. H.C.).

91 *Whitehouse v. Jordan*, [1981] 1 All E.R. 267; *Wilson v. Swanson*, [1956] S.C.R. 804; *Grant Estate v. Mathers* (1991), 100 N.S.R. (2d) 363 (T.D.).

92 *Reibl v. Hughes* (1980), 114 D.L.R. (3d) 1 (S.C.C.); *Buchan v. Ortho Pharmaceuticals (Canada) Ltd.* (1986), 25 D.L.R. (4th) 658 (Ont. C.A.); *Lambert v. Lastoplex Chemicals Co.*, [1972] S.C.R. 569.

93 *Glasgow Corp. v. Muir*, [1943] A.C. 448.

94 *Gellie v. Naylor* (1986), 28 D.L.R. (4th) 762 (Ont. C.A.); *Ware's Taxi Ltd. v. Gilliham*, [1949] S.C.R. 637; *Nespolon v. Alford* (1998), 40 O.R. (3d) 355 (C.A.).

95 *Madalena v. Kuun* (1987), 35 D.L.R. (4th) 222 (B.C.S.C.).

96 *Nespolon v. Alford* (1998), 40 O.R. (3d) 355 (C.A.); *Walmsley v. Humenick*, [1954] 2 D.L.R. 232 (B.C.S.C.).

she owed a duty of care or that what he or she did was a breach of a duty of care. If that is so, then such a person may not be held to be guilty of negligence.[97]

There are other factors, apart from those such as age and incompetence referred to above, that may be taken into account when determining whether a defendant has observed the appropriate standard of care in the circumstances. One is the relation between the possibility of harm and the cost of, or the difficulty entailed in, prevention of that harm. Another is the comparison between the risks involved in what the defendant was doing and the general importance of that activity. A third is whether the defendant was acting in accordance with the usual or customary practices of others engaged in the same activity.

The reasonable person, not being required to act in a superhuman or extraordinary way, is not expected to go to outrageous lengths or extravagant expense in order to avoid harm. If the financial or other cost of averting injury to another would significantly outweigh the extent of the risk of such injury occurring, the failure to undertake such cost will not amount to negligence. Just as, in order to mitigate the effects of a wrong done to the plaintiff the latter is not expected to do anything other than to act "reasonably", so a defendant is not expected to act otherwise than "reasonably" in order to prevent foreseeable harm to another. By way of contrast, to create a risk to another person for the purpose of saving some insignificant cost will usually, if not indeed always, amount to acting negligently.[98]

When determining whether the defendant has behaved "unreasonably", it is also pertinent to assess that behaviour in relation to the purpose being served by the defendant at the material time. Thus a fire engine may be travelling at a speed that is normally unreasonably fast, which might lead to the conclusion that the driver was negligent. However, if at the time the fire engine was rushing to attend to an emergency such as a household fire, the normally excessive speed will not amount to negligent driving.[99] The actions of police in arresting or attempting to arrest criminals or suspected criminals has sometimes led to allegations of negligence on their part. These have not been successful unless the police in question were not acting in accordance with their duties or otherwise could be said to have gone beyond what was necessary and therefore excusable.[100]

A defendant who was acting in a way that was consistent with the usual or customary practices applicable to the defendant's profession or business may be held to have observed the relevant standard of care.[101] However, for a defendant to rely on such argument, it must be proved that the alleged practice existed and was clearly established.[102] Even if that is proved, reliance on such a practice will

---

97 *Fiala v. Cechmanek* (1999), 246 A.R. 120 (C.A.); *Hutchings v. Nevin* (1992), 9 O.R. (3d) 776 (Gen. Div.).

98 *Cf. Arnold v. Teno* (1978), 83 D.L.R. (3d) 609 (S.C.C.).

99 *Kraus v. City of Vancouver* (1964), 47 W.W.R. 364 (B.C.C.A.).

100 *Priestman v. Colangelo & Smythson*, [1959] S.C.R. 615; *Vallery v. Po* (1971), 23 D.L.R. (3d) 92 (B.C.S.C.); *Murphy v. Hollingshead* (1991), 84 Alta. L.R. (2d) 312 (Q.B.).

101 *Vancouver General Hospital v. McDaniel*, [1934] 4 D.L.R. 593 (P.C.).

102 *Lepine v. University Hospital Board* (1965), 50 W.W.R. 709 (Alta. S.C.T.D.), affirmed (1965), 54 D.L.R. (2d) 340 (Alta. C.A.), reversed on other grounds [1966] S.C.R. 561.

not be possible for the defendant if the defendant was instructed by the plaintiff to act otherwise than in accordance with the practice.[103] Moreover, in certain circumstances it may be negligent to adopt the practice and careful, that is to say, consistent with observing the standard of care expected in the circumstances, to deviate from the practice. This will be the case, for example, where considerable danger is involved in the activity undertaken by the defendant,[104] or where the practice is itself careless so that to indulge in it amounts to the failure to fulfil or observe the applicable standard of care.[105]

Although, in general, the plaintiff only has to prove that the defendant was guilty of "negligence", as defined and explained above, there remain, in some Canadian provinces, two situations in which proof of such negligence will not suffice, and the plaintiff must establish that the defendant was guilty of "gross" negligence, which presumably entails more egregious misconduct on the defendant's part. They are: (1) where a municipality is being sued in respect of injuries resulting from snow or ice on a sidewalk;[106] and (2) where a doctor, nurse, or other person (*i.e.*, "good Samaritan") gives emergency medical services or first aid at an accident.[107]

8. QUALIFICATIONS OF LIABILITY

(a) Contributory Negligence

At common law the failure of a plaintiff to exercise reasonable care with respect to his or her own safety, or the safety of his or her property, might deprive the plaintiff of any claim against a defendant alleged to have committed the tort of negligence. Whether such behaviour had that effect depended on whether it could be characterized as "contributory negligence". As will be seen later, as a result of modern legislation, a plaintiff's contributory negligence may only rarely, if at all, have such a drastic effect, but can reduce the responsibility of the defendant for what happened, thereby qualifying to some extent the latter's liability.

In one sense the expression contributory negligence is misleading. It suggests that the plaintiff has been "negligent" in the same way as the defendant. However there is an important distinction between the negligence of a defendant and the contributory negligence of a plaintiff. For the former to be negligent, as previously explained, he or she must have been guilty of a breach of a duty of care owed by the defendant to the plaintiff. For a plaintiff to be guilty of contributory negligence it is not necessary for the plaintiff to have been guilty of the breach

---

103 *Winrob v. Street & Wollen* (1959), 19 D.L.R. (2d) 172 (B.C.S.C.).

104 *James v. River East School Division No. 9*, [1976] 2 W.W.R. 577 (Man. C.A.).

105 *ter Neuzen v. Korn* (1995), 127 D.L.R. (4th) 577 (S.C.C.); *Cavanagh v. Ulster Weaving Co.*, [1960] A.C. 145; *Kaufman v. Toronto Transit Commission*, [1960] S.C.R. 251.

106 *E.g.*, *Municipal Act, 2001*, S.O. 2001, c. 25, s. 44(9).

107 *Emergency Medical Aid Act*, R.S.A. 2000, c. E-7, s. 2.

of a duty of care owed to the defendant.[108] There do not have to have been reciprocal duties of care owed between the parties, although this may sometimes be the case, for example, in cases involving accidents on the highway involving two motor vehicles.

The test of contributory negligence is whether the plaintiff behaved as a reasonable person in the particular situation of, and with the particular capacities of, the plaintiff.[109] This entails the issue of foresight on the part of the plaintiff with respect to the possibility of suffering injury or loss, in much the same way as the determination of whether a defendant has been negligent.[110] Hence the age of the plaintiff may be relevant. A child may not be as capable of taking care of himself or herself, and avoiding injury in a dangerous situation, as an adult. Everything depends on the circumstances and the age and intelligence of the child.[111] So, too, in some situations, where the plaintiff is forced by the defendant's conduct to react on the spur of the moment, in what has been termed "the agony of collision", what might otherwise have been contributory negligence may not be construed as such.[112]

Whether a plaintiff's negligence is "contributory" is a matter of causation.[113] Before the passage of statutes that altered the effect of such negligence in the manner indicated earlier, it might have been said that almost any negligent act by the plaintiff that, in any degree, helped to bring about the injury or loss of the plaintiff sufficed to render the plaintiff guilty of contributory negligence which deprived the plaintiff of a remedy.[114]

Because this often resulted in hardship, the courts in England, from which the law in Canada took its direction, invented rules designed to avoid the harsher consequences of the doctrine of contributory negligence, and treated the issue of "contribution" in an artificial way. Their attitude was to analyze the plaintiff's conduct, in comparison with that of the defendant, and categorize each in terms of which actually *caused* the eventual injury or damage to the victim. In this respect there emerged what became known as the "last opportunity rule".[115] By this rule, the party who had the "last opportunity" of avoiding the ultimate occurrence, whether it was the plaintiff who could have prevented the consequences of the defendant's negligence, or the defendant who could still have

---

108 *Nance v. British Columbia Electric Rly. Co.*, [1951] A.C. 601.

109 *Ibid.*

110 *Abbott v. Kasza*, [1976] 4 W.W.R. 20 (Alta. C.A.).

111 *McEllistrum v. Etches*, [1956] S.C.R. 787; *Wade v. C.N. Railway*, [1978] 1 S.C.R. 1064; *Laviolette v. C.N. Rly.* (1986), 36 C.C.L.T. 203 (Q.B.), affirmed (1987), 40 C.C.L.T. 138 (C.A.), leave to appeal to S.C.C. refused (1987), 86 N.R. 266*n* (S.C.C.).

112 *Jones v. Boyce* (1816), 1 Stark. 493; *Billings & Sons Ltd. v. Riden*, [1958] A.C. 240; *Long v. Owners of Condominium Plan No. 74R40206* (1979), 2 Sask. R. 212 (Q.B.).

113 *Sigurdson v. British Columbia Electric Rly. Co.*, [1953] A.C. 291; *Dennison v. Young* (1998), 169 Sask. R. 77 (Q.B.). Hence, failure to use a seat belt while driving a vehicle, which is now compulsory under statute, will not amount to contributory negligence unless it is proved that use of a seat belt would have prevented or reduced those injuries: *Bishop (Litigation Guardian of) v. Sexsmith*, [1995] 6 W.W.R. 385 (Sask. Q.B.); *Manzer v. Lines* (1990), 98 N.S.R. (2d) 213 (T.D.).

114 *Butterfield v. Forrester* (1809), 11 East 60.

115 *Davis v. Mann* (1842), 10 M. & W. 546; *Long v. Toronto Railway Co.* (1914), 50 S.C.R. 224.

done something to forestall the outcome of his or her own and the plaintiff's prior acts of negligence, was held to be the one and only party responsible.[116] If the plaintiff were the one, his or her action was denied; if the defendant, then he or she was liable, and the plaintiff's conduct albeit amounting to negligence as described above, was not "contributory". Prior to changes in the law, therefore, a plaintiff who was denied a remedy on this ground had not just "contributed" to his or her injury or loss, in a legal sense: he or she had "caused" it. If all the plaintiff had done was to contribute to the circumstances out of which the plaintiff was injured, he or she might retain the right of action.[117] Since the law was changed,[118] the plaintiff's conduct may result in a diminution of the damages payable to him or her, on the basis of the plaintiff's involvement in the eventual loss or injury incurred. The exact proportion of such diminution will be based on the court's assessment of the extent to which the plaintiff caused his or her injury, expressed in percentage terms. The plaintiff may still be the "sole" cause of his or her injury.[119] If not, however, the plaintiff will not lose his or her entire claim, only that part of it which can be said to have been brought about by his or her own neglect. In these circumstances perhaps the plaintiff may accurately be described as having "contributed" to his or her loss. The language of the statutes, which speak of apportionment on the basis of "degree of fault or negligence", and the attitude of the courts suggest that a more descriptive expression for this way of looking at the conduct of plaintiff and defendant is *comparative* negligence, rather than contributory negligence.[120]

(b) Consent

The effect of a plaintiff's consent to a defendant's act has already been noted in relation to the tort of trespass,[121] where reference was made to the maxim *volenti non fit injuria*, which is derived from the Roman law of slavery, under which one who permitted himself to be sold into slavery unlawfully could not afterwards complain of the illegality of the sale, which might have been undertaken in defraud of the innocent purchaser of the so-called "slave".[122] The idea encapsulated in that maxim which results in a victim's consent rendering non-tortious what otherwise would be a trespass, has been extended to apply to the tort of negligence. If a defendant is alleged to have been negligent thereby breaching a duty of care owed to the plaintiff, the consent of the plaintiff to the potentially harmful activity which the defendant is undertaking is considered to amount to

---

116 There was also a doctrine of "notional" last opportunity: *British Columbia Electric Rly. Co. v. Loach*, [1916] 1 A.C. 719.

117 The doctrine of "last clear chance", which was abolished by statute in British Columbia and Prince Edward Island, has been held elsewhere not to have survived the modern "apportionment" legislation: *Wickberg v. Patterson* (1997), 145 D.L.R. (4th) 263 (Alta. C.A.).

118 See, *e.g.*, the *Negligence Act*, R.S.O. 1990, c. N.1.

119 See, *e.g.*, *Haydu v. Calgary (City)* (1991), 81 Alta. L.R. (2d) 107 (Q.B.).

120 If apportionment is not possible, the result may be that both parties are to be held equally at fault: see *Taylor v. Asody*, [1975] 2 S.C.R. 414, applying s. 5 of the Ontario Act.

121 Above p. 47.

122 *Woolridge v. Sumner*, [1963] 2 Q.B. 43 at 69 *per* Diplock L.J.

the plaintiff's assumption of the risk of being injured as a result of that activity.[123] As such it will preclude the liability of the defendant for negligence, either on the ground that the plaintiff is forgoing in advance any right of action he or she might have in the event of the defendant being negligent or on the ground that the consent of, or assumption of risk by the plaintiff relieves the defendant of any duty of care the defendant otherwise would have owed the plaintiff.

Consent given prior to the occurrence of injury by the plaintiff must be distinguished from an agreement after the injury has been incurred under which the plaintiff settles and undertakes not to seek the imposition of any possible liability on the part of the defendant. A post-accident agreement to settle is a compromise, which must be in the form of an express contract, in which the consideration for the plaintiff's agreement is some kind of payment by the defendant.[124] A pre-accident ouster of potential liability may be contained in a contract, in the form of a disclaimer or exclusion clause by the terms of which the plaintiff either: (i) waives any obligation on the part of the defendant to take care of the safety of the plaintiff or the plaintiff's property; or (ii) undertakes not to hold the defendant liable, or limits the defendant's liability, in the event that the defendant by some wrongful act injures the plaintiff or the plaintiff's property. The validity and effect of such clauses depends on the nature of the contract in which such a clause is contained and the operation thereon of applicable principles of the law of contract. For such a clause to be effective to protect the defendant from liability consideration must have been given or promised to the plaintiff by the defendant.[125] However, a plaintiff may expressly agree not to hold a defendant liable even if no consideration has been given by the latter for such agreement, in other words even if there is no contract between the parties to such effect. Moreover, such an agreement, by which the plaintiff assumes the risk of being injured, that is to say is *volens* for the purposes of the maxim, need not be express but may be implied, as a consequence of the conduct of the parties and the surrounding circumstances. Indeed, most of the cases in which the issue of consent has arisen involve an implied, rather than an express agreement.

Implication of an agreement by the plaintiff to assume or accept the risk of being injured at the hands of the defendant involves two major elements.[126] In the first place there must be knowledge on the part of the plaintiff of what is happening and what is likely to occur, namely the possibility or risk of injury by reason of the conduct of the defendant.[127] Second, from that knowledge, coupled

---

[123] *Hall v. Hebert* (1993), 101 D.L.R. (4th) 129 (S.C.C.).

[124] Fridman, *The Law of Contract in Canada*, 4th ed. (Toronto: Carswell, 1999), at 102-105.

[125] *Ibid*., at 608-637.

[126] *Mack v. Enns* (1981), 30 B.C.L.R. 337 (S.C.), varied (1983), 44 B.C.L.R. 145 (C.A.), leave to appeal to S.C.C. refused (1984), 52 N.R. 235 (S.C.C.).

[127] *Miller v. Decker*, [1957] S.C.R. 624; *Car & General Insurance Corp. v. Seymour & Maloney*, [1956] S.C.R. 322; *Stein v. Lehnert*, [1963] S.C.R. 38. Hence a medical or dental patient will not be considered *volens* so as to oust liability for negligence unless such patient has been able to provide the medical or dental practitioner with an "informed consent" as to the risks inherent in a projected procedure: *Reibl v. Hughes* (1980), 114 D.L.R. (3d) 1 (S.C.C.), a doctrine that has been followed in Australia, in *Rogers v. Whittaker* (1992), 175 C.L.R. 479, but not in England, *Sidaway v. Bethlem Royal Hospital Governors*, [1985] A.C. 871.

with the response or behaviour of the plaintiff, it must be possible to conclude that the plaintiff has truly consented to, or assumed the risk involved.[128] Knowledge is insufficient but knowledge is essential.[129] Thus if for some reason the plaintiff is ignorant of the risk, or the risk is one which is not foreseeable by the plaintiff, the maxim *volenti non fit injuria* is inapplicable. A party only consents to, or assumes, known or knowable risks. This clearly means that the test is subjective, *i.e.*, dependent upon the understanding of the actual plaintiff, not the objective reasonable person in the position of the plaintiff. Once the knowledge is proved, it must then be shown that the plaintiff gave consent. This means that if the plaintiff is incapable of consenting, *e.g.*, through youth, or has not validly consented, *e.g.* because of fraud on the part of the defendant, or has not freely consented, *e.g.* because of some duress, the plaintiff will not be considered to have consented or assumed the risk.

It is this last feature of consent which has caused most trouble in the courts. Cases concerned with employees who realize that they are likely to be hurt if they continue to do what they are employed to do, reveal that their refusal to abandon their task does not mean they have consented to being injured if the threatened harm materializes.[130] It is different where a person voluntarily undertakes employment that is inherently dangerous, such as by becoming a firefighter. Only if the dangerous character of the work is increased through the negligence or other tortious conduct of the employer will the latter be liable in respect of injuries incurred during the employment in question. Acceptance of dangerous work is not truly an instance of the maxim *volenti non fit injuria*. That issue will only arise where there is some unusual danger in the performance of the work on a particular occasion. What the courts have held is that the situation of the employee is such that he or she is not fully able to give a free consent, and so cannot be said to have assumed the unusual risk involved. The only choice is to refuse to work and so, perhaps, lose the employment.[131] So, too, in the "rescue" cases, the rescuer does not have a fully free choice whether to attempt the rescue which involves the risk, or leave the threatened third party exposed without protection or assistance to the risk created by the negligent defendant.[132] The courts have expounded the notion of "duress" very widely in this connection, and have been willing to permit a plaintiff to recover even where there would have been no injury if the plaintiff had not interfered, as long as interference was necessary to preserve or protect life (and sometimes property)[133] and was reasonable in all the circumstances, not rash or reckless.[134] In such situations the plaintiff has not consented to the risk of injury or assumed the risk

---

[128] *Hall v. Hebert* (1993), 101 D.L.R. (4th) 129 (S.C.C.); *Eid Estate v. Dumas*, [1969] S.C.R. 668.

[129] *Smith v. Baker*, [1891] A.C. 325.

[130] *Ibid.*

[131] See *Hambley v. Shepley*, [1967] 2 O.R. 217 (C.A.), which involved a policeman.

[132] *Horsley v. MacLaren*, [1972] S.C.R. 441; *Corothers v. Slobodian* (1975), 51 D.L.R. (3d) 1 (S.C.C.); see p. 79.

[133] *Hyett v. Great Western Ry. Co.*, [1948] 1 K.B. 345 (C.A.); *Hutterley v. Imperial Oil Co. and Calder*, [1956] O.W.N. 681 (H.C.).

[134] *Baker v. Hopkins*, [1958] 1 W.L.R. 966 (C.A.); *Chadwick v. British Transport Commission*, [1967] 2 All E.R. 945.

of injury. In other words the notion of "consent" has received an artificial interpretation from the courts, in much the same way as the notions of causation and contributory negligence. They have been prepared to exclude the operation of the maxim *volenti non fit injuria*, where, for reasons of policy, such as the desire to encourage people to rescue others, or the need to protect employees from the consequences of their employers' misconduct, it has been thought undesirable or unreasonable to penalize the victim and deny him or her a remedy against a negligent or otherwise tortious defendant.

(c) The Plaintiff's Illegality

Cases which raise issues of contributory negligence or consent are not usually cases in which the victim has been engaged upon anything unlawful at the material time. In some, however, the victim may have been behaving criminally at that time, *e.g.*, by engaging in dangerous driving, or driving under the influence of drugs or alcohol. There are decisions which suggest that such behaviour will negate liability on the part of the defendant, not because the latter was innocent of any tortious conduct, nor because such conduct did not help to cause the plaintiff's injury, but because it is considered undesirable and indeed, in some respects, illogical, to permit the plaintiff to sue the defendant. At various times, however, different reasons have been given for such decisions. Courts have been willing to decide cases raising such a question on the basis of contributory negligence or consent, without delving more deeply. Other courts have been prepared to state that the true reason for denying liability is something else. This has been described in general terms as a doctrine of public policy. It has been put in terms of there being no duty of care owed to a person who is engaged in criminal activity at the material time. It has also been expressed to be another application of the doctrine *ex turpi causa non oritur actio*. This maxim, which originally applied to prevent suits upon contracts that were illegal or involved an illegal purpose or some illegal performance, has been said to apply equally to prevent actions in tort arising from events which occurred, in part at least, because of the criminal conduct of the victim at the material time. Some judicial criticism of the relevance of this maxim has been expressed. But other judges have as firmly said that the maxim *ex turpi causa* is as relevant in the law of torts as it is in the law of contracts.[135]

The kind of situation in which this problem can arise is where two robbers are engaged in a robbery which involves the use of firearms and one carelessly discharges a gun in such a way that it injures the other. Or the plaintiff steals a car and while driving carefully upon the highway in the stolen vehicle is injured by reason of the negligence of the driver of another car. To what extent does, and should, the criminality of the plaintiff operate to defeat a claim in negligence? While the courts have acknowledged the desirability of preventing an

---

[135] *Cf. Tallow v. Tailfeathers*, [1973] 6 W.W.R. 732 (Alta. C.A.); *Tomlinson v. Harrison*, [1972] 1 O.R. 670 (H.C.J.) with *Canada Cement LaFarge Ltd. v. B.C. Lightweight Aggregates Ltd.*, [1983] 1 S.C.R. 452 at 479; *Norberg v. Wynrib* (1992), 92 D.L.R. (4th) 449 at 483; *Hall v. Hebert* (1993), 101 D.L.R. (4th) 129 at 148, 161 (S.C.C.).

abuse of their process by denying the criminal party recovery, to establish and maintain his or her action such a party would have to admit to behaving criminally at the material time. They have also been anxious to avoid treating such a victim as totally without rights. It is clear that even criminals have rights, so far as the law of torts is concerned. A convict in prison may not be injured with impunity by someone who has no authority or legal right to do so. So too, a person engaged upon some criminal enterprise is not thereby precluded automatically from suing anybody in respect of injuries inccurred during the course of that enterprise.

In *Hall v. Hebert*[136] the Supreme Court of Canada was very critical of the maxim *ex turpi causa* and of the notion that a plaintiff who was doing something illegal at the material time should be deprived of a remedy if injured by a defendant's negligence. In this case the plaintiff was injured in the accident which happened when, with the consent of the defendant who was drunk, the plaintiff, who was also drunk, drove the vehicle after it had stalled and was being started by running it down a hill. When the plaintiff claimed that the defendant was negligent in letting the plaintiff drive on a difficult road, the defendant pleaded that the plaintiff was committing an illegal act at the time, namely driving while drunk. The Court rejected that plea and held both parties equally at fault and to blame. Before the defence could be raised successfully the situation must be one where acceptance of the defence would be necessary and justified to protect the integrity of the legal system, for example, where to ignore the plaintiff's illegality would allow the plaintiff to profit from a wrongful act. The case before the Court did not fall into this category.

It would seem that the conditions under which the plea of *ex turpi* can be raised as a defence to an action for negligence are as follows: (1) the offence in question must be an offence under the *Criminal Code*; (2) there must be a causal connection between the plaintiff's illegality and the plaintiff's subsequent injury; (3) the parties must have been acting jointly, with a common intent, in the commission of the illegal purpose; and (4) the plaintiff must be aware that a criminal offence is being committed.[137]

---

136 Above, note 135.

137 *Tallow v. Tailfeathers*, [1973] 6 W.W.R. 732 (Alta. C.A.); *Tomlinson v. Harrison*, [1972] 1 O.R. 670; *Schill v. Weiner* (1980), 5 Sask. R. 112 (Q.B.), varied in part (1981), 13 Sask. R. 361 (C.A.); *Rodrigue v. Penner* (1970), 74 W.W.R. 96.

Chapter 8

SOME CATEGORIES OF LIABILITY FOR NEGLIGENCE

1. LIABILITY FOR DEFECTIVE CHATTELS

Prior to 1932, the position with respect to damage caused by putting into circulation a chattel which was so defective that it was capable of causing harm, and did cause harm, was that liability would only occur if an operative contract existed between the circulator and the recipient of the chattel, under which contract there might be such liability, *e.g.*, if there was a sale and the condition of the chattel resulted in a breach of an implied condition under a Sale of Goods Act,[1] or if the circulator had been guilty of fraud, *e.g.* by falsely stating that the chattel was safe, with the result that the recipient, or someone else, used the chattel and was injured,[2] or, in some select instances, when the chattel was considered as "dangerous *per se*", which indicated a chattel that was subject to a hidden defect known to the one circulating the chattel but not revealed to the recipient or anyone else.[3] The courts were unwilling, however, to impose any general duty of care with respect to chattels which were only dangerous *sub modo*, because they were subject to a concealed defect, even though normally such a chattel would not be dangerous. This was surprising, since it meant that the law imposed liability in the case of the wolf that was in wolf's clothing, but not where the wolf was in sheep's clothing.[4] An obviously dangerous chattel could lead to responsibility, but not one that appeared harmless but was in fact often more dangerous than something that was obviously so.

With the decision in *Donoghue v. Stevenson*[5] all this was changed. Since 1932, whenever anyone puts into circulation a chattel which is designed for use by people generally, in circumstances in which there is not or is not foreseeably likely to be an opportunity for an intermediate examination of the chattel such as would reveal its defects and dangers, there is a duty on the circulator to take

---

1 Fridman, *Sale of Goods in Canada*, 4th ed. (Toronto: Carswell, 1995), at 174-217.

2 *Langridge v. Levy* (1837), 2 M. & W. 519.

3 *Dixon v. Bell* (1816), 5 M. & S. 198; *George v. Skivington* (1869), L.R. 5 Ex. 1; *Ross v. Dunstall* (1921), 62 S.C.R. 393.

4 *Hodge & Sons v. Anglo-American Oil Co.* (1922), 12 Lloyd's Rep. 183 at 187 *per* Scrutton L. J.

5 [1932] A.C. 532.

reasonable care to ensure that the chattel is reasonably safe for the kind of use by an ultimate transferee, or consumer, that would normally be expected.[6]

Usually what is expected of the one putting a chattel in circulation, whether as manufacturer or otherwise, is that reasonable care will be taken to ensure that the chattel is not dangerous. This entails that the design, condition, and quality of the chattel are such that it is as free from potentially harmful defects as reasonable care can ensure.[7] But there is no guarantee that the chattel is harmless. Nor will the one putting the chattel in circulation be liable if something happens to the chattel while it is outside the control of that person.[8] In this respect, if it is normally expected that the chattel will be inspected or examined, or otherwise dealt with in a way that could expose or preclude the effect of harmful defects, by the ultimate consumer or a third person, prior to the consumer's use of the chattel, the original circulator of the chattel will not be liable should such intermediate examination, inspection or other action not occur, with the result that the chattel causes injury or damage.[9]

The duty of care required of those who put dangerous or potentially dangerous chattels into circulation may be satisfied by providing a warning, as long as such warning suffices to protect the user or consumer of the chattel.[10] However, no warning need be given if the contract under which the chattel was supplied and eventually used by a third party stated that no such duty was imposed on or undertaken by the manufacturer.[11] Furthermore, if the chattel is of such a technical nature that it will only be used when supervised by experts, for example varnish used to polish a floor,[12] a prescription drug to be taken only as and when advised by a doctor,[13] an implant to be put inside a patient's body by a surgeon,[14] a warning to the experts, on the basis of which such experts can determine if, when and how the chattel is to be used, may satisfy the requirements of the duty.

The duty applies to, and is imposed upon, manufacturers of a chattel, repairers, bailors generally, and builders. At one time it was held that if the chattel was fixed to realty and, by reason of its defective condition caused injury, the duty expounded in *Donoghue v. Stevenson* did not apply unless the chattel could be classified, as in the days before that decision, as a thing that was dangerous *per se*.[15] This qualification of the manufacturer's duty set out in 1932 no longer ap-

---

6 See also *Grant v. Australian Knitting Mills*, [1936] A.C. 85; *Shields v. E.V. Larson Co.*, [1962] O.R. 355 (C.A.), affirmed, *sub nom. Hobbs Mfg. Co. v. Shields*, [1962] S.C.R. 716.

7 *Nicholson v. John Deere Ltd.* (1986), 34 D.L.R. (4th) 542 (Ont. H.C.), affirmed (1989), 57 D.L.R. (4th) 639 (Ont. C.A.).

8 *LeBlanc v. Oland Breweries Ltd.* (1992), 130 N.B.R. (2d) 271 (Q.B.), affirmed (1994), 142 N.B.R. (2d) 287 (C.A.).

9 *Christie v. Putherbough Construction Co.* (1959), 18 D.L.R. (2d) 250 (Ont. H.C.).

10 *Lambert v. Lastoplex Chemicals Co.*, [1972] S.C.R. 569.

11 *Bow Valley Husky (Bermuda) Ltd. v. Saint John Shipbuilding Ltd.* (1997), 153 D.L.R. (4th) 385 (S.C.C.).

12 *Schmitz v. Stoveld* (1974), 64 D.L.R. (3d) 615 (Ont. Co. Ct.).

13 *Buchan v. Ortho Pharmaceuticals (Canada) Ltd.* (1986), 25 D.L.R. (4th) 658 (Ont. C.A.).

14 *Hollis v. Birch* (1995), 129 D.L.R. (4th) 609 (B.C.C.A.).

15 *Cavalier v. Pope*, [1906] A.C. 428: *Bottomley v. Bannister*, [1932] K.B. 458; *Otto v. Bolton* [1936] 2 K.B. 46.

plies.[16] Nor does the old distinction between classes of chattels apply except, perhaps, in regard to the degree of care to be expected from the party under the duty to use care.[17]

The duty operates to protect the immediate bailee or transferee of a chattel, whether gratuitous or not; any person to whom such bailee or transferee gives, lends, sells or otherwise disposes of the chattel; anyone else who lawfully obtains possession of the chattel in circumstances in which that person's use of the chattel is foreseeable as being likely;[18] and, any person who, though not a user, consumer or transferee of the chattel, is affected by its use in a defective condition.[19]

2. OCCUPIERS' LIABILITY

Well before 1932 it was accepted that a duty of care might be owed to a visitor coming onto another person's land or other premises. Liability for negligence in this respect developed in a very individual manner. In the first place, such duty as was owed was placed upon the "occupier" of the land or premises concerned. It was not ownership that carried with it responsibilities, but possession or occupation. While an owner of land might be liable for any nuisance which occurred on his or her land to the detriment of a neighbour,[20] the owner, unless he or she was also in possession, was not considered responsible for injuries resulting from "negligence" in the sense of a neglect of the state of the premises or land. Second, there appear to have emerged during the 19th century not one duty of care with respect to visitors, but several distinct ones depending upon the character or status of the visitor concerned. A distinction was made between visitors coming onto land or premises under a contract with the occupier and those who came on with permission, but not under contract. These first categories of visitors, all of whom were lawfully on premises or land, were differentiated from a trespasser who came on without permission and was unlawfully present. Legislative change occurred in England in 1957[21] and subsequently in almost all Canadian provinces.[22] The prior common law must be examined, however, because it continues to apply in Saskatchewan and because the changes made by the

---

16 *Lock v. Stibor* (1962), 34 D.L.R. (2d) 704 (Ont. S.C.).

17 See *e.g.*, *Rae v. T. Eaton Co. (Maritimes) Ltd.* (1961), 28 D.L.R. (2d) 522 (N.S.S.C.); *Dahlberg v. Naydiuk* (1969), 10 D.L.R. (3d) 319 (Man. C.A.); *Ives v. Clare Bros.*, [1971] 1 O.R. 417 (H.C.); *Tanner v. Atlantic Bridge Co.* (1966), 56 D.L.R. (2d) 162 (N.S.S.C.).

18 *Shields v. E.V. Larson Co.*, [1962] O.R. 355 (C.A.), affirmed *sub nom. Hobbs Mfg. Co. v. Shields*, [1962] S.C.R. 716.

19 *Good-Wear Treaders Ltd. v. D. & B. Holdings Ltd.* (1979), 8 C.C.L.T. 87 (Ont. H.C.).

20 Above p. 57.

21 *Occupiers Liability Act*, 1957, c. 31, amended by the *Occupiers Liability Act*, 1984, c. 3.

22 R.S.A. 2000, c. O-4; R.S.B.C. 1996, c. 337; R.S.M. 1987, c. O8; R.S.O. 1990, c. O.2; R.S.P.E.I. 1988, c. O-2; S.N.S. 1996, c. 27. New Brunswick abolished the law of occupiers' liability, and stated that all such cases were to be governed by the general law of negligence, by the *Law Reform Act*, S.N.B. 1993, c. L-1.2.

various provincial Occupiers' Liability Acts can only be understood against the background of that law.

Where a visitor entered under a contract which conferred on him or her a right of entry, the contract itself might stipulate the existence and extent of a duty of care owed to such visitor with respect to the state of the premises. In such event the contract governed all questions of duty and liability. More often than not such a contract did not, and does not specify anything with regard to such matters. In such instances the courts implied into such a contract a warranty that the premises were as safe as a reasonable person could make them for the purpose of the visit. This was not an absolute guarantee of safety for the visitor, nor did it apply unless it was necessary for the purpose of the visit that the premises should be safe. If entry onto premises or land was only incidental to, and not a necessary aspect of the real purpose of the contract, no such warranty could be implied. Where it did apply, however, it meant that the occupier might be liable even if the danger which caused harm to the contractual visitor was produced by the negligence of someone for whom, normally, the occupier would not be liable, namely an independent contractor, as contrasted with a servant or agent of the occupier. While all this may be said to involve liability in tort, its true basis is a breach of contract.[23]

By way of contrast, other lawful visitors are not protected by any contract. Prior to 1932, therefore, the law developed certain rules under which such visitors might still be protected from harm while on premises to which they were admitted by the occupier. To begin with, such a person was originally described as having been admitted under a licence. The distinction was drawn between a contractual licence (which might involve the implication of the kind of term to which reference has earlier been made) and a gratuitous one. In respect of the latter, since the visitor had given no consideration for the permission to come onto the premises or land, all that the law would grant by way of protection was an obligation on the occupier: (a) not to deceive or entrap the licensee; and (b) to warn him or her of any dangers or traps which were known to the licensor and were not obvious to the licensee.[24] The latter requirement was clearly an offshoot or corollary of the first. Thus in the absence of a contract between the parties, the law took the view that an occupier would only be liable for deliberate fraud, *i.e.*, intentionally endangering the gratuitous visitor, or conduct which was tantamount to fraud, in that it involved concealment of a danger which might harm the visitor and was known to the occupier.

---

23 *Maclenan v. Segar*, [1917] 2 K.B. 325; *Bell v. Travco Hotels Ltd.*, [1953] 1 Q.B. 473; *Sinclair v. Hudson Coal & Fuel Oil Ltd.*, [1966] 2 O.R. 256 (C.A.); *Butler v. Scott* (1976), 65 D.L.R. (3d) 692 (N.B.C.A.); *Payne v. Maple Leaf Gardens*, [1949] O.R. 26 (C.A.).

24 *Hambourg v. T. Eaton Co.*, [1935] S.C.R. 430; *Fraser v. Ronsten Developments Ltd.*, [1969] 2 O.R. 106 (H.C.); *Sanders v. Frawley Lake Lumber Co.*, [1972] 2 O.R. 130 (C.A.); *Booth v. City of St. Catharines*, [1948] S.C.R. 564; *Auffrey v. New Brunswick*, [1977] 1 S.C.R. 509.

This underwent some alteration and development in 1866 in the case of *Indermaur v. Dames*.[25] The case was concerned with liability of a visitor who did not come onto premises under contract (the contract in the case being between the occupier and the visitor's employer), but was there with permission, since he was employed as an assistant by the man who was engaged by the occupier to repair something that had gone wrong on the premises. The danger which caused his injury was not something hidden: it consisted in the lack of fencing around a shaft, into which the visitor fell. The argument was raised that this visitor was a bare licensee, who took the premises as he found them save for the possibility of his being deceived or intentionally led into being harmed. This argument did not succeed. The court took the view that the visitor in question belonged to a "special" class or category of lawful visitors, namely, those who were invited onto premises because the occupier had an interest in their being there for his purposes. Thus the notion of "invitees", or as it has sometimes been expressed "business visitors", was introduced into the common law. People in this class were given more protection by the law. The occupier was obliged to do more than warn them of dangers known to him but unrevealed to them. He had to take reasonable care to prevent their being harmed by "unusual dangers" of which he knew or of which he ought to have known. This involved a development of the concept of negligence in cases of visitors entering otherwise than under a contract. It meant that towards certain visitors, those who were there for the benefit of the occupier and not simply, as in the case of a gratuitous licensee, for the benefit of the visitor, the occupier had to exercise some more positive duty of care: the occupier had to take steps to make the premises reasonably safe.

The distinction between invitees and licensees created difficulties in several situations. Thus, if a visitor were the invitee of a person in occupation of one part of premises the courts were uncertain whether such visitor would only be the licensee and not the invitee of someone in occupation of another part of those premises through which the visitor had to go in order to get to the part occupied by his invitor.[26] If a visitor had a "right" to enter premises, for example, as a police officer executing a warrant, or a visitor coming to a public park, or an inspector reading a meter, it was not clear whether such a visitor was an invitee or a licensee.[27] In regard to the duties owed respectively to invitees and licensees, the meaning of, and difference between an "unusual danger" and a

---

25 (1866), L.R. 1 C.P. 274, affirmed (1867), L.R. 2 C.P. 311; *Haseldine v. Daw & Sons Ltd.*, [1941] 2 K.B. 343; *Hillman v. MacIntosh*, [1959] S.C.R. 387; *Smith v. Provincial Motors Ltd.* (1962), 32 D.L.R. (2d) 405 (N.S.S.C.).

26 *Fairman v. Perpetual Investment Building Society*, [1923] A.C. 74; *Jacobs v. London County Council*, [1950] A.C. 361; *Greisman v. Gillingham*, [1934] S.C.R. 375; *Arendale v. Federal Building Corp.*, [1962] O.R. 1053 (C.A.); *Levy v. Wellington Square Ltd.*, [1965] 1 O.R. 289 (Co. Ct.); *Mazur v. Sontowski*, [1952] 3 D.L.R. 333 (B.C.S.C.); *Ottawa v. Munroe*, [1954] S.C.R. 756.

27 *Ellis v. Fulham Borough Council*, [1938] 1 K.B. 212; *Nickell v. Windsor*, [1927] 1 D.L.R. 379 (Ont. C.A.); *Portelance v. Trustees of Grantham Separate School*, [1962] O.R. 365 (C.A.); *Pearson v. Lambeth Borough Council*, [1950] 2 K.B. 353; *Creighton v. Delisle Hospital Board* (1961), 34 D.L.R. (2d) 606 (Sask. Q.B.).

"hidden trap" was not always clear. Moreover after the decision in *Horton v. London Graving Dock Co.*,[28] in which the House of Lords held that, if an invitee was aware of a danger, however such awareness was acquired, it was no longer "unusual", it appeared that an invitor's duty towards an invitee, like that towards a licensee, could be fulfilled by providing a warning and no more.[29]

The statutes which have replaced the common law have resolved many, if not all, of these problems. This has been done by stipulating what is meant by "occupation" and "premises", and by defining the expression "visitor" in such a way as to make older differentiations otiose, or by eradicating such differentiations altogether and stipulating a common duty of care to use reasonable care in the circumstances, while the visitor is expected to take reasonable care for his or her own safety.[30] This common duty of care applies to protect the safety of all lawful visitors and their property, regardless of the arrangements or terms under which such visitors enter the premises. In British Columbia, Manitoba, Prince Edward Island and Ontario, it also applies to unlawful visitors, that is to say, trespassers, unless the trespasser enters with a view to committing a criminal act. In Alberta no duty of care is owed a trespasser. However an occupier will be liable for wilful or reckless conduct that causes the death or injury of a trespasser. Alberta also has special provisions regarding trespassing children, the effect of which would appear to make the occupier obliged to use virtually the same degree of care as towards an adult lawful visitor, if the occupier knows or has reason to know a child trespasser is on the premises.[31]

3. NEGLIGENT MISREPRESENTATION

Nineteenth-century courts drew a sharp, clear distinction between certain kinds of negligent acts and negligence in relation to the spoken or written word. Prior to 1963 the courts were unwilling to equate the latter with the former.[32] For a misrepresentation to result in tortious liability when it led to the occurrence of financial or economic, instead of physical harm, it had to have been a false misrepresentation involving commission of the tort of deceit.[33] Despite the emer-

---

28 [1951] A.C. 737. Hence it was queried whether the invitee's coming on to, or continuing to remain on the premises with knowledge of such danger meant that the visitor was *volens*, *i.e.*, assumed the risk.

29 For other cases which suggest the pre-statutory erosion of the invitee/licensee distinction, see *Mitchell v. C.N. Railway Co.* (1973), 46 D.L.R. (3d) 363 (S.C.C.); *Bartlett v. Weiche Apartments Ltd.* (1974), 55 D.L.R. (3d) 44 (Ont. C.A.).

30 No duty is owed, according to some of the statutes, when a visitor has willingly assumed the risk which results in the injury: *Brautigam v. Orderly Investments Ltd.* (1985), 36 Alta. L.R. (2d) 427 (Q.B.); *Hall v. Sorley* (1980), 23 B.C.L.R. 281 (S.C.); *Blomberg v. Blackcomb Skiing Enterprises Ltd.* (1992), 64 B.C.L.R. (2d) 51 (S.C.); *Peters v. Remer* (1993), 86 Man. R. (2d) 295 (Q.B.), affirmed (1994), 95 Man. R. (2d) 286 (C.A.).

31 See *Houle v. Calgary (City)* (1985), 20 D.L.R. (4th) 15 (Alta. C.A.), leave to appeal refused (1985), 20 D.L.R. (4th) 15*n* (S.C.C.).

32 *LeLievre v. Gould*, [1893] 1 Q.B. 491.

33 *Derry v. Peek* (1889), 14 App. Cas. 337: below p. 165.

gence of a tort of negligence as a result of the decision in *Donoghue v. Stevenson*,[34] the English Court of Appeal held in 1951[35] that a statement that was inaccurate by reason of its maker's negligence, not deliberate fraud, could not give rise to liability in the absence of a contract (or, as an earlier decision had held,[36] a fiduciary relationship) between the maker of the statement and the one to whom it was made who relied on the statement to that person's detriment. In other decisions it was held that there could be liability for a negligently made misstatement or misrepresentation if reliance thereon led to physical injury.[37] But in *Guay v. Sun Publishing Co.*[38] the Supreme Court of Canada held that an action would not lie for nervous shock, not physical injury, resulting from the careless publication of a false report of the death of the plaintiff's husband.

The situation was changed by the decision of the House of Lords in 1963 in *Hedley Byrne & Co. v. Heller & Partners*,[39] which, as seen earlier,[40] introduced the idea that, in the absence of a contract between the parties, there could be liability for economic loss caused negligently as opposed to intentionally. That decision virtually revolutionized the law, by recognizing a new category of liability, "negligence by words" in contrast with "negligent acts". A host of decisions since 1963 have attempted to elucidate and analyze the circumstances under which such liability may ensue,[41] in order to avoid the possibility of creating what was described in an American case[42] as "liability in an indeterminate amount for an indeterminate time to an indeterminate class".

Before such liability can arise the maker of the statement must owe a duty of care to the recipient of such statement. Such a duty, it has been said, is founded on a "special relationship" between the parties,[43] a relationship that has been said to be "equivalent to contract", although not actually contractual.[44] However in Canada, where, as noted earlier,[45] the determination whether a duty of care was

---

34 [1932] A.C. 326, above p. 69.

35 *Candler v. Crane, Christmas & Co.*, [1951] 2 Q.B. 164.

36 *Nocton v. Lord Ashburton*, [1914] A.C. 132; *Bank of Montreal v. Young* (1966), 60 D.L.R. (2d) 220 (B.C.S.C.).

37 See, *e.g.*, *Robson v. Chrysler Corp. (Canada) Ltd.* (1962), 32 D.L.R. (2d) 49 (Alta. C.A.); *Manitoba Sausage Manufacturing Co. v. City of Winnipeg* (1976), 1 C.C.L.T. 221 (Man. C.A.); *Gertsen v. Municipality of Metropolitan Toronto* (1974), 2 O.R. (2d) 1 (H.C.); *Ivo v. Halabura* (1990), 85 Sask. R. 147 (Q.B.).

38 [1953] 2 S.C.R. 216.

39 [1964] A.C. 465.

40 Above p. 81.

41 See, *e.g.*, *Haigh v. Bamford* (1977), 72 D.L.R. (3d) 68 (S.C.C.); *The Pas (Town) v. Porky Packers Ltd.* (1976), 65 D.L.R. (3d) 1 (S.C.C.); *Hofstrand Farms Ltd. v. B.C.*, [1986] 1 S.C.R. 228; *Fletcher v. Manitoba Public Insurance Corp.* (1990), 74 D.L.R. (4th) 636 (S.C.C.); *Queen v. Cognos Inc.* (1993), 99 D.L.R. (4th) 626 (S.C.C.); *Hercules Managements Ltd. v. Ernst & Young* (1997), 146 D.L.R. (4th) 577 (S.C.C.).

42 *Ultramares Corp. v. Touche*, 255 N.Y. 170 at 179 (1931).

43 *Queen v. Cognos Inc.* (1993), 99 D.L.R. (4th) 626 (S.C.C.), where the requirements for a successful action for negligent misrepresentation are set out.

44 *Hedley Byrne & Co. v. Heller & Partners*, [1964] A.C. 465; *Junior Books Ltd. v. Veitchi Co.*, [1983] 3 All E.R. 201.

45 Above p. 72.

owed by one party to the other is based upon the two-stage test propounded in the *Anns* case,[46] the relationship required is one of proximity where it is foreseeable that one party would reasonably rely on information or advice given by the other. Therefore the party on whom reliance is placed must possess some special skill or judgment which, reasonably not unreasonably, leads the other party to rely on the accuracy of the statement that has been made. Moreover the one providing the statement must have known, or in the circumstances, ought to have known or realized that reliance would be placed upon the information conveyed.

Cases since 1963 have applied the concept of liability for negligent misrepresentation to various kinds of business, trades, or professions which involve the provision of information or advice, for example, auditors,[47] real estate agents,[48] stockbrokers,[49] manufacturers,[50] and governmental officials.[51] But it is quite clear that the duty to take reasonable care to make accurate not misleading statements is not confined to those who carry on a business or profession of providing information or advice, as was once erroneously thought by the Privy Council.[52] As long as reliance on the skill or judgment of the maker of a statement was foreseen as being reasonably likely, the duty of care will arise. Indeed, as seen in a previous chapter,[53] a duty of care in the making of statements will also apply as between a solicitor, advising a client about a will, and a potential beneficiary under the will, who is not the solicitor's client, so that the solicitor can be liable if, by reason of his or her negligence, the will is invalid and the beneficiary is prevented from succeeding thereunder.[54]

Since "reasonable reliance" on the part of the recipient of some information or advice is a prerequisite for the liability of the one giving such information or advice, if the recipient's reliance is not "reasonable" it might be thought that no duty and no liability arise. However it has been held that, in such circumstances the recipient may be guilty of contributory negligence, which, as in all instances of negligence, will reduce the amount of damages that may be claimed.[55] Another ground upon which the *prima facie* liability of the negligent party may be affected is if the defendant has provided the statement under a contract, which contains a term excluding, qualifying, or limiting in some way,[56] or, even if no contract governed their relationship, the statement was given, as the statement in *Hedley Byrne*[57] was given, accompanied by a disclaimer that validly ousts any potential liability for the accuracy of the statement. In such circumstances,

---

46 *Anns v. Merton London Borough Council*, [1978] A.C. 728.

47 *Bloor Italian Gift Ltd. v. Dixon* (2000), 48 O.R. (3d) 760 (C.A.).

48 *Olsen v. Poirier* (1978), 21 O.R. (2d) 642 (H.C.), affirmed (1980), 28 O.R. (2d) 744 (C.A.).

49 *Central B.C. Planers Ltd. v. Hocker* (1970), 10 D.L.R. (3d) 689 (B.C.C.A.), leave to appeal refused (1971), 16 D.L.R. (3d) 368*n* (S.C.C.).

50 *Rivtow Marine Ltd. v. Washington Iron Works*, [1974] S.C.R. 1189.

51 *Windsor Motors Ltd. v. District of Powell River* (1969), 4 D.L.R. (3d) 155 (B.C.C.A.).

52 *Mutual Life & Citizen's Assurance Co. v. Evatt*, [1971] 1 All E.R. 150.

53 Above p. 82 note 70.

54 *Whittingham v. Crease & Co.* (1978), 88 D.L.R. (3d) 353 (B.C.S.C.).

55 *Grand Restaurants of Canada Ltd. v. City of Toronto* (1981), 32 O.R. (2d) 757 (H.C.).

56 *Carman Construction Ltd. v. C.P. Rly* (1982), 136 D.L.R. (3d) 193 (S.C.C.).

57 *Hedley Byrne & Co. v. Heller & Partners*, [1964] A.C. 465.

logically speaking, it cannot be said that the recipient is, or perhaps should be, reasonably relying on the statement. If that is so, then the conditions for the existence of a duty and for ultimate liability have not been fulfilled.

4. PROFESSIONAL NEGLIGENCE

Practitioners of professions are usually bound to those for whom they act by a contract by the terms of which they are obliged to perform their professional work with reasonable care and skill. The failure to do so will expose them to an action for breach of contract. However the negligent performance of their professional duties will also give rise to liability in tort which will be concurrent with, and alternate to, their contractual liability. Formerly the existence of a contract governing the relationship between a professional and his or her client or patient excluded the possibility of tortious liability for negligence. This is no longer the situation in Canada,[58] or in England.[59] Thus, if the professional fails to observe the standard of care and skill that would normally and reasonably be expected of someone exercising the profession in question, and causes physical or financial harm to the client or patient, the latter may sue the professional for breach of contract or in tort for negligence, unless a valid, operative term of the contract excludes, or otherwise qualifies or limits, the liability of the professional.[60]

However, unlike other professionals, doctors and dentists are also obliged to inform their patients of the risks involved in any operation, so that the patient can give an "informed" consent to the performance of the procedure. The failure to provide such information may result in a consent by the patient not sufficing to relieve a doctor or dentist from liability for either trespass to the person or negligence.[61]

A professional person who misleads or provides inaccurate information which results in the conclusion of a contract with a client or patient may also be liable for negligent misrepresentation.[62] In the case of some professionals, for example, lawyers or real estate agents, the negligent performance of the

---

58 *Central Trust Co. v. Rafuse* (1986), 31 D.L.R. (4th) 481 (S.C.C.).

59 *Henderson v. Merritt Syndicates Ltd.*, [1995] 2 A.C. 149.

60 *BG Checo International v. B.C. Hydro* (1993), 99 D.L.R. (4th) 577 (S.C.C.); *Canadian Pacific Hotels Ltd. v. Bank of Montreal* (1988), 40 D.L.R. (4th) 385 (S.C.C.).

It is now clear that a lawyer, whether acting as a barrister, *i.e.*, as an advocate, or as a solicitor, *i.e.*, out of court, may be liable for negligence in the performance of his or her professional work: *Demarco v. Ungaro* (1979), 95 D.L.R. (3d) 385 (Ont. H.C.); *Ali v. Sidney Mitchell & Co.*, [1980] A.C. 198; *Arthur J.S. Hill & Co. (a firm) v. Simons*, [2000] 3 All E.R. 673.

61 Above p. 93 note 127.

62 *Carman Construction Ltd. v. C.P. Rly.* (1982), 136 D.L.R. (3d) 193 (S.C.C.); *Rainbow Industrial Caterers Ltd. v. C.N. Railway Co.* (1990), 67 D.L.R. (4th) 348 (B.C.C.A.), affirmed (1991), 84 D.L.R. (4th) 291 (S.C.C.).

professional's contractual duty to a client that results in harm to a third party may also render the professional liable in tort to such third party.[63]

5. EMPLOYERS' LIABILITY

Even before the decision in *Donoghue v. Stevenson*[64] the relationship of employer and employee gave rise to a duty of care that was owed by the employer towards the employee. That duty was both contractual and tortious in character. It was distinct from, as well as more onerous than, any duty owed by an employer to visitors to the employer's premises. It applied for the protection of those who were employed whether for reward, *i.e.,* under a contract of employment, or gratuitously, as volunteers, as where a person of his or her own free will came to the assistance of someone who was working for the employer under a contract of employment.[65] It can also apply where an employee is "transferred" from one employer to another for a limited period or purpose. As where the issue is one of vicarious liability for the acts of such an employee, the question becomes one of determining whether the nature of the arrangement between the two employers is such that the transferred employee has become, for all purposes, the employee of the party to whom the employee has been transferred, which may depend on such matters as "control" and whether along with the employee some equipment for him or her to use has also been transferred *pro tempore*.[66]

The duty imposed on the appropriate employer is to provide the employee with what has been termed "a safe system of work".[67] This entails that the employer must take reasonable care to ensure that the premises where the employee works, the equipment with which the employee works, and the fellow employees with whom the employee works are such as to make the employment reasonably safe for the employee. The employer has to use reasonable care to prevent injury to the employee from danger of which the employer is aware or of which he or she ought reasonably to be aware.[68] In this regard it is to be noted that the employer will not have performed this duty if he or she merely delegates its performance to another employee. The duty is personal to the employer.[69]

As is true of other instances of liability for negligence, the employer may escape, or qualify, liability by a plea of consent or assumption of risk, if it can really be said that the employee has consented to run the risk of being injured by

---

63 *Whittingham v. Crease & Co.* (1978), 88 D.L.R. (3d) 353 (B.C.S.C.), above p. 82; *Dodds v. Millman* (1964), 47 W.W.R. 690 (B.C.S.C.); *Chand v. Sabo Bros. Realty Ltd.*, [1979] 2 W.W.R. 248 (Alta. C.A.); *Olsen v. Poirier* (1978), 21 O.R. (2d) 642 (H.C.), affirmed (1980), 28 O.R. (2d) 744 (C.A.).

64 [1932] A.C. 562.

65 *Huba v. Schulze* (1962), 32 D.L.R. (2d) 171 (Man. C.A.).

66 Above pp. 33-34.

67 *Veronneau v. Gregory* (1979), 11 B.C.L.R. 121 (S.C.).

68 *Shenbansky v. Kapchinsky* (1981), 28 A.R. 451 (Q.B.), varied (1982), 41 A.R. 424 (C.A.).

69 *Marshment v. Borgstrom*, [1942] S.C.R. 374.

the employer's breach of duty,[70] or by a plea of contributory negligence when the employee has been guilty of a failure to look after his or her own safety. There is also the possibility that, if the employee's injury has been caused by the negligence of a fellow employee rather than by the defective state of the premises or equipment, the employer may be able to plead the doctrine of "common employment",[71] that has been abolished in England and in some parts of Canada.[72]

The common law duty of care owed by an employer has been augmented by statutory provisions, often more specific in their content, that have been enacted in respect of various kinds of employment that have the potential of causing injury to employees. Where such provisions exist, their breach gives rise to an action for breach of statute, or statutory negligence.[73] Moreover the common law action for negligence against an employer has been replaced in various Canadian provinces by Workers' Compensation Acts, under which certain employees injured in industrial accidents have an administrative remedy from a board in place of an action in the courts.[74]

6. LOSS OF SERVICES

By way of corollary to the possible liability of an employer for injury to an employee incurred in the course of the latter's employment, reference must be made to the liability of someone who negligently injures an employee to that employee's employer for loss caused to the employer by reason of the employee's inability to perform his or her service because of the injury.[75] The action by an employer is distinct from any action the employee may bring against the negligent defendant.

The action available to the employer for loss of the employee's services, the action *per quod servitium amisit*, emerged several hundred years ago. It has long been recognized as an exception to the notion that, for liability in negligence to arise, a tortfeasor must have owed a duty of care to someone who was foreseeably likely to be affected by the tortfeasor's careless behaviour. It is immaterial to liability under this action whether the negligent party knew or ought to have known that the immediate victim of the negligence was employed by a third person. In this the action *per quod* is different from other actions which were available to an employer whose employee had been enticed away, or was

---

70 *Smith v. Baker*, [1891] A.C. 325.

71 *Carl v. Warren*, [1959] O.R. 485 (H.C.), affirmed (1960), 23 D.L.R. (2d) 156 (Ont. C.A.).

72 *E.g.*, British Columbia, by the *Workers Compensation Act*, R.S.B.C. 1996, c. 492, s. 104(1).

73 Below p. 108.

74 *Ryan v. Ontario (Workmen's Compensation Board)* (1988), 6 O.A.C. 33 (Div. Ct.). See, however, how this can be circumvented, as in *Berger v. Willowdale A.M.C.* (1982), 131 D.L.R. (3d) 585 (Ont. H.C.), affirmed (1983), 145 D.L.R. (3d) 247 (Ont. C.A.).

75 *Canada (Attorney-General) v. Kerr* (1997), 148 D.L.R. (4th) 784 (Ont. Gen. Div.). But it has been abolished in British Columbia, by the *Law Reform Amendment Act, 1988*, S.B.C. 1988, c. 42, s. 4.

harboured after leaving the employer, by another person. For the latter to be liable it was necessary to prove knowledge by such a party that the one enticed or harboured was in the service of someone else.[76]

The action *per quod* may be brought when the necessary relationship of employer and employee between the injured party and the plaintiff is established. Once again the test of whether that relationship existed at the material time is "control", the same test used to determine whether someone is an employer who will be liable vicariously for the tortious act of another.[77] In England the availability of the action has been limited to those employees who are "domestic" or "menial" servants, namely, those employed in a house or farm.[78] Some Canadian provincial courts have adopted the same approach. Others appear to hold that the action is also available to employers employing others in the fields of commerce and industry. However, even those courts which adopt the more limited approach appear to accept that the action will be available if the injured party is in the military:[79] but not if that party is in a police force.[80] The action is not available if the employee has been killed outright by the defendant's negligence, but it is available, in respect of the intervening period, if the employee is injured and later dies. It may not be available once the employee's employment is terminated. Nor can the employer sue unless the employee himself or herself has a cause of action against the defendant.[81]

The damages recoverable in this action are restricted to what has been paid to someone to substitute for the affected employee.[82] An employer will not be able to claim loss of profits caused by the absence of the employee from employment by reason of the injuries inflicted by the negligent defendant. Such "relational economic loss" is outside the limits of what is foreseeable.[83]

7. STATUTORY NEGLIGENCE

For the protection of the public at large, statutes frequently impose duties and make the breach of such duties an offence punishable by fine, imprisonment, or both. Examples of this can be found in legislation dealing with the regulation of highway traffic. If the breach of such a statutory duty also causes harm to a particular individual it may be possible for such a party to maintain an action in tort for damages against the offender, an action that is distinct from any criminal penalty to which the offender may be exposed. In such instances the latter will be guilty of a tort that has been variously known as breach of statutory duty or statutory negligence.

---

76 *Jones Bros. (Hunstanton) v. Steven*, [1955] 1 Q.B. 275.

77 Above p. 33.

78 *Inland Revenue Commissioners v. Hambrook*, [1956] 2 Q.B. 641.

79 *R. v. Richardson & Adams*, [1948] S.C.R. 57; *R. v. Buchinsky*, [1983] 1 S.C.R. 481.

80 *Myers & City of Guelph v. Hoffman*, [1955] O.R. 965 (H.C.).

81 *Canada (Attorney-General) v. Jackson*, [1946] S.C.R. 489.

82 *Genereux v. Petersen, Howells & Hunter (Canada) Ltd.* (1973), 34 D.L.R. (3d) 614 (Ont. C.A.).

83 *D'Amato v. Badger* (1996), 137 D.L.R. (4th) 129 (S.C.C.).

Not all statutes that impose duties the breach of which invites criminal liability will permit such an action. Whether a statute does so will depend upon the way it is interpreted. Several factors affect such interpretation. One is whether the duty that is in issue was imposed to protect the public generally or only a particular section of the public to which the injured individual plaintiff belonged. Only a duty of the second type will support a civil action for breach of statute. Another is whether the nature of the penalty imposed by the statute is such that it is clear that the legislature that enacted the statute intended that such penalty should be the sole consequence of a breach. The more serious the penalty the less likely will it be that a civil action will be regarded as permissible. A further factor, of more recent origin, is whether the statute as well as imposing duties also creates an administrative structure to investigate complaints of breach of statute, impose sanctions on offenders, and award damages.[84]

Even if the statute can be construed or interpreted as allowing a civil action for its breach, the plaintiff must establish: (a) that what occurred was foreseen by the statute as a probable consequence of its breach; (b) that the plaintiff belonged to the class of persons that it was foreseen would be likely to be affected by a breach of the statute; (c) that the breach of the statute was the effective cause of the plaintiff's injury or damage.

One aspect of this liability underwent change as a result of the decision of the Supreme Court of Canada in *Canada v. Saskatchewan Wheat Pool.*[85] Prior to that case it was most frequently considered, although not in the United States, that, in contrast with the situation under the law of negligence which required proof of the relevant standard of care and evidence that the conduct of the defendant amounted to a failure to observe such standard, where a plaintiff alleged an injury caused by the breach of a statutory duty proof that the duty had been breached was enough to satisfy the allegation that the defendant had acted negligently. The statutory duty, in other words, set out the standard of care that was required of a defendant in the appropriate circumstances. In the United States liability for breach of statute, or statutory negligence, was assimilated into the general law of negligence. Thus proof of a breach of statutory duty *might*, but might not, establish that the defendant was negligent so as to be liable civilly. The *Wheat Pool* case adopted the American approach and held that breach of a statutory duty was some, but was not conclusive, evidence of negligence. In consequence, while, under certain conditions, a breach of statute can result in liability in negligence, it may not be entirely accurate to speak of breach of statutory duty or statutory negligence as a distinct variety of negligence liability.[86]

---

84 *Board of Governors of Seneca College of Applied Arts & Technology v. Bhadauria* (1981), 124 D.L.R. (3d) 193 (S.C.C.).

85 (1983), 143 D.L.R. (3d) 9 (S.C.C.).

86 But see *Whistler Cable TV Ltd. v. Ipec Canada Ltd.* (1992), 75 B.C. L. R. (2d) 48 (S.C.).
Note that an *intentional*, not negligent, breach of statute designed to inflict injury is governed by different principles, those involved in the law of conspiracy; below p. 181.

Chapter 9

Liability under the Rule in Rylands v. Fletcher

1. THE RULE STATED

An important principle was stated in England shortly after the middle of the 19th century in the famous case of *Rylands v. Fletcher*.[1] Although what was enunciated in that decision was said to be derived from the earlier law of trespass to land and nuisance, in effect what was achieved in that case was the creation of a new instance of liability where the carrying on of a potentially dangerous activity on the defendant's land led to damage to the defendant's neighbour. The circumstances of the case made it necessary to establish such a new form of liability because (a) neither the defendant nor the defendant's independent contractor had been negligent; and (b) what occurred did not give rise to tortious liability for trespass to land or nuisance. What happened was that the plaintiff's mines were flooded by the escape of water from the land of the defendant when the latter employed a contractor to build a reservoir on the defendant's land to provide water for the defendant's mills. On the basis of the doctrine for which the case is authority, the defendant was held liable for what happened. In the Court of Exchequer Chamber, Blackburn J. stated the doctrine in these words:

> We think that the true rule of law is that the person who, for his own purposes, brings on his land and collects and keeps there anything likely to do mischief if it escapes, must keep it at his peril; and if he does not do so, is prima facie answerable for all the damage which is the natural consequence of its escape.[2]

This statement of the principle was accepted and approved by the House of Lords in that case, with one significant addition: namely, that the defendant, in order to attract liability under this principle, must have been making what was called a "non-natural use" of his land when he brought, collected, and kept there the thing which escaped and caused the mischief.[3] This added a new dimension to the doctrine expounded in the lower court, by requiring that the use of the land by the defendant would have to be something that was out of the ordinary,

---

[1] (1866), L. R. 1 Ex. 265, affirmed (1868), L.R. 3 H.L. 330.

[2] (1866), L.R. 1 Ex. at 279.

[3] (1868), L.R. 3 H.L. at 340.

something that was ultrahazardous, something that was not previously regarded as necessary and usual for normal living.[4] The courts in Canada, as well as England, have utilized this notion in order to differentiate what might be called simple, domestic, essential, everyday use of the land, such as farming and maintaining a house, from extraspecial, more dangerous uses of land that carry with them some imbalance of the normal risks inherent in landowning,[5] for example, erecting an electric generator or a factory that handles radioactive material, building a reservoir, or operating a sewage disposal plant.[6] But there are many other examples of the sort of activity that has been held to involve a "non-natural" user of land for the purposes of the doctrine.[7] An examination and analysis of the multitude of decisions on this point reveal that, while the general idea of the distinction between natural and non-natural uses of land may be understood, the application of that distinction is sometimes not so easy to understand.

2. NUISANCE DISTINGUISHED

The requirement that liability under *Rylands v. Fletcher* can only arise if a non-natural use of land is being undertaken by the defendant distinguishes such liability from liability for a nuisance that causes interference or inconvenience. The latter, as noted in an earlier chapter,[8] requires that the defendant's use of the land in question be "unreasonable". This does not have the same connotation as "non-natural". A use of land may be both unreasonable and non-natural: or it could be natural but unreasonable or non-natural but reasonable. A further mark of differentiation between liability under *Rylands v. Fletcher* and liability for certain kinds of nuisance lies in the fact that the former can arise where a single incident has occurred: whereas, except where physical damage to the plaintiff or the plaintiff's property is concerned, nuisance involves the existence of a continuing situation. *Rylands v. Fletcher* liability also entails the escape of something dangerous from the defendant's land to the plaintiff's.[9] In many instances of nuisance it is unnecessary for anything substantial to have escaped as long as what is being done on the defendant's land interferes with the plaintiff's enjoyment of his or her land. Moreover what is collected by the defendant may cause a nuisance to a neighbour but might not qualify as the collection of a dangerous

---

4 *J. Porter Co. v. Bell*, [1955] 1 D.L.R. 62 (N.S.C.A.); *Chu v. District of North Vancouver* (1983), 139 D.L.R. (3d) 201 (B.C.S.C.). But see the remarks of Krever J. in *North York v. Kert Chemical Industries Inc.* (1985), 33 C.C.L.T. 184 (Ont. H.C.J.).

5 *Aldridge v. Van Patter*, [1952] O.R. 595 (S.C.); *Heintzman & Co. v. Hashman Construction Co.*, [1973] 1 W.W.R. 202 (Alta. T.D.).

6 *Saccardo v. Hamilton*, [1971] 2 O.R. 479 (H.C.); *Lickoch v. Madu* (1973), 34 D.L.R. (3d) 569 (Alta. C.A.); *Richard v. New Brunswick Power Corp.* (1993), 131 N.B.R. (2d) 153 (Q.B.).

7 See, *e.g.*, *Gertsen v. Municipality of Metropolitan Toronto* (1974), 41 D.L.R. (3d) 646 (Ont. H.C.); *O'Brien v. Newfoundland Light & Power Co.* (1984), 51 Nfld. & P.E.I.R. 30 (Nfld. Dist. Ct.); *Ira Berg Ltd. v. Skrow's Produce (1971) Ltd.* (1990), 76 D.L.R. (4th) 431 (Ont. Gen. Div.).

8 Above p. 60.

9 *Read v. J. Lyons & Co.*, [1947] A.C. 156.

thing for the purposes of the rule in *Rylands v. Fletcher*. Finally, a landowner may be liable in nuisance even if the landowner has not created the nuisance but has "continued" or "adopted" it.[10] For a defendant to be liable under *Rylands v. Fletcher* the landowner, or someone for whom the landowner is vicariously liable, must have brought the dangerous thing, the escape of which causes harm, onto the defendant's land. And this must have been done for the defendant's own purposes, which means that if what the defendant did was to benefit the defendant and, *inter alia*, the plaintiff,[11] the defendant may not be liable under *Rylands v. Fletcher*, whereas it is no excuse in a case of nuisance for the defendant to plead that what was being done was for the benefit of others, such as the plaintiff or the public at large (unless some applicable statutory authority empowers the defendant to carry on the offending activity).[12]

3. STRICTNESS OF LIABILITY

As the facts and decision in the case of *Rylands v. Fletcher* demonstrate, liability under the rule is strict. Neither an intent to injure nor negligence, whether on the part of the defendant or someone for whom the defendant is responsible (which, by way of exception to the usual principles, includes an independent contractor) is relevant to the imposition of liability if the requirements of such liability are met.[13] However, negligence may become an ingredient of liability in certain circumstances. Thus it is accepted that a defendant can escape liability under *Rylands v. Fletcher* if it is proved that the escape that caused the harm or damage was the result of: (a) the act of a stranger, *i.e.* one who is neither servant, agent nor independent contractor;[14] (b) an act of God or *vis major*, *i.e.* some event over which the defendant did not have, and could not have had control, nor could have foreseen;[15] or (c) some default or conduct on the part of the plaintiff.[16] Nor may the defendant be liable where the defendant was acting under the authority of some statute.[17] However, if the defendant was negligent in not foreseeing the possible occurrence of what happened and not taking reasonable

---

10 Above p. 63.

11 *Elfassy v. Sylben Investments Ltd.* (1978), 21 O.R. (2d) 609 (H.C.).

12 Above p. 64.

13 A different view seems to have been adopted in England and Australia, where a closer connection between the doctrine of *Rylands v. Fletcher*, nuisance and negligence has been enunciated: see *Cambridge Water Co. v. Eastern Counties Leather plc*, [1994] 2 A.C. 264 (with respect to the extent of liability, which, as decided in relation to nuisance in *The Wagon Mound (No. 2)*, [1967] 1 A.C. 617, was limited to foreseeable consequences); *Burnie Port Authority v. General Jones Pty Ltd.* (1994), 179 C.L.R. 520.

14 *Northwestern Utilities Ltd. v. London Guarantee Accident Co.*, [1936] A.C. 108 (P.C.); *Hale v. Jennings Bros.*, [1938] 1 All E.R. 579 (C.A.); *Balfour v. Barty-King*, [1957] 1 Q.B. 496 (C.A.).

15 *Rylands v. Fletcher* (1866), L. R. 1 Ex. at 279.

16 *Pattison v. Prince Edward Region Conservation Authority* (1984), 30 C.C.L.T. 304 (Ont. H.C.).

17 *Turpin v. Halifax-Dartmouth Bridge Commission* (1960), 21 D.L.R. (2d) 623 (N.S.C.A.); *Gertsen v. Municipality of Metropolitan Toronto* (1974), 41 D.L.R. (3d) 646 (Ont. H.C.); *Tahsis Co. v. Canadian Forest Products Ltd.* (1968), 70 D.L.R. (2d) 376 (B.C.S.C.). See also above p. 64.

steps to guard against its occurrence, or if the defendant was negligent in the manner in which what was authorized by statute was performed (unless the statute gave the defendant "absolute immunity"), none of these excuses or exemptions from liability will be applicable.[18]

4. THE COLLECTION OF DANGEROUS THINGS

Liability under the doctrine of *Rylands v. Fletcher* depends upon the collection or accumulation of things considered to be "dangerous". This means that the defendant must bring the "dangerous" object or objects on to the land: if something grows there naturally any liability that may ensue will rest upon the tort of nuisance or, where appropriate, negligence. What is "dangerous" for the purposes of this doctrine is debatable. Almost anything can be dangerous, particularly if it is collected in bulk. Some things can be dangerous when accumulated singly, such as a motor vehicle leaking petrol.[19] The accumulation of gas, electricity or water, which, in small quantities, may not be dangerous, may result in the collection of a dangerous thing under the doctrine (as well as rendering the use of the land by such accumulation a "non-natural" use).

Whatever the defendant has done, as previously noted, must have been done solely for the defendant's own purposes. This will be the situation when the defendant brings, collects or keeps[20] the dangerous, or mischievous (as it is sometimes termed) object in order to attain the defendant's own economic, financial, hedonistic, or aesthetic advantages. Despite one decision to the contrary,[21] the generally accepted view would appear to be that if the defendant argues that what was being done benefited the community at large this will not exempt the defendant from liability.[22] If those doing things beneficial to the community wish to be exempted or excused from liability they must be able to rely on some statutory authority, just as in cases of nuisance.[23]

5. THE SCOPE OF LIABILITY

Originally the doctrine of *Rylands v. Fletcher* applied to afford protection to adjoining landowners in respect of damage to their property. It covered injuries to land and things on the land, including chattels belonging to the landowner. As a result of subsequent judicial development, the doctrine now can be applied to

---

18 *Rickards v. Lothian*, [1913] A.C. 263; *Holinaty v. Hawkins*, [1966] 1 O.R. 9 (C.A.); *Greenock Corp. v. Caledonian Rly.*, [1917] A.C. 556.

19 *Cf. Ira-Berg Ltd. v. Skrow's Produce (1971) Ltd.* (1991), 76 D.L.R. (4th) 431 (Ont. Gen. Div.); *Musgrove v. Pandelis*, [1919] 2 K.B. 63.

20 *Canada (Attorney-General) v. Diamond Waterproofing Ltd.* (1974), 4 O.R. (2d) 489 (C.A.).

21 *Danku v. Town of Fort Frances* (1977), 14 O.R. (2d) 285 (Dist. Ct.).

22 *J. Porter & Co. v. Bell*, [1955] 1 D.L.R. 62 (N.S.C.A.); *Lawrysyn v. Town of Kipling* (1964), 50 W.W.R. 430 (Sask. Q.B.), affirmed (1965), 55 W.W.R. 108 (Sask. C.A.).

23 Above p. 64.

situations where what has occurred, following the escape of the dangerous thing collected by the defendant, is damage to the property of someone who is not a landowner but has a licence to go or put things on or under the land of another party:[24] and to the causing of damage, including personal injury, to someone who is neither a landowner nor an occupier of the land on which the damage or injury occurred.[25]

Thus the pristine narrowness of the doctrine, justified by the strictness of its nature, has been subjected to a process of enlargement as a result of which the doctrine is potentially capable of dealing with many different situations. This might make the scope of strict liability very wide. However, the manner in which courts have interpreted and applied the notions of "dangerous things" and "non-natural use", as well as the extreme importance of an escape from the defendant's land[26] before there can be liability under this doctrine, reveals the limitations of the doctrine. Although *Rylands v. Fletcher*, like the law of nuisance, may be of great value in assisting the law of negligence to provide a remedy for injuries to property and personal injuries, there is no question of the law of negligence, or of nuisance, being displaced by, or incorporated in that doctrine.

---

24 *Charing Cross Electric Supply Co. v. Hydraulic Power Co.*, [1914] 3 K.B. 772 (C.A.); *Eastern & S.A. Telegraph Co. v. Cape Town Tramways*, [1902] A.C. 381.

25 *Aldridge v. Van Patter*, [1952] O.R. 595 (S.C.).

26 *Read v. J. Lyons & Co.*, [1947] A.C. 156; *Deyo v. Kingston Speedway Ltd.*, [1954] O.R. 223 (C.A.), affirmed [1955] 1 D.L.R. 718 (S.C.C.).

Chapter 10

LIABILITY FOR FIRE

1. POSSIBLE ACTIONS

Where the victim or the victim's property is damaged by fire, whether or not the victim is the occupier of property, the conduct of the alleged wrongdoer (whose acts are responsible for the fire or the consequential damage it produces) may be tortious on a variety of grounds. He or she may have acted deliberately, with the intention of creating the fire in order to damage the victim's property or spreading it for such purpose. In such circumstances the wrongdoer may be guilty of trespass (where appropriate) or nuisance, depending upon such factors as the directness or indirectness of the invasion of and damage to the victim's property.[1] The wrongdoer may have acted negligently, either as to the creation of the fire or its movement onto the property of the victim. In such a case the wrongdoer may be liable in negligence, if a duty of care was owed by him or her to the victim.[2] Another possibility is that the fire started or spread to the victim's property accidentally. Such situations raise the question whether there can be liability in those cases without proof of an intent to injure or negligence.

2. STRICT LIABILITY

At common law, even before the advent of the doctrine of *Rylands v. Fletcher*,[3] there was strict liability for damage caused by a fire which started on the defendant's land (whether caused by the defendant, his servant or agent, or even a stranger who was on his premises).[4] This was altered in England by a statute passed during the 18th century,[5] under which liability for fire or its consequences would only arise where the fire was commenced through negligence, or it spread as a result of such misconduct on the part of the defendant. Those statutes would seem to be applicable in Canada either as a consequence of their reception into the law of the provinces when they acquired separate legal status,

---

1 See above pp. 39, 58.

2 See above p. 69.

3 (1866), L.R. 1 Ex. 265, affirmed (1868), L.R. 3 H.L. 330.

4 *Beaulieu v. Fingham* (1401), Y.B. Pach. 2, Hen. IV Fo. 18, pl. 6; *Balfour v. Barty-King*, [1957] 1 Q.B. 496. This was known as liability for *ignis suus*. It no longer applies in Australia: *Burnie Port Authority v. General Jones Pty Ltd.* (1994), 179 C.L.R. 520.

5 *Fire Prevention (Metropolis) Act*, 1774, 14 Geo. 3, c. 78, s. 86.

or as a result of the enactment of similar legislation by the provinces.[6] At first sight, therefore, it would appear that only where there was negligence in relation to the handling of fire will there be liability in tort. However, the English courts have held that there will be liability if the defendant can be shown to have committed some specific tort, such as nuisance, from which the fire occurred.[7] Moreover, where the fire was the consequence of the collection of something within the doctrine of *Rylands v. Fletcher*, or the fire itself can be treated as such an object, that doctrine will apply and there is no need to establish negligence on the part of the defendant. Thus, if the defendant brings combustible material onto his or her land in sufficiently large quantities, and for his or her own purposes, and a fire results and spreads to the land of the plaintiff, even though no negligence can be proved against the defendant, he or she will be liable. So too, if he or she has a fire on the land other than in pursuance of a "natural" use of the land, and the fire "escapes". For example, a domestic fire in a grate in a room of the defendant's house will not attract the operation of the doctrine of *Rylands v. Fletcher*. But a fire which was commenced for industrial purposes, such as a blast furnace in a factory, or a fire which was started in order to burn off stubble in a field, will invite the application of the doctrine in appropriate circumstances. The latter instances, therefore, may be cases of strict liability. Where the fire is a purely domestic, normal one, it will only give rise to liability if there is proof of negligence in the way it was kept or allowed to get out of control.[8]

---

6 See, for Ontario, the *Accidental Fires Act*, R.S.O. 1990, c. A.4.

7 *Filliter v. Phippard* (1847), 11 Q.B. 347; *Spicer v. Smee*, [1946] 1 All E.R. 489; *Mason v. Levy Auto Parts of England Ltd.*, [1967] 2 Q.B. 530.

8 *Sochaki v. Sas*, [1947] 1 All E.R. 344; *Ayoub v. Beaupré* (1964), 45 D.L.R. (2d) 411 (S.C.C.); *Gogo v. Eureka Sawmills*, [1944] 4 D.L.R. 689, varied [1945] 4 D.L.R. 127 (B.C.C.A.); *Musgrove v. Pandelis*, [1919] 2 K.B. 43 (C.A.); *Canada (Attorney General) v. Diamond Waterproofing Ltd.* (1974), 4 O.R. (2d) 489 (C.A.). See also *Maritime Telegraph v. Joseph Neiff Land Surveyors Ltd.* (1975), 15 N.S.R. (2d) 575 (T.D.).

Chapter 11

Liability for Harm Caused by Animals

1. IN GENERAL

There are various ways in which an animal may cause harm, and various grounds upon which liability may arise in respect of such harm. Liability can arise even if the animal that has caused the harm did not belong to a species that is normally regarded as dangerous, a categorization that, as will be seen,[1] has an important legal connotation. A domestic, or normally tame animal, such as a cat or a dog, which is used or kept in a certain way, may be the cause of liability.[2] For example, trespass, nuisance, or negligence may be committed as a result of conduct involving the use of such an animal. Thus a cat may be used as an instrument to cause harm, as when it is picked up and thrown at the plaintiff. That would amount to trespass to the person, in the same way as if the defendant had thrown a stick at the plaintiff. Or the defendant may keep a noisy or smelly animal or group of animals on his or her land resulting in the commission of a nuisance to the plaintiff, a neighbouring landowner who is upset by, or inconvenienced by the noise or smell. So, too, a defendant may be careless in the manner an animal, such as a dog or a horse, is controlled, leading to the plaintiff's suffering injury or damage to property. If, in the circumstances, the defendant owed a duty of care to the plaintiff, the defendant might be liable in negligence. By way of illustration, anyone who brings an animal onto the highway owes a duty of care to other users of the highway: hence, if the animal, through the defendant's negligence, causes harm to someone or someone's property, liability for negligence will ensue.[3] According to the decision of the Supreme Court of Canada in

---

1 Below p. 121.

2 See, *e.g.*, *Acheson v. Dory* (1993), 8 Alta. L.R. (3d) 128, affirmed (1994), 24 Alta. L.R. (3d) 187 (C.A.); *Lucas v. Pettit* (1906), 12 O.L.R. 448. The defendant might also be liable as an employer where the employee's injury is caused by the employer's animal: *Gilmour v. Mossop*, [1951] S.C.R. 815.

Liability for what is done by an animal may also arise under the rule in *Rylands v. Fletcher* (1866), L.R. 1 Ex. 265, affirmed (1868), L.R. 3 H.L. 330, see above chapter 9, p. 111, in the event of the escape of a dangerous animal, or a collection of otherwise not dangerous animals. But an escape is necessary for such liability: *Lewis v. Oeming* (1983), 24 C.C.L.T. 81 (Alta. Q.B.).

3 See, *e.g.*, *Carnivet v. Brown's Bread Ltd.* (1929), 64 O.L.R. 580; *Moffet v. Downing* (1981), 120 D.L.R. (3d) 560 (Ont. C.A.); *Buold v. Dempsey* (1996), 181 N.B.R. (2d) 111 (Q.B.).

Fleming v. Atkinson[4] such liability for negligence will also ensue should an animal escape from the defendant's land onto the highway and there injure a plaintiff or damage a plaintiff's property.

Over and above such situations, there exist two important forms of liability that apply exclusively where harm has been caused by an animal. Both, except to the extent that provincial statutes have made changes with respect to particular kinds of animals or to particular kinds of damage perpetrated by animals,[5] involve strict liability, that is liability in the absence of proof that the defendant intended to cause harm or was negligent in not preventing harm.

2. CATTLE TRESPASS

This ancient variety of the tort of trespass, which has been abolished in Manitoba,[6] and modified by statutes in British Columbia, Nova Scotia and Saskatchewan,[7] involves strict liability on the part of a defendant whose straying cattle wander on to the plaintiff's land and there cause damage. It applies only to animals that fall within the rubric "cattle", for example, horses, cows, bulls, and pigs. It does not apply to cats or dogs.[8]

Usually the damage perpetrated by the straying cattle takes the form of damage to property, for example, by uprooting plants, spoiling grass, injuring another animal such as a horse belonging to the plaintiff.[9] But no actual damage need be shown, since as with all trespasses, the mere fact of the trespass by the cattle suffices to impose liability on the cattle's owner. However, there is some authority for the proposition that if personal injury is inflicted on the owner of the property on which the cattle was trespassing, such injury may also be remedied in an action for cattle trespass.[10] It is more unlikely, however, that liability for such an injury would arise if the injury were suffered by someone other than the owner of the property on which the trespass occurred, such as a visitor on the property. Since cattle trespass, like trespass to land, is a wrong against the possessor, whether or not he or she is the owner, of the land in question, a claim by a visitor or other non-possessor of the land who is the victim of trespassing cat-

---

4 [1959] S.C.R. 513, which has sometimes been rejected by provincial courts in favour of the opposite English rule laid down in *Searle v. Wallbank*, [1947] A.C. 341.

5 *E.g.*, *Dog Owners' Liability Act*, R.S.O. 1990, c. D.16; *Dogs Act*, R.S. Nfld. 1990, c. D-26; *Dogs Act*, R.S.P.E.I. 1988, c. D-13.

6 *Animal Liability Act*, S.M. 1998, c. A.95, s. 4, and in England by the *Animals Act*, 1971, c. 22, s. 1(1).

7 *Livestock Act*, R.S.B.C. 1996, c. 270; *Stray Animals Act*, R.S.N.S. 1989, c. 488; *Stray Animals Act*, R.S.S. 1978, c. S-60.

8 *Buckle v. Holmes*, [1926] 2 K.B. 125 (C.A.). The liability of dog owners for straying dogs is dealt with by statute in many, if not all provinces: see, for example, the statutes referred to above in note 5.

9 *Ellis v. Loftus Iron Co.* (1874), L.R. 10 C.P. 10.

10 *Whalley v. Vandergrand* (1918), 12 Sask. L.R. 14; *McKay v. Loucks* (1920), 53 D.L.R. 394 (Sask. C.A.); *Wormald v. Cole*, [1954] 1 Q.B. 614 (C.A.) (which presumably will not now apply in England after the *Animals Act* 1971, c. 22).

tle would have to be founded on negligence, or on the ancient *scienter* action, which has been abolished in Manitoba,[11] and modified in some other provinces.[12]

3. THE SCIENTER ACTION

Liability under this action did not, and does not depend either on whether the animal causing the harm came within the definition of "cattle" nor upon any actual trespass by the animal. The old writ applied and the modern action applies to all animals and it could be, and may now be invoked whether the injury occurred on the defendant's land, the plaintiff's land, or elsewhere. Nor is it necessary for the plaintiff to be the owner or possessor of land. Whomsoever the animal injures can sue, as long as the facts establish that the *scienter* action is otherwise applicable.

For the purposes of the *scienter* action it is necessary to distinguish between two categories of animals. The first consists of those which are *ferae naturae*: the second consists of those which are *mansuetae naturae*. This ancient distinction may be put in other ways. It may be expressed as the difference between "wild" animals, *i.e.*, those not normally kept for domestic purposes, and "tame" animals, *i.e.*, those normally kept as pets or for useful purposes, *e.g.*, horses, and sheep. It may be put as the difference between "harmless" and "dangerous" animals, in the sense that usually such animals fall within one class even though an individual animal may have been tamed or may have become wild, as the case may be. Thus elephants are "wild" animals, even though some elephants may be tamed and used in circuses to perform, or may be used in their native habitat for commercial purposes, *e.g.*, to haul logs.[13] But it was held in one case in England[14] that a camel was a domestic animal even though not indigenous to England, since in their native lands camels are used for purposes of transportation, and to such extent may be regarded as tamed or domesticated. So too, cats and dogs are tame, harmless or domestic animals, even if a particular cat or dog has reverted to its ancient "wildness" for one reason or another. It may be that the distinction is based upon the difference between animals that were and those that were not indigenous to England, but some native English animals, would probably be called wild, *e.g.* foxes,[15] even if kept ostensibly as pets.

The importance of the distinction lies in the question of liability. If the animal is *ferae naturae*, knowledge of its dangerous or harmful character is presumed, and the owner or keeper is liable without proof of knowledge of any dangerous

---

11 *Animal Liability Act*, S.M. 1998, c. A.95, s. 4 (but s. 2 seems to reintroduce strict liability). The *scienter* action was earlier abolished, and replaced by other provisions as to liability, in England: *Animals Act*, 1971, c. 22.

12 See, for example, the statutes referred to above in notes 5 and 7.

13 *Filburn v. People's Palace & Aquarium Co.* (1890), 25 Q.B.D. 258. Or, like the tiger in the game farm in *Lewis v. Oeming* (1983), 24 C.C.L.T. 81 (Alta. Q.B.) had been kept in captivity and raised by humans since it was a kitten.

14 *McQuaker v. Goddard*, [1940] 1 K.B. 687 (C.A.).

15 *Cf.* the animal in the Saskatchewan case of *Temple v. Elvery*, [1926] 3 W.W.R. 652 (Sask.).

propensity or any neglect or other wrongful conduct in respect of its control. If the animal is normally *mansuetae naturae*, before there can be liability for harm caused by its conduct, it must be shown that the owner or keeper knew that this particular animal possessed an unusual dangerous propensity not normal for its species, in other words, that the owner or keeper "knowingly" (*scienter*) kept a dangerous animal.[16] With wild animals there was presumed knowledge of their dangerous character: with others such knowledge had to be established. This could be achieved by showing that the animal in question had done something of a similar character to what it was accused of having done, *e.g.* biting the plaintiff, or someone else, on a previous occasion, and that the owner or keeper knew of this or his or her servant or agent[17] possessed the requisite knowledge.

In neither instance is negligence on the part of the owner or keeper a prerequisite of liability. Even where a tame animal is involved, the knowledge of its propensity is not required to establish negligence. Even if the animal caused the harm without there having been any negligence on the part of its owner or keeper, *e.g.* without the defendant having let the animal out of his control so that it could injure the plaintiff, there may be liability. And this is especially true in the case of a wild animal. Owners or keepers of such animals do so at their peril.[18] This does not mean that they will be liable whatever the cause of the harm. There are limitations upon such liability, *e.g.* the consent of the victim (as where the plaintiff puts his or her head in the lion's mouth);[19] contributory negligence (as where the plaintiff strokes a dog which he or she knows has a tendency to bite);[20] the act of a stranger over whom the defendant has no control (as where a trespasser looses the tiger who then escapes and hurts the plaintiff);[21] an act of God (as where lightning shatters the animal's chain so that it can escape and do harm).[22] Subject to such possibilities, however, the owner or keeper will incur responsibility for injury caused by a wild animal acting in accordance with its normal nature, or a tame one acting in accordance with a dangerous unnatural propensity of which the defendant was aware.

The animal does not have to harm the victim directly, *e.g.* by biting or scratching. If as a result of the conduct of the animal the victim incurs injury, for example by suffering shock at seeing the animal loose, or running away from the animal and falling and breaking a leg, there will be liability.[23] It is all a question of causation. Unlike trespass, therefore, the injury does not have to be directly inflicted upon the victim, as long as it is directly caused or, possibly, is a foreseeable result of the keeping of, the animal. Nor does the animal have to "escape" from control for there to be liability, as is the situation under the doctrine

---

16 See, *e.g.*, *Janota-Bzouska v. Lewis* (1997), 43 B.C.L.R. (3d) 352 (C.A.); *Fitzgerald v. E.B. & A.D. Cooke Bourne (Farms) Ltd.*, [1964] 1 Q.B. 249 (C.A.).

17 *Norton v. Fitzgerald* (1928), 62 O.L.R. 314.

18 The test of liability is not ownership of the animal, but possession or control of it at the time it causes injury: *Purcell v. Taylor* (1994), 120 D.L.R. (4th) 161 (Ont. Gen. Div.).

19 See, *e.g.*, *Hall v. Sorley* (1980), 23 B.C.L.R. 281 (S.C.).

20 See, *e.g.*, *Dowler v. Bravender* (1968), 67 D.L.R. (2d) 734 (B.C.S.C.).

21 *Baker v. Snell*, [1908] 2 K.B. 352.

22 *Ibid.*

23 *Cf. May v. Burdett* (1846), 9 Q.B. 101.

of *Rylands v. Fletcher*. A chained bear that bites the plaintiff will produce liability for its owner or keeper as much as one that has freed itself from its fetters and is running wild in the streets.[24]

---

[24] *Besozzi v. Harris* (1858), 1 F. & F. 92.

Chapter 12

CONVERSION

1. DEFINITION

Conversion, like trespass, involves interference with goods. It is distinct from trespass, however, in that it is not merely an invasion of the possessory rights of the plaintiff but occurs whenever a defendant perpetrates an act that denies another person's title to goods.[1] A further difference from trespass is that conversion can be committed even though the defendant originally obtained possession of the goods lawfully, for example by way of loan by the plaintiff to the defendant, should the defendant then wrongfully give or sell the goods to a third person. In cases of conversion there may be no damage to the goods nor any physical violence to them. However there must be a "dealing" with the goods. If a defendant simply permits a third person to take goods belonging to the plaintiff, for example, where a parking attendant gives the keys to a parked car to the wrong person in error, the defendant will not be guilty of conversion.[2] But there may be a "dealing" with the goods, for this purpose, even though the defendant is not in physical possession of the goods.[3]

2. ACTS OF CONVERSION

Any act which indicates that the defendant was denying the plaintiff's title to the goods, or asserted a title of the defendant, will amount to conversion. This will be the case if the defendant disposes of the goods of another by delivering, selling or pledging them to a third party.[4] Conversion may also be committed by destroying the plaintiff's goods so as to prevent the plaintiff from having them.[5] If a bank honours a forged cheque, by giving the amount of the cheque to the forger who presented the cheque to the bank for payment, the bank, by so doing,

---

1 *384238 Ontario Ltd. v. Ontario* (1983), 8 D.L.R. (4th) 676 (F.C.A.). Note the effect of the owner's consent: *Robertson v. Stang* (1997), 38 C.C.L.T. (2d) 62 (B.C.S.C.).

2 *Ashby v. Tolhurst*, [1937] 2 K.B. 242 (C.A.). But if the one handing over the keys was negligent in doing so, that party may be liable in negligence.

3 *Douglas Valley Finance Co. Ltd. v. Hughes (Hirers) Ltd.*, [1969] 1 Q.B. 738; *Oakley v. Lyster*, [1931] 1 K.B. 148.

4 Unless the action of the defendant is protected by legislation that is referred to below p. 126.

5 *Federal Business Development Bank v. T. & T. Engineering Ltd.*, [1982] 4 W.W.R. 126 (B.C.S.C.).

commits conversion.[6] Even a mere refusal to return the plaintiff's goods to the plaintiff may amount to conversion, unless the defendant has a valid reason for such refusal, such as that a third party has laid claim to such goods and the defendant has reasonable grounds for believing the claim to be genuine and well-founded.[7]

3. STRICT LIABILITY

The innocence of the defendant will not excuse him or her from liability. If the defendant mistakenly believes that the goods are his or hers, or are goods which he or she is entitled to handle on behalf of another (as where the defendant is a factor selling on behalf of a principal, or an auctioneer undertaking a sale by auction on behalf of the person whom he or she believes is the owner of the goods) he or she will not be excused from liability in conversion. Anyone who deals with goods inconsistently with the ownership of a true owner is guilty of conversion. Hence a *bona fide* purchaser of goods to which the seller had no title or was not authorized by the true owner to sell, will be guilty of conversion. However, at common law, and under statutes such as the Sale of Goods Act and the Factors Act, a *bona fide* purchaser for value without notice, in certain circumstances, may be protected from liability to the true owner of such goods.[8] Much depends upon whether the seller of the goods to such *bona fide* purchaser obtained them by a contract induced by mistake, by fraud, from an agent of the owner acting without authority but in circumstances giving rise to an estoppel against the true owner, under a judicial sale, *etc*. Thus the position of the defendant may depend upon facts of which he or she was ignorant at the material time, and of which he or she could not reasonably be expected to be aware. There is no doubt, however, that subject to these special and very limited exceptions, liability in conversion is strict.[9] However, a distinction has been drawn by the courts between exercising an independent possession to the goods, so as to establish the necessary kind of conduct, and simply acting as an instrument of some third party, a mere "conduit-pipe" as it has been called, serving to bring about a transfer of possession from one person to another without in any way acting independently.[10] The conversion may come about by reason of the intervention of a third party, such as customs officials seizing a car which was carrying contraband, when the prospect of such intervention was reasonably fore-

6 *Boma Manufacturing Ltd. v. C.I.B.C.* (1996), 140 D.L.R. (4th) 493 (S.C.C.).

7 *Clayton v. LeRoy*, [1911] 2 K.B. 1031.

8 For details see Fridman, *Sale of Goods in Canada*, 4th ed. (Toronto: Carswell, 1995), pp. 123-148.

9 *Boma Manufacturing Ltd. v. C.I.B.C.* (1996), 140 D.L.R. (4th) 463 (S.C.C.) at 475 *per* Iacobucci J.; *Hollins v. Fowler* (1875), L.R. 7 H.L. 754.

10 *Cf. National Mercantile Bank v. Rymill* (1881), 44 L.T. 767 (C.A.); *Barker v. Furlong*, [1891] 2 Ch. 173; *Consolidated Co. v. Curtis & Son*, [1892] 1 Q.B. 495; *Re Samuel (No. 2)*, [1945] Ch. 408 (C.A.).

seeable as a consequence of some act of the defendant, even though he or she did not intend to commit conversion.[11]

4. WHO MAY SUE

Normally the plaintiff in an action of conversion will be the owner or co-owner of the goods. If this is the case, then there is no opportunity for the defendant to plead *jus tertii*. Possession alone, or even the right to possession without actual possession of the goods, may suffice to found an action of this kind.[12] Thus the finder of goods, or the unlawful possessor of them, may bring the action for conversion against another person unless that other is the true owner, or was acting on behalf of such owner. In respect of finders, as already noted in connection with trespass to goods,[13] there may be a problem where the owner of land, premises, or some other chattel is unaware of the presence thereon of the chattel which has been found. Although the finder may have sufficient possession to maintain an action for trespass, if dispossessed by such owner, or some third party, what if he or she surrenders possession to such owner and then seeks to recover the chattel, asserting some "title" as a finder? His or her action would then be founded on an alleged conversion by the owner of the land, *etc*. It has been held in several cases that the finder will have a better title than the owner of the land, *etc*., as long as the chattel found was lying on top of, and was not attached to the land in question. In other situations it would seem that the latter has the better right.[14] However, a person in possession lawfully, as the bailee of the goods, cannot plead the *jus tertii* in an action for conversion brought by the bailor against him or her, unless the bailee has been evicted by the true owner, or the bailee is defending the action by and on behalf of the true owner.[15] An owner out of possession, under a bailment, may sue for conversion where the act of the defendant operates to destroy the owner's title in such a way as to make it impossible for the owner to recover ownership (as well as possession) of the goods at some future time.

---

[11] *Moorgate Mercantile Co. v. Finch*, [1962] 1 Q.B. 701 (C.A.), but unforeseeability of the consequences may not be a defence to liability: see *Hiort v. Bott* (1874), L.R. 9 Ex. 86; *Elvin & Powell Ltd. v. Plummer Roddis Ltd.* (1933), 50 T.L.R. 158.

[12] *Federal Business Development Bank v. T. & T. Engineering Ltd.*, [1982] 4 W.W.R. 126 (B.C.S.C.).

[13] Above p. 52.

[14] *Armory v. Delamirie* (1722), 1 Stra. 505; *Bridges v. Hawkesworth* (1851), 21 L.J.Q.B. 75; *Elwes v. Brigg Gas Co.* (1886), 33 Ch. D. 562; *South Staffordshire Water Co. v. Sharman*, [1896] 2 Q.B. 44; *Hannah v. Peel*, [1945] K.B. 509; *London Corp. v. Appleyard*, [1963] 1 W.L.R. 982. But the true owner can always recover: *Moffat v. Kazana*, [1969] 1 Q.B. 152.

[15] *Biddle v. Bond* (1865), 6 B. & S. 225; *Rogers, Sons & Co. v. Lambert & Co.*, [1891] 1 Q.B. 318; *Kahler v. Midland Bank*, [1950] A.C. 24.

5. REMEDIES

In case of conversion, the usual remedy is damages.[16] The measure of such damages is the value to the plaintiff of the goods converted by the defendant,[17] the relevant time for calculation of such damages being the date of the conversion, even though the action may have been brought, and the judgment rendered, some time after such conversion.[18] This may give rise to problems where the goods have been improved in value, or may have depreciated, since the date of the conversion. It is clear that where the converter acted in bad faith, *i.e.* with knowledge that he or she was converting, the courts will award damages at the highest possible rate, and will not permit the defendant to plead either that he or she added value to the goods or that they are not now as valuable as they were when they were converted. On the other hand, an innocent but technically liable converter may be given credit for improvements that have been made to the goods. In the latter instance the owner may be ordered to compensate the defendant for the improvements, *e.g.*, where a converter has repaired goods that were damaged or faulty at the time of the conversion, in circumstances in which the converter was an innocent purchaser or otherwise obtained the goods without knowledge that they belonged to someone other than the party from whom he or she obtained them.

Where the plaintiff has obtained judgment for the value of the goods in accordance with what has been said above, and that judgment has been satisfied by payment of the damages, but not before,[19] the effect of that judgment will be to transfer title in the goods from the plaintiff to the defendant. In effect what has happened has been a forced, judicial sale of the goods. Hence the defendant may prefer to return the goods to the plaintiff. Or the plaintiff may prefer to claim their return. Specific restitution of converted goods is a matter of discretion for the court: and normally will not be granted unless the goods are of unique, irreplaceable value.[20]

---

16 Including, when appropriate, punitive or exemplary damages.

17 Usually the market price: *Borden Chemical Co. (Canada) Ltd. v. J.G. Benkers Ltd.* (1973), 29 D.L.R. (3d) 337 (B.C.S.C.).

18 *Asamera Oil Corp. v. Sea Oil & General Corp.*, [1979] 1 S.C.R. 633. Note, however, the duty of the plaintiff to mitigate his or her loss, for example, by purchasing alternative goods on the market, as long as this is a reasonable thing to do.

19 *Sadler v. Scott*, [1947] 1 D.L.R. 712 (B.C.C.A.).

20 *Pusey v. Pusey* (1684), 1 Vern. 273; *Netupsky v. Dominion Bridge Co.* (1969), 9 D.L.R. (3d) 182 (B.C.C.A.).

Chapter 13

DETINUE

1. DEFINITION

An action for detinue is appropriate where the wrongdoer has not damaged the goods of another, nor is denying the owner's title to such goods, but is retaining the goods unlawfully and refusing to return them to their lawful owner. That includes a person who is entitled to the immediate possession of such goods, (*e.g.* a bailee under a bailment that has not yet been determined by the bailor).[1] No handling of the goods is necessary. Nor need the defendant have obtained them wrongfully at the outset. Indeed detinue is the appropriate action where a bailee holds goods improperly after the bailment has ended or been terminated by the bailor. Another difference between detinue on one hand and trespass to goods and conversion on the other is that the latter can be committed by a single act, not repeated, whereas detinue involves some continuous wrongdoing. That wrongdoing may or may not involve a denial of the plaintiff's title. If there is no denial of title, it may be that the plaintiff must prove a demand for the return of the goods, and a refusal by the defendant to return them, before an action may be maintained.[2] If the detention of the goods involves, and is based upon, a denial of the plaintiff's title, then such a prior demand and refusal is not necessary. Indeed, if it is clear from the evidence that if a demand had been made the defendant would have refused delivery of the goods to the owner, the latter is excused from the requirement of such prior demand. As was said in an Albertan case, involving detinue of shares: "To require such a formality in circumstances which show it would have been futile is empty of any merit, and is reminiscent of the discarded formalities of the past century".[3]

2. INTENT

Intention and negligence do not seem to be relevant. Thus an innocent party who genuinely believes that he or she is entitled to retain possession of the goods,

---

1 Note that in some jurisdictions the appropriate action is *replevin*, to recover immediate possession: see *MacKenzie v. Somers*, [1954] 1 D.L.R. 421 (N.S.S.C.).

2 *Schentag v. Gauthier* (1972), 27 D.L.R. (3d) 710 (Sask. Dist. Ct.).

3 *Baud Corp. N.V. v. Brook* (1974), 40 D.L.R. (3d) 418 at 423 (Alta. C.A.), varied [1979] 1 S.C.R. 633.

may still be liable in detinue if in fact he or she is not so entitled. This may not apply, however, where the defendant has some good cause or reason for doubting whether the plaintiff is the true owner, and is refusing delivery on the ground that if the goods are delivered to the claimant, the defendant, may be exposed to the risk of action for conversion brought by the true owner. In acting in this way, however, the defendant undertakes the risk of liability to the claimant, since the latter does not have to prove ownership of the goods, merely the right to possession, as long as such right is superior to any such claim on the part of the defendant. However, the defendant may plead the *jus tertii*, unless the defendant is the bailee of the claimant, when that plea cannot be raised, except when the bailee has been evicted by title paramount, *i.e.*, by the true owner, or the defendant is defending for and on behalf of the true owner. Detinue, like trespass to goods, is a wrong to possession more than it is a wrong to ownership. The right to possession gives the plaintiff title to claim against the party wrongfully detaining the goods. The plaintiff is not required to prove title to, *i.e.* ownership of, the goods in issue. The defendant has to establish either *jus tertii* or some other personal claim.

3. REMEDIES

In cases of detinue, damages may be awarded, to be calculated on the basis of the value of the goods at the date of judgment[4] (not the original detention, since detinue is continuous) *plus* any consequential loss to the plaintiff, such as the rent of the goods lost to the plaintiff while they were out of possession, where they were goods normally hired out by the plaintiff, or the loss of a sale which would have been made if the plaintiff had not been deprived of their possession.[5] However, instead of claiming the value of the chattel and damages for its detention, the plaintiff may claim *either* the return of the chattel or recovery of its value and damages for its detention *or* the return of the chattel and damages for its detention. Thus detinue is a claim in respect of which a suit for specific restitution will be entertained by the courts. But such restitution will only be ordered, as already noted, where damages would not be an adequate remedy, *i.e.*, in cases involving an extraordinary, unique, article, not normally in commerce.[6] Moreover, it would seem, delay in bringing the claim may remove the plaintiff's right to specific restitution. The equitable doctrine of laches — unreasonable delay in pursuing a claim — has been held to apply to an action for detinue (even though it is a common law, not equitable action), where it would be unjust to the defendant to require him or her to return the goods.[7]

---

4 *Asamera Oil Corp. v. Sea Oil & General Corp.* (1978), 89 D.L.R. (3d) 1 at 16 (S.C.C.).

5 *Strand Electric Co. v. Brisford Entertainments Ltd.*, [1951] 1 Q.B. 246.

6 Above p. 128.

7 *Baud Corp., N.V. v. Brook* (1974), 40 D.L.R. (3d) 418 at 425-426 (Alta. C.A.), varied [1979] 1 S.C.R. 633.

Chapter 14

DEFAMATION

1. THE MEANING OF DEFAMATION

For an actionable defamation to occur the defendant must publish to one or more persons an untrue statement about the plaintiff that injuriously affects the latter's reputation or character, lowers right-minded people's opinion about the plaintiff, or causes them to hate, shun or avoid the plaintiff.[1] There is no specific form in which a defamatory statement can be made. Any mode of expression can involve the publication of something defamatory. However, the nature of that mode can be important, not from the point of view of whether the statement is defamatory but for the purpose of determining whether the defamation in question is in the form of a libel or a slander.[2]

In whatever form it appears, the statement in question must be false: it must tell a lie about the plaintiff. However it need not be made maliciously, that is with the intent to harm the plaintiff. Nor need the defendant know or realize that the statement was both untrue and defamatory. Publication of such a statement is *per se* treated as a malicious act: the malice is "implied".[3] At the same time publication of such a statement is *prima facie* proof that it is false.[4] The lack of any intent on the part of the defendant to defame the plaintiff is irrelevant in Canada, unless the defendant was a newspaper or broadcaster. Such defendants have been provided with a statutory defence to liability under certain conditions[5] (which resemble those contained in English legislation of 1952[6] that reversed the effect of certain earlier decisions that created very strict liability for defamation).

---

1 *Botiuk v. Bardyn* (1995), 156 D.L.R. (4th) 609 (S.C.C.); *Sim v. Stretch*, [1936] 2 All E.R. 1237 at 1240.

2 Below p. 135.

3 But "express" malice may become relevant if the defendant pleads that the statement was a fair comment or was made on a privileged occasion: below pp. 139-142.

4 *Elliott v. Friesen* (1984), 6 D.L.R. (4th) 338 (Ont. C.A.).

5 See, *e.g.*, R.S.O. 1990, c. L.12, s. 9; R.S.A. 2000, c. D-7, s. 1: see *Munro v. Toronto Sun Publishing Co.* (1982), 39 O.R. (2d) 100 (H.C.). Other statutory provisions limit the damages recoverable by the plaintiff from such a defendant in certain circumstances: see, *e.g.*, *Fulton v. West End Times Ltd.* (1998), 45 B.C.L.R. (3d) 288 (S.C.).

6 *Defamation Act* 1952, 15 & 16 Geo. 6 & 1 Eliz. 2, c. 66, s. 4.

2. DEFAMATORY STATEMENTS

The law distinguishes between mere insults or abuse and statements which are derogatory and damaging to reputation or character. Vulgar abuse, while it may involve criminal liability of a minor kind, is not necessarily defamation. Nor are statements which every reasonable person knows are simply intended to annoy or upset rather than reflect upon the person about whom they are made, and cause others to think the less of him or her. Nor are statements which will not affect the standing of the plaintiff in the eyes of reasonable people however they might prejudice his or her position in a particular group, *e.g.*, thieves, prostitutes, or members of a golf club. The nature of the language used, and the context in which it is spoken or written may often reveal whether the statement in question is to be characterized as forming the basis for an action. It is a question of the natural and ordinary meaning of the words.[7]

Sometimes a statement will be defamatory without need for any further explanation: it is quite obviously derogatory of the victim. On other occasions, however, a statement will only be defamatory if it is understood in its deeper, more subtle sense: it requires some analysis or explanation. On yet other occasions, a statement will not seem to be defamatory either as it stands or with some exposition: only those who know some *other* facts will realize that the statement is intended to have, or could have a defamatory meaning. Formerly it was said of both these last two situations that the statement was defamatory by innuendo, *i.e.*, as a result of making explicit the nuances of the statement. In *Lewis v. Daily Telegraph Ltd.*[8] the House of Lords explained that only the latter of these two situations involved a true innuendo. Where the statement contained something defamatory within itself, but this required some explanation of the intrinsic meaning of the words, without going to external circumstances to establish that words apparently innocent did have a defamatory meaning and intent, there was no innuendo in a legal sense. There may have been innuendo, colloquially speaking, but this was "false" innuendo, legally speaking. Only where a plaintiff had to plead and prove that the statement was made against a background of facts or circumstances of which recipients of the statement would be aware so that they would interpret and understand the statement in a defamatory sense, was the case one which involved an innuendo. Thus, even where what is said by the alleged wrongdoer is not obviously defamatory, it may become so in some circumstances.[9]

The courts have not been willing to treat a statement as defamatory only because the victim alleges that it could possibly have been defamatory, or even that it was understood in a defamatory sense by some people, however reasonable such people may have been. Where statements can have more than one

---

7 *Sykes v. Fraser*, [1974] S.C.R. 526. Thus the words were not defamatory in *George's Tavern Ltd. v. Fundy Broadcasting Co.* (1975), 10 N.B.R. (2d) 592 (Q.B.); *Gouzenko v. Harris* (1977), 72 D.L.R. (3d) 293 (Ont. H.C.). Contrast *A.U.P.E. v. Edmonton Sun* (1987), 49 Alta. L.R. (2d) 141 (Q.B.); *Mitchell v. Nanaimo District Teachers' Assn.* (1994), 94 B.C.L.R. (2d) 81 (C.A.).

8 [1964] A.C. 234.

9 *Bonham v. Pure Water Assn.* (1970), 14 D.L.R. (3d) 749 (B.C.S.C.).

meaning or interpretation, a party who alleges that he or she has been the victim of defamation cannot single out the one and only possibly defamatory meaning of the statement and successfully maintain an action. Only if the statement can be interpreted solely in a defamatory sense will it be potentially actionable.[10] Hence, whether a statement is capable of bearing such meaning is a matter of law.[11] Whether it *does* bear such meaning is a question of fact, to be determined in the light of whether reasonable people did understand it in such sense (as compared with whether such people could possibly have so understood or interpreted it).[12]

3. REFERENCE TO THE PLAINTIFF

The alleged defamatory statement must refer to the plaintiff, the person bringing the action.[13] There cannot be defamation in the air, anymore than there can be negligence in the abstract. A statement is only defamatory if it defames a particular person. This has given rise to a number of issues. What if the statement was not intended to refer to the plaintiff, but was understood to do so? What if the statement was not believed to be defamatory, but in fact, unknown to the alleged wrongdoer, because of facts of which he or she was ignorant, the statement was defamatory of the plaintiff? What if the statement was made very generally, of a number of people, but was alleged to refer to the plaintiff? These questions fall to be answered by reference to the nature of innuendo. A statement that clearly and on its face refers to the plaintiff, and can only have done so, is manifestly defamatory and actionable (if it satisfies the other criteria of actionability). One that is not so obviously an attack upon the plaintiff will only become actionable if reasonable people reasonably and legitimately associated the statement with the plaintiff.[14]

In some instances an allegedly defamatory statement was not intended to refer to the person subsequently claiming to be the victim of defamation, but was either (a) about somebody else; or (b) about some fictitious personage. The statement might have been true and valid about the other person, or, if it were

---

10 *Lewis v. Daily Telegraph Ltd.*, [1964] A.C. 234. See, *e.g.*, R.S.A. 2000, c. D-7, s. 3 (and other provincial statutes to like effect) permitting an allegation of a defamatory sense without alleging how the statement was used in such a sense. Note also that the *defendant* may allege alternative defamatory meanings for the purposes of raising a defence such as fair comment: *Pizza Pizza Ltd. v. Toronto Star Newspapers Ltd.* (1998), 42 O.R. (3d) 36 (Div. Ct.); *Asper v. Lantos* (2000), 51 O.R. (3d) 215 (Div. Ct.), following earlier English authority.

11 *Hodgson v. Canadian Newspapers Co.* (1998), 39 O.R. (3d) 235 (Gen. Div.).

12 This is a jury question where the trial is with a jury (*e.g.*, in Manitoba where jury trial is mandatory). But the jury's decision may be upset on appeal: see *Laufer v. Bucklaschuk* (1999), 181 D.L.R. (4th) 83 (Man. C.A.), with which contrast *Morrissey v. MacNeil* (1997), 150 Nfld. & P.E.I.R. 80 (P.E.I.C.A.).

13 *Sykes v. Fraser*, [1974] S.C.R. 526.

14 *Morgan v. Odhams Press Ltd.*, [1971] 2 All E.R. 1156 (H.L.); *Church of Scientology of Toronto v. International News Distributing Co.* (1974), 4 O.R. (2d) 408 (H.C.); *Elliott v. C.B.C.* (1993), 16 O.R. (3d) 677 (Gen. Div.), *Aiken v. Ontario (Premier)* (1999), 45 O.R. (3d) 266 (S.C.J.).

intended to be fictional, it could not have been made "falsely" vis-à-vis the actual plaintiff. Because of the requirement that a defamatory statement be made *falsely*, it was argued in a number of English cases that the mere fact that the statement unintentionally referred to, and defamed the plaintiff, did not render the statement actionable. This argument was rejected by the courts.[15] Despite the absence of any intent on the part of the defendant, or even any negligence in failing to ensure that the statement could not refer to, or was not defamatory of the actual plaintiff, liability was imposed upon a defendant who had published a statement that was in fact defamatory of the plaintiff and was taken by other people to refer to him. The same occurred where a defendant published a statement that was not realized to be defamatory of the plaintiff, but became so because of unknown circumstances. There was no intent to say anything defamatory about the plaintiff; indeed the statement did not refer to the plaintiff, but to someone else. However, because the statement carried the inference that there was something disreputable about the plaintiff, by reason of what was said about X, the statement became actionable. This very strict position was alleviated in England by the *Defamation Act* 1952 so far as newspapers and broadcasters were concerned: and similar relief of such defendants has been provided by provincial statutes in Canada.[16] However, where the defendant is a private person, not someone covered by the statutes, it would seem that the strictness of the common law still applies, adding what has been called "a terror to authorship".

Another issue that has arisen with respect to the problem of establishing reference to the plaintiff emerges where the defendant spreads his or her attack very broadly by making a statement about the members of a class of persons, *e.g.*, "all lawyers are thieves", "all the doctors on X street are charlatans", "every detective called Lee on the X police force is a liar". If the category of affected persons is sufficiently large, then the statement, albeit possibly defamatory in character, is not actionable at the suit of any member of the group, since it does not reasonably identify him or her as the person intended to be defamed specifically by the statement, and indeed might be characterized as mere abuse, not defamation, because it is of such wide application that no reasonable person would take it seriously. On the other hand, if the group is small enough, it may well be that *every member* of the group to which the statement is capable of referring, and referring in a defamatory sense, will be able to sue. Once again it all depends upon whether a reasonable person could, and would, associate the statement with the individuals concerned, and not simply dismiss it as too broad, general, and vague to have any real meaning or force. It is question of degree, or perhaps one of certainty and the specific quality of the statement.[17]

---

15 *Hulton & Co. v. Jones*, [1910] A.C. 20; *Cassidy v. Daily Mirror Newspapers Ltd.*, [1929] 2 K.B. 331 (C.A.); *Newstead v. London Express Newspaper Ltd.*, [1940] 1 K.B. 377 (C.A.); *Hough v. London Express Newspapers Ltd.*, [1940] 2 K.B. 507 (C.A.).

16 Above, p. 131 note 5.

17 *Knupffer v. London Express Newspapers Ltd.*, [1944] A.C. 116; *A.U.P.E. v. Edmonton Sun* (1987), 39 C.C.L.T. 143 (Q.B.); *Kenora (Town) Police Services Board v. Savino* (1995), 36 C.P.C. (3d) 46 (Ont. Gen. Div.).

4. PUBLICATION

A defamatory statement is not actionable unless and until it is published. The essence of defamation is the publication of a derogatory statement about the plaintiff.[18] Publication does not necessarily mean publication to the world at large, or to any sizable portion of it, but rather to any person other than the plaintiff. Thus a publication to the spouse of the plaintiff would create a potentially actionable situation.[19] But a publication to the spouse of the defamer would not do so at common law, by reason of the ancient fiction of the unity of husband and wife.[20] That fiction having been abolished by statute, either specifically or as a consequence of the equalization of husband and wife in the law of torts, it may well be now that if a defendant publishes a defamatory statement about the plaintiff to the defendant's spouse, that would be actionable (assuming that the publication in question could be proved, which might depend on the availability of the evidence of the defendant's spouse).

A publication may be unintentional, as where the defendant, speaking to the plaintiff is overheard by a third party. Such a publication will not be actionable unless the defendant was negligent in not realizing that the conversation might be overheard.[21] A similar problem arose, in the days before employers used personal computers and did not require the services of a secretary, where a defendant dictated to a secretary, for it to be typed so as to be sent to the plaintiff or someone privileged to receive the communication, a document defamatory of the plaintiff. On this there were conflicting decisions.[22]

Every publication or republication of a defamatory statement is a separate tort.[23]

5. LIBEL AND SLANDER

Although the most frequent way in which a defamatory statement is published is by the written or spoken word, as previously noted, any mode of expression can be employed to publish a defamatory statement, including putting an effigy of the plaintiff in a place which invites opprobrious comment,[24] a film,[25] or

---

18 *McNabb v. Equifax Canada Inc.* (2000), 143 Man. R. (2d) 72 (Q.B.).

19 *Skomar v. Rachinski* (1991), 88 Sask. R. 177 (Q.B.).

20 *Wennhak v. Morgan* (1888), 20 Q.B.D. 635.

21 *McNichol v. Grandy*, [1931] S.C.R. 696.

22 *Simons v. Carr & Co.* (1997), 189 A.R. 87 (Q.B.); *Riddick v. Thames Board Mills Ltd.*, [1977] 3 All E.R. 677.

23 Every publisher is independently liable unless he has a valid defence such as privilege, below p. However, some "innocent" disseminators are not publishers for this purpose: *Sun Life Assurance Co. of Canada v. W.H. Smith & Son Ltd.*, [1933] 150 L.T. 211; contrast *Vizetelly v. Mudie's Select Library Ltd.*, [1900] 2 Q.B. 170. See also, in England, the *Defamation Act*, 1996, c. 31, s. 1.

24 *Monson v. Tussauds Ltd.*, [1894] 1 Q.B. 671 (C.A.).

25 *Yousoupoff v. M.G.M. Ltd.* (1934), 50 T.L.R. 581 (C.A.).

a cartoon or caricature.[26] Although from the point of view of whether a statement is defamatory, the nature of the form in or by the use of which the defendant defames the plaintiff is immaterial, it becomes important in relation to the question whether the alleged defamation is actionable as a libel or a slander.[27] Broadly speaking libel relates to defamatory statements that are written or in more permanent form: slander to spoken statements or those which are more transitory in nature.

Formerly this caused many problems, particularly in respect of a radio or television broadcast that contained defamatory matter about the plaintiff. These have been dealt with in some jurisdictions by statutory provisions making any form of broadcasting libel,[28] and in others by abolishing the distinction between libel and slander.[29] Where the distinction survives the importance of determining whether the defamation is published in the form of a libel or a slander lies in the fact that a libel is actionable *per se* without proof that the plaintiff has incurred any damage (although damages, other than nominal damages, will not be recoverable except where the plaintiff can establish some loss). Whereas a slander is not actionable, with some exceptions, without proof of what is termed "special damage", that is some specific material loss distinct from the damage to the plaintiff's reputation that would ordinarily be sustained by such a victim. The most important exception was where the slander imputed unfitness on the part of the plaintiff to hold an office or carry on a trade, business, or calling.[30] Modern legislation in some jurisdictions, such as Ontario,[31] has provided that it will suffice if the alleged slander is "calculated to disparage the plaintiff" in relation to the holding of an office or the carrying on of a trade, business or calling.

6. THE SCOPE OF LIABILITY

(a) Plaintiffs

Only live people may bring an action alleging that they have been defamed. The personal representatives of a deceased person may not sue in respect of an alleged defamation of the deceased. However not only natural persons may be defamed. A juridical person, that is a non-profit organization or a business corporation, may sue for defamation if the defamatory statement alleges something of which the organization could be guilty or affects the property or the trading or

---

26 *Tolley v. J.S. Fry & Sons Ltd.*, [1931] A.C. 333; *Vander Zalm v. Times Publishers Ltd.* (1980), 12 C.C.L.T. 81 (B.C.C.A.).

27 Note that libel, but not slander, may be punished as a crime: *Criminal Code*, R.S.C. 1985, c. C-46, ss. 297-317.

28 For example, Ontario: R.S.O. 1990, c. L.12, s. 2.

29 For example, Alberta: R.S.A. 2000, c. D-7, ss. 1(b), 2(1).

30 See *Caldwell v. McBride* (1988), 45 C.C.L.T. 150 (B.C.S.C.); *Hicks v. Stephens* (1997), 40 C.C.L.T. (2d) 223 (Ont. Gen. Div.).

31 R.S.O. 1990, c. L.12, s. 16.

business reputation of the business concerned.[32] The House of Lords, for reasons stemming from the European Convention of Human Rights, since incorporated into English law by the *Human Rights Act*,[33] held that a municipality could not allege that it had been defamed (as contrasted with its individual members).[34] This, however, may not be the case in Canada.

(b) Defendants

Every publisher of a defamatory statement is liable for his or her publication.[35] Each time a defamatory statement is disseminated, albeit innocently and in ignorance that it is defamatory, the culprit will be held liable.[36] However, as noted earlier, there is a defence for newspapers and broadcasters who defame innocently, and, according to decisions which draw a distinction between parties acting "mechanically" and those knowingly putting defamatory matter into circulation, the former cannot be held liable while the latter can.[37]

Just as a corporation may sue for defamation so it can be liable, if the defamatory statement is published by a servant or agent of the corporation acting within the course or scope of his or her employment or authority.[38]

7. REMEDIES

(a) Damages

If the defamation is published in the form of a libel, the victim will have an action in respect of (a) the damage to reputation; and (b) any financial loss which is directly attributable to the publication.[39] All such damages are calculated in accordance with the general principles applicable to the assessment of material loss. While the primary purpose of the action is to vindicate the plaintiff's reputation and provide him or her with some compensation for the invasion of personal life and the attack upon personal integrity, honour and good name, it is clear that the courts will also take into account substantial economic or similar loss suffered by the victim as a consequence of the defamation (as long as it is

---

32 *Church of Scientology of Toronto v. Globe & Mail Ltd.* (1978), 19 O.R. (2d) 62 (H.C.); *Safeway Stores Ltd. v. Harris*, [1948] 4 D.L.R. 187.

33 1998, c. 42.

34 *Derbyshire County Council v. Times Newspapers Ltd.*, [1993] A.C. 534.

35 Including someone who could, but does not remove a defamatory statement on his or her property: *Byrne v. Dean*, [1937] 1 K.B. 818: *cf.* continuing or adopting a nuisance, above p. 63.

36 *Menear v. Miguna* (1997), 33 O.R. (3d) 223 (C.A.).

37 *Allan v. Bushnell T.V. Co.* (1969), 4 D.L.R. (3d) 212 (Ont. C.A.).

38 *Citizen's Life Assurance Co. v. Brown*, [1906] A.C. 423.

39 But note (i) mitigation of damages where the defamation is innocent and there is an apology; (ii) the possibility of claiming only actual loss in certain circumstances, *i.e.*, no damages for effect of the defamation upon the plaintiff's reputation: see the statutes cited, *supra*, p. 131 note 5. In the case of slander, unless within one of the exceptions, "special damage" must be proved: above p. 136.

not too remote, in legal terms). It should be noted, therefore, that the nature of the victim's character is very much in issue in any action of defamation. Even if the defendant has published something defamatory about the plaintiff, any lack of desert on the latter's part vis-à-vis a good reputation will thereby diminish a claim to substantial damages for loss of reputation.[40] By the same token, it is not open to the defendant to argue that others also at the same time published similar attacks upon the plaintiff, such that his or her reputation was lowered as much by the proliferation of defamations as by the nature of the defamation for which the defendant was responsible.[41]

In suitable cases, *e.g.*, where the nature of the defamation was particularly offensive, or the circumstances of the victim especially deserving, a court may award damages in excess of the actual loss suffered by the victim, by way of "aggravated" damages, to mark the excessive nature of the defendant's wrongdoing.[42] Furthermore, a court may award a plaintiff "exemplary", "punitive", or "vindictive" damages, not based upon any actual loss sustained by the victim, but designed to penalize the defendant for the egregious, outrageous, contumelious character of his or her defamation and its form or content, or possibly his or her disregard of the rights, personality, and privacy of the victim for the deliberate purpose of making a profit at the expense of the latter's reputation.[43]

(b) Injunctions

There are situations in which a plaintiff, with advanced knowledge that what may be a defamatory statement is going to be published, would prefer to halt or prevent such publication, on the ground that the harm that would follow would not be susceptible to being remedied by a subsequent award of damages, even including aggravated and/or punitive damages. This could be achieved by the plaintiff's obtaining an injunction to prohibit such publication. However courts are reluctant to award such injunctions, as to do so might amount to an interference with freedom of speech or expression (if, in the event, it turned out that the statement was not actionable as defamation). Such an injunction can be awarded if (a) there is no doubt that the statement is defamatory; (b) it is untrue so that the defence of justification would be unavailable; or (c) neither would the defence of fair comment or privilege.[44]

---

40 *Plato Films Ltd. v. Speidel*, [1961] A.C. 1090.

41 *Associated Newspapers Ltd. v. Dingle*, [1964] A.C. 371.

42 *Walker v. CFTO Ltd.* (1987), 59 O.R. (2d) 104 (C.A.).

43 *Manning v. Hill* (1995), 126 D.L.R. (4th) 129 (S.C.C.).

44 *Wagner v. Lim* (1994), 22 Alta. L.R. (3d) 169 (Q.B.); *Coltsfoot Publishing Ltd. v. Harris* (1999), 180 N.S.R. (2d) 238 (S.C.); *Soprēma Inc. v. N.B. Roofing Contractors Assn. Ltd.* (1995), 181 N.B.R. (2d) 223 (Q.B.).

8. PERMITTED, PROTECTED, OR EXCUSED DEFAMATION

Not all published defamatory statements will be actionable. In some circumstances, and under some conditions, a person who defames another will be exempted or excused from liability. The onus will be on such party, however, to establish that he or she comes within the scope of such exemption or excuse.

One way of achieving this is by proving the truth of the allegedly defamatory statement. Such a plea of justification is in effect a denial of the defamatory nature of the statement, in view of the requirement that to be defamatory a statement must be made "falsely", *i.e.*, it must be untrue. Hence a true statement about someone, even though its publication may be harmful to the victim, and affect his or her reputation and character, is not actionable as defamation. Where justification or truth is raised as an answer to a charge of defamation, the defendant was formerly obliged to make good his or her allegations against the victim in every particular. Legislation in some jurisdictions, *viz.* Ontario, and Nova Scotia,[45] has made it possible for this defence to be raised successfully, even if every matter contained in the defamatory statement is not proved to be true, as long as the gravamen of the alleged defamation is substantially true, such that the victim's reputation has not been seriously damaged.[46]

However, even a false statement about the victim may not give rise to liability. This will be so (a) where the occasion on which the statement was made was privileged; and (b) where the statement is not a statement of fact but takes the form of comment, and the comment is fair.

Privilege in the law of defamation is of two kinds, absolute and qualified. The difference between them lies in the fact that an occasion which is absolutely privileged has the effect of granting protection to the defamer even if he or she is deliberately telling something untrue about the party defamed, and even if he or she is going out of his or her way to defame: whereas on occasions of qualified privilege, the defamer will only be protected when acting without malice, a term which, as already noted,[47] is difficult to define in general, but has a more specific connotation in this context. The concept of absolute privilege, as might be expected, is kept within narrow confines, and only appertains to those kinds of activities which (a) affect the general public interest directly and vitally, and (b) involve situations in which there may be said to be other methods of controlling people who might otherwise give vent to defamatory statements, so as to preclude, or forestall as much as possible, any possibility of deliberate, improper abuse of the law and the privilege which the law confers. The most important examples of this are proceedings in the federal or provincial legislatures; proceedings in court; transactions between different officers of state; and, though this may possibly be a matter of qualified privilege, communications between a lawyer and his or her client. Parliamentary business, the trial of matters in

---

45 R.S.O. 1990, c. L.12, s. 22; R.S.N.S. 1989, c. 122, s. 6.

46 What is more, the defendant need only prove the truth of his statement "on the balance of probability" and not "beyond a reasonable doubt": *York v. Okanagan Broadcasters Ltd.*, [1976] 6 W.W.R. 40 (B.C.S.C.).

47 Above p. 14.

court, executive matters, and the proper representation of accused persons and litigants, could not properly be effected if the parties involved were always having to worry about the possibilities of actions for defamation. In the interests of free speech, good government, unhampered trial process, and proper legal representation of parties, the law covers such situations with the cloak of absolute privilege, leaving the discipline and control of potential offenders against propriety to the sanctions imposed by Parliament itself, the judge and the appropriate law society, and senior officers of state. This protection, therefore, extends to members of any legislature (but only while speaking in the course of their parliamentary or legislative duties), judges, witnesses, counsel, jurors (while acting in the course of judicial proceedings), executive officers of government when communicating with each other on affairs of state, and lawyers and their clients when consulting about the client's affairs. In addition to these it must be added that by the *Defamation Act* in some provinces, *e.g.*, Ontario, Alberta, Nova Scotia, British Columbia, absolute privilege (except where the matter published is obscene or blasphemous) has been accorded to fair and accurate contemporaneous reports of judicial proceedings in newspapers and other media. Again the reason for this protection is the public interest in the knowledge of what occurs in the courts and the need to protect those who properly (*i.e.* by giving fair and accurate reports) inform the public of statements which would be privileged if they were heard by members of the public were they present in court at the time. This is, therefore, an extension of the absolute privilege which already existed at common law with respect to proceedings in court.

At common law qualified privilege extended to reports of judicial proceedings, as long as such reports were fair and accurate, even if the report was not contemporaneous, even if the proceedings took place before a tribunal which was not a court of record, and even if it were a foreign court.[48] Equally, at common law fair and accurate reports of parliamentary proceedings are covered by such privilege. In various jurisdictions, *e.g.*, Ontario, Nova Scotia, Alberta, and British Columbia, there are also statutory provisions dealing with the application of qualified privilege to many different sorts of publications by the media, in all of which there may be some sort of public, general interest deserving of promotion even at the risk that defamatory matter might be publicized more widely than at the meeting or other gathering at which it is originally spoken.[49] The removal of such protection in cases of a malicious publication, as will be seen shortly, provide

---

48 *Webb v. Times Publishing Co.*, [1960] 2 Q.B. 535, as long as the issue was of public interest in the place where the report was read.

49 An attempt was made, unsuccessfully, in Canada in *Manning v. Hill* (1995), 126 D.L.R. (4th) 129 (S.C.C.). In England in *Reynolds v. Times Newspapers Ltd.*, [1999] 3 W.L.R. 1010, in Australia in *Lange v. Australian Broadcasting Commission* (1997), 145 A.L.R. 96 (H.C.A.), and in New Zealand in *Lange v. Atkinson and Australian Consolidated Press NZ Ltd.*, [1998] 3 N.Z.L.R. 424 (N.Z.C.A.), to apply the doctrine enunciated by the Supreme Court of the United States in *New York Times v. Sullivan*, 376 U.S. 254 (1963) by which public figures may be defamed with impunity in the media on the basis of privilege unless it can be proved that the defendant acted maliciously without regard for the truth. However, the Australian and New Zealand courts did extend the scope of qualified privilege somewhat beyond the common law range on grounds of constitutional law.

what is probably an adequate control over possible abuse. Before dealing with this it is also important to mention that at common law, matters which a party was under a duty to communicate, or had an interest in receiving, might also be protected by such privilege. In every such instance the question to be considered is whether, in the circumstances, it was reasonably necessary and whether the person sending the defamatory communication to someone else was morally or socially (even if not legally) bound to inform that other of the statement about the person defamed; and whether there was a corresponding interest in the recipient of the information. As the cases reveal, this can sometimes be a very difficult and subtle question.[50]

In all these situations of qualified privilege, however, there will be no protection, and no exemption from liability, if the publisher of the statement was actuated by malice. The common law will not protect the publication of a defamatory statement not made for some genuine reason, within the ambit of the situation covered by the privilege, but intended to cause harm to the person defamed, out of feelings of spite or ill-will. This might be shown by the intemperate nature of the statement itself. Did it go beyond what was necessary to achieve the legitimate purpose of the privilege?[51] Was it a fair and accurate report? It might be shown by the extent of the publication. Was it published to people other than those to whom it might legitimately have been published[52] or in a form that was excessive in the circumstances, *i.e.*, in a journal of somewhat wider circulation that might be thought reasonable? It might even be shown by some other, extrinsic facts which went to establish the true motive of the defendant, to hurt rather than to inform the public or an individual who had a right to know. Since the plea of privilege, if successful, will avail to defend an untrue statement from being actionable, it is not surprising that the courts have always been anxious not to let this privilege get out of bounds. However, it remains a difficult question whether a defendant was guilty of malice.[53] So too, where there are several co-authors or co-publishers, some of whom may, and others who may not be actuated by malice. It would seem now that the latter are protected, while the former are not.[54] If the defendant, on a privileged occasion, intended to publish only to a person to whom the publication would be privileged, but also made the statement known to others, not within the scope of the protection, the occasion would cease to be privileged if the excessive publication were deliberate. If it were accidental, the opposite would probably be the case. If the

---

50 See, *e.g.*, *Watt v. Longsdon*, [1930] 1 K.B. 130 (C.A.); *Globe & Mail Ltd. v. Boland*, [1960] S.C.R. 203; *Boland v. Globe & Mail Ltd.*, [1961] O.R. 712 (C.A.); *Jones v. Bennett* (1968), 66 D.L.R. (2d) 497 (B.C.C.A.), reversed [1969] S.C.R. 277; *Fisher v. Rankin* (1972), 27 D.L.R. (3d) 746 (B.C.S.C.); *Clarke v. Austin* (1974), 51 D.L.R. (3d) 598 (B.C.S.C.).

51 *Botiuk v. Toronto Free Press Publications Ltd.* (1995), 126 D.L.R. (4th) 609 (S.C.C.).

52 *Seguin v. Brooker* (1998), 211 A.R. 216 (Q.B.).

53 See *Sun Life Assurance Co. of Canada v. Dalrymple*, [1965] S.C.R. 302, 50 D.L.R. (2d) 217 at 222, *per* Spence J.; *Netupsky v. Craig*, [1973] S.C.R. 55. As to the effect of *reckless* or *negligent* conduct by the defendant, see *Fraser v. Sykes*, [1974] S.C.R. 526; *Horrocks v. Lowe*, [1974] 1 All E.R. 662 (H.L.). Knowledge that the statement was untrue will evidence malice: *Gillett v. Nissen Volkswagen Ltd.*, [1975] 3 W.W.R. 520 (Alta. T.D.).

54 *Egger v. Viscount Chelmsford*, [1965] 1 Q.B. 248 (C.A.).

defendant were negligent, but did not actually intend to exceed his or her privilege, then, given the strict attitude of the law towards defamation it is likely that the courts would treat this as something tantamount to malice, or at least an excessive publication, so as to destroy the privilege that would otherwise cover the occasion.

What has been said above applies to misstatements of fact. Where the defendant has defamed another by making some injurious comment about his character, an expression of opinion that is derogatory, rather than an untrue allegation of something factual about the victim, the defendant may yet be protected from liability if the comment was fair, in the circumstances, and the comment was on a matter of public interest.[55] It is not possible to make false statements of fact and claim protection on the basis of fair comment, by dressing the statements in the guise of comment. Indeed if the comment, though fair, is founded upon false statements of fact, the defence of fair comment will not succeed.[56] The defendant must show that the comment was fair on the basis of facts which were true. What is fair is clearly a matter for the court to determine. A comment may be fair even though made maliciously. It may be unfair and yet not be actuated by malice. Possibly, however, proof that the defendant was malicious towards the victim, or that the comment was published in a malicious form, *i.e.*, too widely or using overly forceful language, may help to determine that the comment was unfair. In the absence of such factors, it would appear that comment will be fair if it is such that a reasonable person could hold such opinions about the plaintiff, even if such opinions were invalid or incorrect.[57] Even this will not protect the defendant, however, if the matter on which he or she was commenting cannot be described as something of public interest. This would cover reviews of books, art exhibitions, plays, political activities (even if not covered by privilege), even social behaviour if it were of general concern. It will not cover something that is of private concern, or of only very limited interest.[58]

No action for defamation will be available to a plaintiff who has agreed, before or after the event, to the publication of what is later alleged to be a defamatory statement. Proof of such agreement, however, may not be easily established.[59]

Under provincial legislation any defendant may be able to plead, in mitigation of damages that would otherwise be awarded for defamation, that the defendant offered a written or printed apology before or soon after the action be-

---

55 *Vander Zalm v. Times Publishers Ltd.* (1980), 12 C.C.L.T. 81 (B.C.C.A.); *Carter v. Gair* (1999), 170 D.L.R. (4th) 204 (B.C.C.A.).

56 *Van Baggen v. Nichol* (1963), 42 W.W.R. 248 (B.C.S.C.); *Hicks v. Stephens* (1997), 40 C.C.L.T. (2d) 223 (Ont. Gen. Div.). Some relief of this strict rule has been introduced by the *Libel and Slander Act* in Ontario, R.S.O. 1990, c. L.12 and the *Defamation Act* in Nova Scotia, R.S.N.S. 1989, c. 122.

57 It was held in *Chernesky v. Armadale Publishers Ltd.* (1979), 90 D.L.R. (3d) 321 (S.C.C.) that the defendant had to prove that the comment expressed the honest opinion of the maker of the comment. But this was changed by statute in Ontario and some other jurisdictions to apply an objective, not subjective, standard: R.S.O. 1990, c. L.12, s. 24; R.S.Y. 1986, c. D-1, s. 1(1); R.S.A. 2000, c. D-7, s. 9(1).

58 *Jones v. Bennett*, [1969] S.C.R. 277: *Kerr v. Conlogue* (1992), 65 B.C.L.R. (2d) 70 (S.C.).

59 See *Burnett v. C.B.C.* (1982), 48 N.S.R. (2d) 181 (T.D.).

gan.[60] A newspaper or broadcaster has a special plea of apology to mitigate damages where the statement was published without malice or gross negligence and a full and fair retraction was published or offered.[61]

---

60 See, *e.g.*, R.S.A. 2000, c. D-7, s. 4.

61 See, *e.g.*, R.S.O. 1990, c. L.12, s. 9, on which see *Munro v. Toronto Sun Publishing Co.* (1982), 39 O.R. (2d) 100 (H.C.).

Chapter 15

INVASION OF PRIVACY

1. INTRODUCTION

A recent development in the law of torts, in Canada largely, but not exclusively, as a result of provincial legislation, is the emergence of civil liability for conduct which can best be described as an invasion of a person's privacy.[1] In a sense the law of defamation provides remedies for certain aspects of privacy and the protection of an individual's private life, although it does not apply where the information that is disseminated, while intrusive and harmful to a person's privacy, is true, since to publish a true, though damaging statement about someone is not defamatory. The law of trespass, insofar as it protects someone from physical restraint or interference, loss of property or the invasion of his or her land, is also concerned with aspects of privacy. So, too, is the law of nuisance, to the extent that it applies to provide a remedy in the case of conduct that interferes with a person's use and enjoyment of his or her land. However, there are situations that cannot be dealt with by the invocation of the law of trespass, nuisance or defamation.

The issue that has been raised in the courts and, to a certain extent has been dealt with by the legislation to which reference has been made, is whether the law can and should go further than what is contemplated by trespass, nuisance or defamation, and provide a remedy in respect of conduct that affects someone's personal, private life without constituting a nominate, well-established tort such as trespass, nuisance, libel or slander. Resolution of this issue depends on how the idea of privacy, in legal terms, is to be understood.[2]

---

1 This book is not concerned with criminal law provisions about privacy, nor with legislation dealing with consumer privacy.

2 There is a considerable literature on this topic: see, *e.g.*, Burns, "The Law and Privacy: The Canadian Experience" (1976) 54 Can. Bar Rev. 1; Marshall, "The Right to Privacy: A Sceptical View" (1976) 21 McGill L.J. 262; Gibson, "Common Law Protection of Privacy" in Klar, ed., *Studies in Canadian Tort Law*; Ontario Law Reform Commission, *Report on Protection of Privacy in Ontario*, 1968; Wacks, "The Poverty of Privacy" (1980) 96 L.Q.R. 73; Todd, "Protection of Privacy" in Mullany, ed., *Torts in the Nineties* (Sydney: LBC, 1997).

2. THE MEANING OF PRIVACY

At one time privacy was said to mean "the right to be let alone".[3] That idea was at the root of an early discussion of the topic in 1890.[4] Attempts have been made to make this nebulous concept more specific and precise.[5] Two problems have arisen in this context.

The first is whether it is possible, in a general way, to specify, or delimit what ideally should be included within the scope of any notion of privacy. What elements of life, in the abstract, forgetting any other considerations which, as will be noted, might be relevant, go to make up the concept of privacy or a private life? In this respect, on one hand it might be valid to speak of the "right to be let alone" as a principle giving guidance in a specific case, and to accept, at least as a basic working guide, the four major categories once suggested by the American jurist Prosser,[6] on the basis of American authority: (a) freedom from intrusion upon an individual's physical seclusion or solitude; (b) freedom from public disclosure of private facts; (c) freedom from publicity placing the plaintiff in a false light; and (d) no appropriation of the plaintiff's name or likeness for the defendant's benefit. Other instances or situations may be added from time to time, such as surveillances of the kinds already mentioned. In time, therefore, the gradual accretion of situations in which a right is recognized and a remedy given, all founded upon the basic principle, *i.e.*, the right to be let alone, may build up into a formidable structure of law, evidencing and constituting a new area for the operation of the law, and especially the law of torts.

The second problem is that of balancing the individual's "right" to privacy against the "rights" of other individuals or the public at large to indulge in certain conduct, or to the exposure of certain facts about the person claiming a right to privacy. It is a matter of possibly submitting the individual's interests to the greater, more powerful or important interests (at least in the eyes of the law) of the general public, society at large. It is, perhaps, the fear that this might be impossible, or the reluctance to become involved in the measurement of one set of interests against another that has led the courts to refrain from a general recognition of any right or rights to privacy. If this is the case, then their reluctance is hard to accept in view of the fact that courts are faced with similar tasks in other areas of the law, and have fulfilled them successfully. It is part of the function of the law and the courts, in the context of tort. Why then should the law excuse itself from responsibility in this regard? Perhaps, by way of alternative, the reason is the difficulty of identifying exactly what ought to be protected, or what conduct ought to be penalized, that has led the courts to refuse recognition to claims fundamentally based upon invasion of privacy, in circumstances in which

---

3 *Cooley on Torts*, 1888, at p. 29.

4 Warren & Brandeis, "The Right to Privacy" (1890) 4 Harvard L.R. 191, on which see Zimmerman, "Requiem for a Heavyweight: A Farewell to Warren & Brandeis's Privacy Tort" (1983) 68 Cornell L.R. 291.

5 See, *e.g.*, Prosser, "Privacy" (1960) 48 Calif. L.R. 83; Australian Law Reform Commission, *Privacy*, 1983.

6 Prosser, *loc. cit.*

the plaintiff has been unable to bring his or her case under a settled, accepted rubric of liability.

The two questions, therefore, are somewhat intertwined. Once the categories of privacy are recognized, the courts will be obliged, and will be able to limit the extent to which conduct will fall within or under one of those categories, by reference, *inter alia*, to the demands and legitimate interests of others or of society in general. At the moment, it can be said that there are some common law and legislative strands from which some crude, elementary concept of privacy can be woven. It is not elaborate, nor is it very well developed, but it does exist to a limited extent. Much more remains to be done, whether by legislatures or by the common law. However, the idea that a person's private life in itself is something worthy of protection from invasion has begun to be accepted.

3. PROTECTION AT COMMON LAW

At common law, it would seem, there is no right of privacy *per se* and no protection from an alleged invasion of privacy, at least not in so many words.[7] What courts have done is to permit the bringing of an action, for example, for trespass, nuisance, passing-off, *etc.*, in circumstances in which the plaintiff's real substantial claim is not for damages for the trespass, nuisance or other nominate wrong as for its consequences, namely the invasion of the plaintiff's privacy or personal life.

For this to occur the plaintiff must establish the basic elements of the appropriate cause of action; mere allegations that he has been damaged or injured will not suffice. Thus in a famous recent case, *Krouse v. Chrysler Canada Ltd.*,[8] although at first instance Edson Haines J. was willing to give the plaintiff a remedy when his features were improperly used by the defendants in an advertisement of theirs, so as to assist them to sell their products and make money, the Ontario Court of Appeal held that the tort of passing-off, in its strict sense, involving inducing people to believe that the defendants' product was that of the plaintiff, so that they would buy it on that false premise, did not apply. By way of contrast an action was allowed for "appropriation of personality", as it has become known as, in several later decisions,[9] but denied, in the case of a book

---

7 *R. v. Gill*, [1995] 7 W.W.R. 61 (Man. Q.B.); *Peters-Brown v. Regina District Health Board* (1995), 136 Sask. R. 126 (Q.B.), affirmed (1996), 148 Sask. R. 248 (C.A.); but contrast *Roth v. Roth* (1991), 4 O.R. (3d) 740 (Gen. Div.); *Dawe v. Nova Collection Services (Nfld.) Ltd.* (1998), 160 Nfld. & P.E.I.R. 266 (Nfld. Prov. Ct.). See the discussion by the High Court of Australia in *ABC v. Lenah Game Meats Pty Ltd.* (2001), 208 C.L.R. 199.

8 (1972), 25 D.L.R. (3d) 49 (Ont. H.C.), reversed (1974), 40 D.L.R. (3d) 15 (Ont. C.A.).

9 *Racine v. C.J.R.C. Radio Capitale Ltée* (1977), 80 D.L.R. (3d) 441 (Ont. Co. Ct.); *Athans v. Canadian Adventure Camps Ltd.* (1977), 80 D.L.R. (3d) 583 (Ont. H.C.); *Heath v. Weist-Barron School of Television (Canada) Ltd.* (1981), 18 C.C.L.T. 129 (Ont. H.C.); *Baron Philippe de Rothschild S.A. v. La Casa de Habana Inc.* (1987), 19 C.P.R. (3d) 114 (Ont. H.C.).

about the famous Canadian pianist Glenn Gould, on the ground that he was a person in the public eye in whose life and work the public had an interest.[10]

In *Motherwell v. Motherwell*,[11] the Appellate Division of the Supreme Court of Alberta was able to utilize the law of nuisance to grant a remedy, by way of injunction, to restrain the defendant from making objectionable, but not obscene or criminal, telephone calls to the house of one defendant, the result of which was to upset that defendant as well as his wife and others who were not, strictly speaking, parties who should have come within the protection of the law of nuisance (since they were not themselves landowners or people with some interest in the land that was being injuriously affected). To some extent the court in that case was making imaginative, innovative use of the law, in this instance the law of nuisance, to cope with an entirely unprecedented situation.

An Ontario case, *Poole v. Ragen and Toronto Harbour Commission*[12] is another illustration of imaginative application of the law, also possibly the law of nuisance, in which a court awarded damages to a plaintiff whose boat was followed across Toronto Harbour for a period of three months by the police. While it may be possible to sympathize with the plaintiff and with the court which wanted to castigate the police for their injurious behaviour, which was totally unjustified on the facts, it is nonetheless debatable whether what had occurred was a nuisance in any previously accepted sense.

4. STATUTORY REMEDIES

Some statutes not primarily designed to deal with any issue of "privacy" have been utilized by courts to provide protection in respect of what was, in effect, an invasion of someone's personal private life.[13] More direct statutory recognition of these matters is contained in the Privacy Acts of the provinces of Manitoba, Newfoundland, Saskatchewan and British Columbia,[14] and the amendments to the federal *Criminal Code* contained in the *Privacy Act*,[15] which although part of the criminal law, appears to have civil, or *quasi*-civil consequences, in that it permits recovery of damages for what is, or is treated as a criminal offence. Hence, possibly, its relevance to the issue of tortious recovery for invasion of privacy.

In the provinces just named, a statutory right of action has been created in respect of the unreasonable violation of the privacy of another person, wilfully and without a claim of right. Where an action is successful the court can award dam-

---

10 *Gould Estate v. Stoddart Publishing Co.* (1996), 30 O.R. (3d) 520 (Gen. Div.), affirmed (1998), 39 O.R. (3d) 545 (C.A.), leave to appeal refused (1999), 236 N.R. 396*n* (S.C.C.).

11 [1976] 6 W.W.R. 550 (Alta. C.A.), criticized in *Hunter v. Canary Wharf Ltd.*, [1997] A.C. 655.

12 [1958] O.W.N. 77. Contrast *286880 Ontario Ltd. v. Parke* (1974), 6 O.R. (2d) 311 (H.C.).

13 *E.g.*, *Re MacIsaac and Beretanos* (1971), 25 D.L.R. (3d) 610 (B.C. Prov. Ct.); *Re Copeland and Adamson*, [1972] 3 O.R. 248 (H.C.); *R. v. Penner* (1973), 12 C.C.C. (2d) 35 (Man. C.A.).

14 R.S.M. 1970, c. 74; R.S.S. 1979, c. P-24; R.S.B.C. 1996, c. 373; R.S.N. 1990, c. P-22.

15 R.S.C. 1985, c. P-26, which added what is now s. 194, dealing with criminal surveillance, to the *Criminal Code*, R.S.C. 1985, c. C-46.

ages, grant an injunction, or make the defendant account for profits made by the violation of the plaintiff's privacy. In British Columbia there is also a separate tort, namely, using the name or portrait of another person for advertising or promotional purposes without his or her consent; and in the other provinces a tort committed by the unauthorized use of someone's name, likeness or voice for advertising purposes. The statutes contain some significant differences with respect to the nature of privacy and the kinds of conduct which may constitute an invasion. Manitoba includes a negligent invasion of privacy within the scope of the tort, the other provinces require the conduct to be deliberate or intentional. The British Columbia statute enumerates certain defences, *e.g.*, consent of the plaintiff, lawful defence of person or property, *e.g.*, consent of the plaintiff, lawful defence of person or property, *etc.* Under the Manitoba statute, ignorance that a violation of privacy was involved may also be a defence. A study of the statutes will reveal other similarities and differences in their wording, scope, and effects. Basically, however, the statutes are intended to fill in gaps which the common law has revealed exist in its fabric or structure. All four statutes give a cause of action in the Supreme Court of the province, a stipulation which has been criticized on the ground that it means litigation will be expensive, thereby perhaps precluding many people to whom the statutes would and should afford protection from going to court when they may have a valid case. When the fact that the damages awarded will not be large is added to this, taking into account the considerations which the court must observe when calculating damages, and the fact that punitive damages may not be awarded, even though such an award is possible, it has been argued that "these Acts do not grant real protection to the privacy interests they were set up to safeguard, at least at the most visible level".[16]

In a number of decisions various provisions of these Acts have been examined and considered by the courts of the provinces concerned. In very few of these was the plaintiff successful.[17] For the most part the claims failed either because the conduct did not amount to an invasion of privacy within the meaning of the relevant statute[18] or because a defence that was given by such statute was applicable on the facts.[19] The experience of the years since these statutes were first enacted suggests, in the words of one commentator,[20] either that the

---

16 Burns, "The Law and Privacy: The Canadian Experience" (1976) 54 Can. Bar Rev. 1 at 38.

17 See, *e.g.*, *Lee v. Jacobson* (1992), 87 D.L.R. (4th) 401 (B.C.S.C.), reversed (1994), 99 B.C.L.R. (2d) 144 (C.A.); *F. (J.M.) v. Chapell* (1998), 45 B.C.L.R. (3d) 64 (C.A.); *Ferguson v. McBee Technographics Inc.* (1989), 58 Man. R. (2d) 119 (Q.B.).

18 See, *e.g.*, *Davis v. McArthur* (1971), 17 D.L.R. (3d) 760 (B.C.C.A.), reversing (1969), 10 D.L.R. (3d) 250 (B.C.S.C.); *Milton v. Savinkoff* (1993), 18 C.C.L.T. (2d) 288 (B.C.S.C.); *Silber v. B.C. Broadcasting System Ltd.* (1986), 25 D.L.R. (4th) 345 (B.C.S.C.); *Parasiuk v. Canadian Newspapers Co.*, [1988] 2 W.W.R. 737 (Man. Q.B.); *Bingo Enterprises Ltd. v. Plaxton* (1986), 26 D.L.R. (4th) 604 (Man. C.A.); *Peters-Brown v. Regina District Health Board* (1995), 136 Sask. R. 126 (Q.B.), affirmed (1996), 148 Sask. R. 248 (C.A.).

19 *Hollinsworth v. BCTV* (1996), 34 C.C.L.T. (2d) 95 (B.C.S.C.), affirmed (1998), 59 B.C.L.R. (3d) 121 (C.A.); *Druken v. R.G. Fewer & Associates Inc.* (1998), 171 Nfld. & P.E.I.R. 312 (Nfld. T.D.).

20 Burns, above note 16 at 38.

statutes are a "dead letter" or that they have created a type of "preventive legal" situation whereby people regulate their activities to take account of them.

Chapter 16

MALICIOUS PROSECUTION

1. ABUSE OF LEGAL PROCEDURE

In certain situations, and under certain conditions, to institute criminal proceedings against another person improperly will be actionable on the part of the person subjected to prosecution. The law gives the right to one person to prosecute another, but this right, if abused, may give rise to liability. The privilege to ensure that crimes are not unprosecuted may be enjoyed only for the proper motive of seeing that criminals are brought to justice. It may not be exercised for personal spite or for any other improper, illegitimate object or purpose.

Other aspects of legal procedure can be abused and so give rise to liability. For example, an abuse of the right to arrest another can lead to liability for false imprisonment.[1] Indeed, frequently, actions for false arrest or imprisonment and for malicious prosecution arise out of the same fact-situation. However the application of these torts differs. False imprisonment or arrest may occur when the defendant, personally or by employing the services of a police officer, seizes the plaintiff and puts him or her under restraint with a view to subsequent proceedings. Malicious prosecution may be committed when a false charge is brought against the plaintiff, setting in motion the criminal process and leading to the plaintiff's being subjected to, or to the risk of a trial.[2] Hence the same person may not be liable for both false arrest or false imprisonment and for malicious prosecution.

There are other kinds of abuse involving liability that may, but do not necessarily, occur when legal proceedings are improperly set in motion, such as abuse of a power given by statute, an abuse of authority or an abuse of office.[3] Moreover an action resembling the action for malicious prosecution may be available to the victim of a claim to obtain a search warrant,[4] or where a civil, not criminal proceeding has been instituted against the plaintiff, such as to secure his or her adjudication in bankruptcy.[5] As with malicious prosecution, proof

---

1 Above p. 42.

2 *Austin v. Dowling* (1870), L.R. 5 C.P. 534 at 540 *per* Willes J. See *Wiche v. Ontario* (2002), 9 C.C.L.T. (3d) 72 at 83-95 (Ont. S.C.J.).

3 *Milgaard v. Kujawa* (1994), 118 D.L.R. (4th) 653 (Sask. C.A.). See also below Chapter 18.

4 *Gibbs v. Rea*, [1998] A.C. 786.

5 *Flame Bar-B-Q Ltd. v. Hoar* (1979), 106 D.L.R. (3d) 438 (N.B.C.A.). *Re Down* (1999), 178 D.L.R. (4th) 294 (B.C.S.C.), reversed (1999), 196 D.L.R. (4th) 114 (B.C.C.A.). But there are

of an improper motive is vital.[6] It is not certain, however, whether, as with malicious prosecution, the proceedings have to terminate in the plaintiff's favour, or whether lack of reasonable and probable cause for such proceedings existed.[7] The scope of such actions is uncertain. What is certain, however, is that their availability depends upon the use, or the threat of use, of the process of a court for an improper purpose or motive.[8]

Actions of that kind are rarely successful. Where malicious prosecution is concerned, although the possibility of such an action is well-recognized in appropriate circumstances, the law is cautious in allowing an action lest people are discouraged from attempting to enforce the law by reason of the threat of legal proceedings against them should the prosecution fail. Hence before a defendant can be made liable for malicious prosecution, various stringent requirements must be fulfilled.

2. ESSENTIALS OF LIABILITY

In *Nelles v. Ontario*[9] the Supreme Court of Canada set out what are the essential ingredients of a successful modern day action for malicious prosecution. They are as follows:

1. Initiation of a prosecution by the defendant;
2. Termination of the prosecution in the plaintiff's favour;
3. Initiation of the prosecution without reasonable cause or in the absence of reasonable and probable cause;
4. Bringing of the prosecution by the defendant acting out of malice or for a purpose other than enforcement of the law.

Although this was not mentioned by the court, proof that the plaintiff suffered damage is also essential.

The defendant need not actively engage in the process of prosecution. But he or she must start the process by an appropriate legal act. This means that the prosecution offence must have been begun by the laying of an information or the proffering of a charge against the plaintiff by the defendant. Merely by telling his or her story to a magistrate in consequence of which the magistrate decides that an offence has been committed may not suffice.[10] However, the actual

---

limits upon this; see *Johnston v. Prince Edward Island* (1995), 128 Nfld. & P.E.I.R. 1 (P.E.I. T.D.); *Gregory v. Portsmouth City Council*, [2000] 1 A.C. 619.

6 *Trinh v. Chan* (1997), 34 C.C.E.L. (2d) 293 (B.C.S.C.); *Atland Containers Ltd. v. Macs Corp.* (1974), 7 O.R. (2d) 107 (H.C.).

7 *Grainger v. Hill* (1838), 4 Bing. N.C. 212; *Geo. Cluthe Manufacturing Co. v. ZTW Properties Inc.* (1995), 23 O.R. (3d) 370 (Div. Ct.).

8 *Speed Seal Products Ltd. v. Paddington*, [1986] 1 All E.R. 91 at 97 (C.A.).

9 (1989), 60 D.L.R. (4th) 609 at 615 (S.C.C.) *per* McIntyre J., 639 *per* Lamer J. Their language differed in some details but was, in essence, to the same effect.

10 *Carnahan v. Coates* (1990), 47 B.C.L.R. (2d) 127 (S.C.).

charge need not be laid by the defendant personally.[11] Thus if a charge is laid by the police, even if this is the result of a complaint by the defendant, the defendant cannot be sued for malicious prosecution.[12] The same will be the case if all the defendant has done is make a statement to the police, unless the defendant knew that this would lead to the laying of a charge against the plaintiff by the police.[13] However, the effect of what the defendant does must be to initiate the requisite criminal proceedings, which is what occurred in *Romegialli v. Marceau*,[14] in which the prosecution of the plaintiff after issuance of a warrant for his arrest was later withdrawn without prejudice to later proceedings if desired.

Termination of the prosecution in favour of the plaintiff means the acquittal of the plaintiff at trial or on appeal.[15] If the conviction stands, no action for malicious prosecution can be maintained. Hence a discharge after conviction will not satisfy this requirement. However abandonment of the prosecution by the defendant will, unless it is the result of a compromise or arrangement between the parties.[16]

The onus is on the plaintiff to establish that the prosecution was begun without reasonable and probable cause. This means that the prosecution must not have been begun in good faith on the part of the defendant. Curiously, and unusually for the law, the burden is on the plaintiff to prove a negative. The defendant is not obliged to prove affirmatively that he or she had reasonable cause for the prosecution. As to what constitutes reasonable and probable cause, it was said in one 19th-century English case[17] that the expression meant such reasonable cause as would operate on the mind of a discreet and reasonable man making the charge. In another English case of the same period[18] it was stated that a reasonable basis for a prosecution is "an honest belief in the guilt of the accused based on a full conviction, founded upon reasonable grounds, of the existence of a state of circumstances which, assuming them to be true, would lead any ordinarily prudent and cautious man, placed in the position of the accuser, to the conclusion that the person charged was probably guilty of the crime imputed." This statement may be a little elaborate for modern times. It may be enough for the plaintiff to show that the defendant lacked sufficient grounds for thinking that there was a case fit to be tried. Everything turns on what facts the defendant knew and believed when he or she began the prosecution not on whether those facts were true.[19] Whether the defendant took legal advice as to the reasonableness of the prosecution may also be relevant. As long as the defendant truthfully

---

11 *Hinde v. Skibinski* (1994), 21 C.C.L.T. (2d) 314 (Ont. Gen. Div.).

12 *Frigault v. Canada (Armed Forces)* (1995), 167 A.R. 216 (Q.B.).

13 *Wood v. Kennedy* (1998), 165 D.L.R. (4th) 542 (Ont. Gen. Div.).

14 [1964] 1 O.R. 407 (C.A.). Contrast *Casey v. Automobiles Renault Canada Ltd.*, [1965] S.C.R. 607.

15 *Herniman v. Smith*, [1938] A.C. 305 at 315.

16 But not where a charge was withdrawn on condition that the plaintiff enter into a peace bond: *Beardsley v. Ontario* (2001), 57 O.R. (3d) 1 (C.A.), reversing (2000), 50 O.R. (3d) 491 (S.C.J.).

17 *Lister v. Perryman* (1870), L.R. 4 H.L. 521, cited in *Wytinck v. DeGrouwe* (1925), 6 W.W.R. 97 (Man. C.A.).

18 *Hicks v. Faulkner* (1881), 8 Q.B.D. 167 at 171 *per* Hawkins J.

19 *Kinloch v. T. (T.)* (1984), 33 Sask. R. 66 (Q.B.).

puts the facts known to him or her to an experienced counsel from whom he or she sought advice, that may suffice to show that the defendant acted with reasonable and probable cause.[20] If the defendant did not act in good faith, for example, if he or she did not believe in the justice of the prosecution, absence of reasonable and probable cause may be established. However, the fact that the defendant acted out of malice or ill-will towards the plaintiff will not of itself establish a lack of reasonable and probable cause, although it may go to prove that he or she did not have a genuine belief, based on reasonable grounds, in the rightness of the prosecution.

It is also incumbent on the plaintiff to prove, in addition to and quite distinctly from proof of a lack of reasonable and probable grounds for the prosecution, that the defendant acted out of malice. Both requirements must be established. Normally malice cannot be inferred from a lack of reasonable and probable cause any more than such a lack can be inferred by proof of malice. If the plaintiff fails to prove one or other of these elements, the action will fail.[21] Malice in this context means an intent to employ the legal process for an improper, wrong or indirect motive,[22] such as spitefulness, to cause harm to the plaintiff, to make a personal gain or to enjoy revenge.[23] It is not easy to prove, as is evidenced by many cases in which an allegation of malice could not be substantiated, with the result that the action failed.

Whether there was reasonable and probable cause for a prosecution is a question of law, although if issues of fact arise in this context they are determined by the jury, or, in the absence of a jury, by the judge acting as a trier of fact not law. Whether the defendant acted out of malice is a question of fact.

Before an action can succeed, the plaintiff must also establish that he or she has suffered damage in consequence of the prosecution. In the old case of *Savile v. Roberts*[24] it was held that there were three kinds of damage in this context: (1) damage to a man's fame if he is accused of something scandalous, which suggests something akin to defamation;[25] (2) damage to the person which normally means physical injury but may include emotional harm; and (3) damage to property in that the plaintiff has incurred financial loss such as the cost of defending himself. The explanation of these three forms of damage has not been without some difficulty or complexity. For example, it has been suggested[26] that the first two of the categories in the old case are really only one, so that only a crime that involved imputations against the character of the accused will suffice

---

20 *Meyer v. General Exchange Insurance Corp.*, [1962] S.C.R. 193.

21 *Glinski v. McIver*, [1962] A.C. 726.

22 *Kendall v. Gambles Canada Ltd.*, [1981] 4 W.W.R. 718 (Q.B.); *Oniel v. Metropolitan Toronto (Municipal) Police Force* (2001), 195 D.L.R. (4th) 59 (Ont. C.A.).

23 *Carroll v. Montsion* (1991), 74 Man. R. (2d) 63 (Q.B.); *Kinloch v. T. (T.)* (1984), 33 Sask. R. 66 (Q.B.). It may be inferred from continuation of a prosecution with reckless indifference to the truth or to right: *Klein v. Seiferling*, [1999] 10 W.W.R. 556 (Sask. Q.B.).

24 (1698), 1 Ld. Raym. 374.

25 See, *e.g.*, *Wiffen v. Bailey & Romford Urban Council*, [1915] 1 K.B. 600.

26 *Berry v. British Transport Commission*, [1961] 1 Q.B. 149.

to support an action. The crime must carry with it the serious possibility of imprisonment, not just the payment of a fine. [27]

3. WHO MAY BE LIABLE

Someone against whom a prosecution has been brought improperly, so as to support an action for malicious prosecution, can hold liable the person who commenced the proceedings, in the sense in which the phrase "commenced the proceedings" has previously been explained. If such person is a private individual no difficulties arise. That person's abuse of the right to institute criminal proceedings against another renders him or her susceptible to liability. Should the prosecution be commenced by an officer of the Crown, such as the Attorney-General of Canada or of a province, or by a Crown Attorney acting on behalf of an Attorney-General, which is more frequently the case, it was considered that such officials enjoyed absolute immunity from liability, even if the prosecution led to the acquittal of the accused.[28] In this respect such officials were equated with, and treated in the same way, as certain judges.[29]

At common law, it was a long established doctrine, based upon the idea that justice should be administered fearlessly, that judges of superior courts, such as the Supreme Court of Canada or a provincial High Court, were immune from all civil liability,[30] including liability for malicious prosecution or abuse of process, even if an accused was wrongly convicted by such court, and even if the judge is alleged to have acted maliciously or with bias.[31] Until recently, the same immunity covered judges of inferior courts, such as Provincial Courts only if the judge in question was acting in the honest if mistaken belief that the case was within his or her jurisdiction. That distinction, and its effects, were challenged in England in 1974 by the Court of Appeal in *Sirros v. Moore*.[32] Some provincial legislation, the language of which differs between provinces, now protects lower court judges from liability for trespass if they were acting within their jurisdiction unless they acted maliciously and without reasonable and probable cause.[33] However nothing is said in the legislation about liability for malicious prosecution or abuse of process. Nevertheless the situation today may be that all judges will be immune from suit unless it can be proved that the judge deliberately

---

27 *Ibid.*, on appeal which reversed the original judgment, [1962] 1 Q.B. 306.

28 *Unterreiner v. Wilson* (1982), 142 D.L.R. (3d) 588 (Ont. H.C.), affirmed (1983), 146 D.L.R. (3d) 322 (Ont. C.A.). Irvine, "The Limitations of Prosecutorial Immunity in Tort" (1986), 34 C.C.L.T. 286.

29 Even though the immunity of the Crown from suit for tort was abolished by legislation: see, *e.g.*, *Proceedings Against the Crown Act*, R.S.O. 1990, c. P.27.

30 *Bosada v. Pinos* (1984), 5 D.L.R. (4th) 334 (Ont. H.C.).

31 *Prefontaine v. Gosman* (2000), 78 Alta. L.R. (3d) 120 (Q.B.).

32 [1974] 3 All E.R. 776 (C.A.): *Re Clendenning and Board of Police Commissioners for City of Belleville* (1976), 75 D.L.R. (3d) 33 (Ont. Div. Ct.).

33 See, *e.g.*, *Public Authorities Protection Act*, R.S.O. 1990, c. P.38, s. 2.

acted without jurisdiction, maliciously and without reasonable and probable cause, all of which will be hard to prove.[34]

The position of the officials referred to above was changed by the decision of the majority of the Supreme Court of Canada in *Nelles v. Ontario*.[35] The majority held that although the Crown was still absolutely immune from suit for malicious prosecution, on the ground of public policy no such absolute immunity was given to the Crown's agents, Attorneys-General and Crown Attorneys. They could be held liable for malicious prosecution or abuse of office in appropriate instances. Hence if such an agent of the Crown acted without reasonable and probable cause and with malice, no immunity was applicable.[36] The immunity of such agents of the Crown is now qualified not absolute.

---

34 See, generally, Feldthusen, "Judicial Immunity: In Search of an Applicable Limiting Formula" (1980) 29 U.N.B.L.J. 73. On the possible immunity of witnesses, see *Carnahan v. Coates* (1990), 47 B.C.L.R. (2d) 127 (C.A.); *Roy v. Prior*, [1971] A.C. 470; *Darker v. Chief Constable of the West Midland Police*, [2000] 4 All E.R. 193.

35 (1989), 60 D.L.R. (4th) 609 (S.C.C.).

36 See *Walker v. Ontario* (1997), 40 C.C.L.T. (2d) 197 (Ont. Gen. Div.); *Osborne v. Ontario (Attorney-General)* (1998), 115 O.A.C. 291 (C.A.); *McTaggart v. Ontario* (1991), 86 D.L.R. (4th) 556 (Ont. Gen. Div.).

Chapter 17

MAINTENANCE AND CHAMPERTY

1. DEFINITIONS

Maintenance is the officious intermeddling in the litigation of others, for an improper motive, when the maintainer has no personal interest in such litigation and the assistance, which usually takes the form of financial support, is unjustified. Champerty occurs when, in return for such support, the parties to the arrangement agree that any profits of the action will be shared between them. Champerty is an "aggravated"[1] or "egregious"[2] form of maintenance, in which there is the added element that the maintainer shares the profits of the litigation. Without maintenance there can be no champerty.[3]

2. SCOPE

At common law maintenance and champerty were crimes as well as torts. In Canada they are no longer crimes,[4] although in Ontario the *Champerty Act* of

---

1 *Giles v. Thompson*, [1993] A.C. 321 at 328 *per* Steyn L.J., at 357 *per* Lord Mustill.

2 *McIntyre Estate v. Ontario (Attorney-General)* (2002), 218 D.L.R. (4th) 193 at 204 (Ont. C.A.).

3 Hence when the conduct involved was not maintenance because the support of the litigation was justified and allowed, as discussed below, the fact that the supporter obtained a financial gain, *e.g.*, by the assignment of the proceeds of the action, did not render such assignment champertous: *Galati v. Edwards Estate* (1999), 27 C.P.C. (4th) 123 (Ont. Gen. Div.); *cf. American Home Assurance Co. v. Brett Buick Pontiac GMC Ltd.* (1992), 116 N.S.R. (2d) 328 (C.A.). However, in *Thai Trading Co. v. Taylor*, [1998] Q.B. 781, Millett L.J., at 786, suggested that, even if the maintenance were "lawful", the agreement to share proceeds would be champertous. The decision in that case was repudiated as wrong and not followed by the English Court of Appeal in *Hughes v. Kingston Upon Hull City Council*, [1999] Q.B. 1193, on the ground that the earlier case ignored the remarks in *Swain v. The Law Society*, [1983] 1 A.C. 598 on the legal effect of the provisions of rules of practice made by the Law Society under the powers given by the *Solicitors Act*. The law has since been changed in England by the *Courts and Legal Services Act*, 1990, c. 41, amended by the *Access to Justice Act*, 1999, c. 22.

4 Nor in England as a result of the *Criminal Law Act*, 1967, c. 58, s. 14(1). The crime of barratry was also abolished, but there appears to be a very rare *tort* of barratry, on which see *McIntyre Estate v. Ontario (Attorney-General)* (2003), 14 C.C.L.T. (3d) 223 at 230-231 (Ont. C.A.).

1897[5] makes champerty "illegal". It would seem, however, that, whether in Ontario or elsewhere in Canada, an action in tort may be brought for maintenance or champerty,[6] although in modern times such actions are rare, and, when brought, seem to be unsuccessful.[7] Their relevance today is more to the question whether a contract is illegal, and therefore invalid, on the ground that it offends the law against maintenance or champerty.[8] For such reason "contingency fee" agreements between a lawyer and a client, under which the lawyer would be paid a percentage of any damages awarded to the client in an action or be paid nothing if the client were unsuccessful were considered unacceptable, until more recent times when by legislation in various provinces such arrangements were validated if made under the supervision of a court.[9]

The rationale for making such conduct tortious[10] was that an abuse of the legal process might be committed, for example, by the bringing of unjustified actions to harass a defendant,[11] the suppression or manufacture of evidence, the subornation of witnesses.[12] However, in exceptional cases maintenance, and hence champerty,[13] was accepted as being "privileged" and therefore neither criminal nor tortious. Such would be the case if there was a common interest in the action brought by the person maintained or the parties were members of the

---

5 R.S.O. 1897, c. 327, which, though not to be found in subsequent revisions of the Ontario statutes remains part of Ontario law: *Buday v. Locator of Missing Heirs Inc.* (1993), 16 O.R. (3d) 257 (C.A.); *George Biro Real Estate Ltd. v. Sheldon* (1965), 46 D.L.R. (2d) 610 (Ont. C.A.).

6 *155569 Canada Ltd. v. 248524 Alberta Ltd.* (1999), 247 A.R. 239 (Q.B.).

7 See *American Home Assurance Co. v. Brett Buick Pontiac GMC Ltd.* (1992), 116 N.S.R. (2d) 319 (T.D.), *Re Down* (1999), 178 D.L.R. (4th) 294 (B.C.S.C.), reversed (1999), 196 D.L.R. (4th) 114 (B.C.C.A.).

8 See, *e.g.*, *453416 Ontario Inc. v. White* (1984), 42 C.P.C. 209 (Ont.), with which contrast *Fredrickson v. Insurance Corp. of B.C.* (1986), 28 D.L.R. (4th) 414 (S.C.), affirmed (1988), 49 D.L.R. (4th) 160 (B.C.C.A.).

9 See the discussion of such fees, and of agreements by which in addition to the regular fee a lawyer might be paid an extra amount if the case were successful, in *McIntyre Estate v. Ontario (Attorney-General)* (2002), 218 D.L.R. (4th) 193 (Ont. C.A.) where, it would seem, the Ontario Court of Appeal was prepared, in certain circumstances, to permit or recognize as valid a contingency fee agreement. See the changes in the *Justice Statute Law Amendment Act, 2002*, S.O. 2002, c. 24, Schedule A.

10 *McIntyre Estate v. Ontario (Attorney-General)* (2002), 218 D.L.R. (4th) 193 (Ont. C.A.), at 201-203.

11 Hence if the litigation was already in progress when the agreement with respect to fees that might otherwise be a contingency fee arrangement, there would be no maintenance and no champerty: *Bergel & Edson v. Wolf* (2001), 50 O.R. (3d) 777 (S.C.J.).

12 In this regard, namely, tampering with evidence, it should be noted that it has been suggested, and disputed, that there is a distinct tort of "spoliation" that may lie when relevant evidence is alleged to have been concealed or destroyed: see *St. Louis v. R.* (1896), 25 S.C.R. 649; *Endean v. Canadian Red Cross Society* (1998), 157 D.L.R. (4th) 465 (B.C.C.A.); *Coriale (Litigation guardian of) v. Sisters of St. Joseph of Sault Ste. Marie* (1998), 41 O.R. (3d) 347 (Gen. Div.); *Robb Estate v. St. Joseph's Health Care Centre* (1998), 166 D.L.R. (4th) 158 (Ont. Gen. Div.); *Spasic Estate v. Imperial Tobacco Ltd.* (1998), 42 O.R. (3d) 391 (Gen. Div.), reversed (2000), 49 O.R. (3d) 699 (C.A.).

13 *Bulli Coal Mining Co. v. Osborne*, [1899] A.C. 351; *Galati v. Edwards Estate* (1999), 27 C.P.C. (4th) 123 (Ont. Gen. Div.).

same family or master and servant, or the one providing the support did so out of charity or because of religious empathy.[14]

3. RELEVANT FACTORS

If maintenance or champerty is alleged the plaintiff must prove that he or she has incurred actual loss. It is not necessary, however, that the plaintiff prove that the person providing the financial support was acting out of malice[15] or lacked reasonable and probable cause for promoting or defending the action in respect of which that support was provided. Nor will a plaintiff be barred from bringing an action alleging maintenance or champerty if the party being maintained was successful.[16]

---

[14] *Hill v. Archbold*, [1968] 1 Q.B. 686; *Ilic v. Calgary Sun* (1998), 61 Alta. L.R. (3d) 322 (Q.B.). *Cf. Finlayson v. Roberts* (2000), 136 O.A.C. 271 at 275.

[15] But malice, the intent to harm, is an essential element of barratry: *McIntyre Estate v. Ontario (Attorney General)* (2003), 14 C.C.L.T. (3d) 223 at 231 (Ont. C.A.).

[16] *Neville v. London Express Newspaper Ltd.*, [1919] A.C. 308; *Margetts (Next Friend of Estate) v. Timmer Estate* (1999), 244 A.R. 114 (C.A.).

Chapter 18

MISFEASANCE IN PUBLIC OFFICE

1. ANOTHER TYPE OF ABUSE

Previous chapters have been concerned with various forms of abuse of the legal process that can lead to liability in tort. Some of these, such as malicious prosecution or false imprisonment, may entail an abuse of office or power that can lead to harmful economic, and possibly physical, consequences. Another type of abuse that can result in liability in tort is one that has been growing in importance in recent years, as evidenced by the number of cases reported in several common law jurisdictions, is what has been referred to as "misfeasance in public office". The basic idea underlying this tort is that someone who is invested with a certain statutory power[1] by virtue of his or her occupation of a given public office or position does not use or wield such power legitimately, in accordance with the nature, scope and purpose of the power, but unlawfully and improperly, for a purpose that is, in fact, malicious, in other words to cause harm to another person. Such harm, judging by recent decisions, is usually financial or economic.

The tort appears to have been recognized for some considerable time and to be well established,[2] although, in Canada, until the past few years, the most famous illustration of its operation was the case of *Roncarelli v. Duplessis*.[3] This concerned the cancellation of a liquor licence by the Premier of Quebec because the licence holder was a Jehovah's Witness who had aided another member of the sect charged with transgressing a municipal bylaw about the distribution of pamphlets. It was held that the action of the Premier was discriminatory and punitive, and did not constitute a valid, legitimate exercise of a statutory power. As this case, and later ones in Canada[4] reveal, the essence of the tort, in which respect it resembles some instances of the torts of malicious prosecution and false imprisonment, is the misuse of a legal right by a public, not a private, person or

---

1 Or perhaps other powers: *per* Feldman J.A., dissenting, in *Odhavji Estate v. Woodhouse* (2000), 52 O.R. (3d) 181 (Ont. C.A.) at 207-215.

2 See the cases referred to in *Farrington v. Thomson*, [1959] V.R. 286, an Australian case, and at first instance, in *Bourgoin SA v. Ministry of Agriculture, Fisheries and Food*, [1986] 1 Q.B. 716; *Dunlop v. Woollhara Municipal Council*, [1982] A.C. 158.

3 [1959] S.C.R. 121.

4 *Gershman v. Manitoba (Vegetable Producers' Marketing Board)* (1976), 69 D.L.R. (3d) 114 (Man. C.A.); *Gerrard v. Manitoba* (1992), 98 D.L.R. (4th) 167 (Man. C.A.).

body. Therefore, although, like other torts,[5] it gives a private right of action to an individual or organization that has been damnified by its commission, the tort of misfeasance in public office can be looked upon as an aspect of public rather than private law.

Those who have been accused of commission of this tort include police officers,[6] prison guards,[7] officers of state and government departments,[8] municipal councillors, mayors and municipalities,[9] law societies charged with governance of the profession,[10] inspectors,[11] social workers,[12] customs officers,[13] tax officials,[14] and many others holding official positions created under statute.[15] Hence the scope of this tort is extremely wide: its application appears to be potentially limitless. It is surprising, therefore, to find that there is some disagreement about the conditions that must be satisfied before this tort can be held to have been committed.

2. ESSENTIALS OF LIABILITY

Some of these are generally agreed upon. Others, however, seem to be unsettled. With respect to the latter, what has been termed the "orthodox" approach to this tort was recently embraced by the House of Lords, contrary to the views of the English Court of Appeal, in *Three Rivers District Council v. Bank of England (No. 3)*,[16] and by the British Columbia Court of Appeal in *National Properties Ltd. v. Highlands (District)*.[17] A variation from this is found in an Albertan

---

5 *Cf.* the right to sue for special damage suffered as a result of the breach of a statutory duty: above p. 108. Note also, in Canada, the power of a court, under s. 24 of the *Canadian Charter of Rights and Freedoms*, Part I of the *Constitution Act, 1982*, being Schedule B to the *Canada Act 1982* (U.K.), 1982, c. 11, to grant damages for the infringement of a person's *Charter* rights.

6 *Calveley v. Chief Constable of Merseyside Police*, [1988] 3 All E.R. 335; *Simson v. Attorney-General (Baigent's Case)*, [1994] 2 N.Z.L.R. 667.

7 *Racz v. Home Office*, [1994] 2 A.C. 45.

8 *Bennett v. Commissioner of Police of the Metropolis*, [1995] 1 W.L.R. 488; *Cheticamp Fisheries Co-Operative Ltd. v. Canada* (1995), 123 D.L.R. (4th) 121 (N.S.C.A.).

9 *First National Properties Ltd. v. Highlands (District)* (1999), 178 D.L.R. (4th) 505 (B.C.S.C.), reversed (2001), 198 D.L.R. (4th) 443 (B.C.C.A.); *Namusa Enterprises Ltd, v. Etobicoke (City)* (1990), 3 M.P.L.R. (2d) 227 (Ont. Gen. Div.).

10 *Little v. Law Institute of Victoria (No. 3)*, [1990] V.R. 287.

11 *White Hatter Limousine Service Ltd. v. Calgary (City)*, [1994] 1 W.W.R. 620 (Alta. Q.B.); *Northern Territory of Australia v. Mengel* (1996), 185 C.L.R. 307 (H.C.A.).

12 *E. K.*, [1995] 2 N.Z.L.R. 239.

13 *Francoeur v. R.* (1994), 78 F.T.R. 109 (T.D.), affirmed (1996), 110 F.T.R. 321 (C.A.).

14 *Longley v. Minister of National Revenue* (1999), 176 D.L.R. (4th) 445 (B.C.S.C.), affirmed (2000), 184 D.L.R. (4th) 590 (B.C.C.A.).

15 Such as the executive director of the Manitoba Agricultural Lands Protection Board: *Gerrard v. Manitoba* (1992), 98 D.L.R. (4th) 167 (Man. C.A.); a Superintendent of Brokers: *Stenner v. British Columbia (Securities Commission)* (1996), 141 D.L.R. (4th) 122 (B.C.C.A.).

16 [1996] 3 All E.R. 558, affirmed [1999] 4 All E.R. 800*n*, affirmed in part, [2000] 3 All E.R. 1.

17 (2001), 198 D.L.R. (4th) 443.

case,[18] which was decided prior to the appearance of the speeches in the House of Lords in *Three Rivers*. That judgment was subsequently approved by the Manitoba Court of Appeal.[19] The result of this divergence of opinion is that, in Canada at any rate, the definition or explanation of important elements of this tort remains to be authoritatively determined.

The following features of this tort are generally agreed upon. In the first place, as previously noted, the alleged wrong must have been committed by a public officer acting, or purporting to act, in the exercise of his or her public powers. Second, there must have been misconduct, an improper exercise of those powers. Third, that misconduct must have caused the damage or loss alleged by the plaintiff (which may be inferred from the pleadings).[20] What has been the subject of disagreement is the fourth element, namely, that the defendant public officer must have acted as he or she did with a certain state of mind.

The orthodox view states that, for the purposes of liability, the defendant should have acted with what has been termed "targeted malice", or, if he or she acted without such malice, knowing that he or she was acting in abuse of the relevant power, even though he or she had no intention of harming the plaintiff. According to the orthodox view, therefore, there exist two categories or "limbs" of liability for misfeasance in public office. Malice, in the orthodox view denotes " bad faith",[21] that is from, spite or ill-will, purely with intent to harm the plaintiff or a class of persons of which the plaintiff is a member.[22] However, in contrast it has sometimes been asserted that a person who has acted not out of malice, in the sense just set out, but with knowledge of the invalidity of the exercise of the power and with knowledge that its exercise will, or will be likely to cause harm to the plaintiff, will be considered to have acted maliciously.[23] It has also been suggested that malice can be inferred from the fact that the defendant acted with reckless indifference or deliberate blindness as to the effect of what he or she was doing.[24] To adopt this alternative meaning of malice, it may be suggested, would have the effect of coalescing the two "limbs" of the tort, contrary to the orthodox view.

In the absence of malice, in the orthodox sense, liability will depend, according to the orthodox view, on the knowledge of the defendant. This should mean knowledge that the exercise of the power was invalid or improper. But in

---

18 *Alberta (Minister of Public Works, Supply and Services) v. Nilsson*, [1999] 9 W.W.R. 203 (Alta. Q.B.), which is under appeal after leave to appeal was given by the Alberta Court of Appeal: (1999), 74 Alta. L.R. (3d) 205 (C.A.).

19 *Uni-Jet Industrial Pipe Ltd. v. Canada (Attorney-General)* (2001), 198 D.L.R. (4th) 527 (Man. C.A.).

20 *Columbus Investment Corp. v. Alberta (Minister of Public Works, Supply and Services)* (2000), 259 A.R. 299 (Q.B.).

21 *Stenner v. British Columbia (Securities Commission)* (1996), 141 D.L.R. (4th) 122 (B.C.C.A.).

22 *Simpson v. Chiropractors' Assn. (Saskatchewan)* (1999), 185 Sask. R. 7 (Q.B.), reversed on other grounds (2001), 203 Sask. R. 231 (C.A.).

23 *Northern Territory of Australia v. Mengel* (1996), 185 C.L.R. 307 at 370 *per* Deane J.; *Three Rivers District Council v. Bank of England (No. 3)*, [1996] 3 All E.R. 558 at 582 *per* Clarke J.

24 *Northern Territory of Australia v. Mengel* (1996), 185 C.L.R. 307 (H.C.A.).

an English case[25] prior to *Three Rivers* it was said that the requisite knowledge also included foresight of injury to the plaintiff. This appears to introduce the element of negligence into a tort which has always been thought of as a tort that can only be committed intentionally. Hence it would seem that foresight of harm, the hallmark of a duty of care, has no place in the definition of this tort.

What is "knowledge" for the purposes of this tort has also been explained as meaning (1) actual knowledge that the act was unlawful or (2) suspicion or belief that the act was outside the powers of the official accompanied either by a failure to ascertain the truth or by the failure to take reasonable steps to ascertain the truth.[26] The Albertan judge, Marceau J., whose view was adopted later by the Manitoba Court of Appeal, seems to have equated the latter two situations with the idea of reckless indifference or willful blindness to the lack of authority to perform the act in question. If such extension of the meaning of "knowledge" is accepted as valid, the scope of this tort will have been widened beyond its definition according to the orthodox view that can be traced back to the language of Lord Diplock in *Dunlop v. Woollhara Municipal Council.*[27] There knowledge, that is actual knowledge, of the invalidity of the exercise of the power was given as the alternative to acting out of malice.

The exposition of what is an "intentional illegal act" capable of supporting an action for misfeasance in public office is, for Canadian courts, uncertain. A recent critical examination of the Canadian decisions[28] appears to favour the orthodox view. It remains to be seen whether, in the future, other Canadian courts will conform to the definition of this tort by the House of Lords, which would confine its scope to malicious or otherwise deliberate misconduct, or will adopt a broader approach, which would make it apply even if the defendant did not act maliciously or with appreciation that he or she was acting illegally in order to cause harm to the plaintiff.

---

25 *Bourgoin SA v. Ministry of Agriculture, Fisheries and Food*, [1986] 1 Q.B. 716 at 740 *per* Mann J.

26 *Three Rivers District Council v. Bank of England (No. 3)*, [1996] 3 All E.R. 558.

27 [1982] A.C. 158 at 172.

28 See Irvine, "Misfeasance in Public Office: Reflections on Some Recent Developments" (2002), 9 C.C.L.T. (3d) 26.

Chapter 19

DECEIT

1. THE CONSEQUENCES AND NATURE OF FRAUD

Dishonesty in the course of making a contract was recognized as affecting the validity of such a transaction long before the making of a false statement that led to harm or loss was accepted as giving rise to liability in tort. In the modern law of contract a false or fraudulent misrepresentation that induces someone to enter into a contract with the maker of such misrepresentation will entitle the victim to avoid the transaction.[1] Since the decision in *Pasley v. Freeman*[2] in 1789 it can also entitle the victim to sue for damages. There are situations in which the consequence of the victim's reliance upon a fraudulent misrepresentation has been that the victim incurs physical injury. Long before the law recognized liability for negligence in relation to defective chattels it was held that if someone fraudulently misrepresented that a chattel was safe to be used that person would be liable to the victim who relied thereon and was injured because of the defect in the chattel, even though the chattel was transferred gratuitously not under a contract.[3] So, too, where someone suffered nervous shock as a result of another person's making a deliberately false statement about the health of a third party, liability in tort would be imposed on the one guilty of making the statement.[4] However, in most situations the harm that results from such fraud will be economic or financial loss. Hence the tort of deceit is more usually included within the category of what are referred to as the "economic torts".

To constitute fraud that will amount to the tort of deceit the defendant must have made a false statement or misrepresentation of fact with the intent that the victim should act upon it, and the victim must act in reliance upon the statement to his or her detriment.[5] The defendant, to be liable in deceit, must be guilty of moral as well as legal fraud.

---

1 Fridman, *The Law of Contract in Canada*, 4th ed. (Toronto: Carswell, 1999), pp. 309-315.

2 (1789), 3 Term Rep. 51.

3 *Langridge v. Levy* (1837), 2 M. & W. 519.

4 *Wilkinson v. Downton*, [1897] 2 Q.B. 57. But such cases are more like trespass to the person than deceit: above p. 42.

5 *Parna v. G. & S. Properties Ltd.*, [1968] 1 O.R. 626 at 629 (H.C.).

2. STATEMENTS OF FACT

The tort of deceit is only concerned with statements of fact. Moreover the fact in question must relate to something in the past or present. A statement regarding some future fact, event, or action will not qualify as a misrepresentation for the purposes of the tort of deceit. Such a statement may amount to a promise which will have legal effect only if it is supported by consideration, *i.e.*, constitutes a contractual promise, or permits the invocation of the doctrines of promissory or proprietary estoppel.[6] However a statement that seems to be a statement about the future, *i.e.*, a promise, may be a statement of fact if it amounts to a false representation about the *present* state or condition of the mind of the one making the representation. As it was once said: "the state of a man's mind is as much a matter of fact as the state of a man's digestion".[7]

A statement of fact must be distinguished from a statement of law. It must also be differentiated from an opinion. However, even if what has been said appears to be a matter of opinion rather than fact, if it involves some comment or statement about matters which are within the expert knowledge of the person making the statement, by reason of that person's business, profession or knowledge of a certain locality, the statement may be considered to be one of fact and so susceptible of leading to liability if the other conditions of such liability are met.[8]

3. FALSITY

The statement must be untrue.[9] Everyone is obliged not to be deliberately dishonest. Hence a statement that is half-true can amount to a false statement.

To conceal a fact that affects the validity of what has been said will amount to deceit, because the maker of the statement has given a false picture of the true situation by reason of what has been omitted.[10] However, unless this is the effect of the omission of something, there will be no liability on the part of the maker of the statement for deceit, because, in general, silence is not deceit and a person is under no duty to speak except where some statute imposes such a requirement or the relationship between the parties is special involving what has been referred to as *uberrimae fides*, the utmost good faith. This is the situation, for example, where the parties are solicitor and client, banker and customer, or a person applying for insurance and the insurance company.

---

6 Fridman, *op. cit.* at pp. 131-147.

7 *Edgington v. Fitzmaurice* (1884), 29 Ch. D. 459 at 483 *per* Bowen L.J.

8 *Bisset v. Wilkinson*, [1927] A.C. 177; *Northern & Central Gas Corp. v. Hillcrest Collieries*, [1976] 1 W.W.R. 481 (Alta. T.D.).

9 *Dixon v. Deacon Morgan McEwan Easson* (1993), 102 D.L.R. (4th) 1 (B.C.C.A.).

10 Fridman, *op. cit.* at pp. 326-327.

If the statement is true when first made but becomes untrue later, to the knowledge of the person making it, such person is bound to correct the earlier statement. The failure to do so will constitute both moral and legal fraud.[11]

4. KNOWLEDGE AND INTENT

The making of an untrue statement of fact will not lead to liability for deceit unless the person making the statement knew that it was false either when he or she made it or when it later became false, or the maker of the statement was reckless with respect to whether it was true or false. This is the effect of the decision of the House of Lords in *Derry v. Peek*[12] in 1889. The person making the statement must have lacked belief in the truth of the statement. Mere carelessness or negligence as to whether the statement was true or false will not suffice for liability in deceit. Not until 1963 was it accepted that there could be liability in tort for a misrepresentation that was made negligently not fraudulently with awareness and knowledge that the statement was untrue.[13] But *Derry v. Peek* also held that one who acted with reckless indifference to the truth or falsity of a statement made with the intent that the person to whom it was made should act upon it to his or her detriment would also be guilty of deceit.

Knowledge of the statement's falsity is not enough. The tort of deceit also involves the intent to deceive.[14] The statement must be designed or intended to deceive the person to whom it is made. This means that the one making the statement must have intended that the person receiving the statement should act upon it. The fact that the one making the statement knew that the statement was false will usually lead to the conclusion that he or she had the intent to deceive. Lack of such knowledge will mean that the necessary intent was absent.

5. RELIANCE

Although it can be proved that the defendant had the requisite knowledge and intent when he or she made the statement in question, liability will not ensue unless the victim, directly or indirectly, acted in reliance upon the truth of the statement.[15] The essence of the tort is the reliance placed upon the statement by the party to whom it was communicated. Reliance by someone else will not result in liability on the part of the fraudulent person, unless that person made the statement with the intent that it should be communicated to the third party who

---

11 *Ibid.*, at pp. 324-325.

12 (1889), 14 App. Cas. 337.

13 Above pp. 102-105.

14 *BG Checo International Ltd. v. BC Hydro & Power Authority*, [1993] 1 S.C.R. 12.

15 *Elmy v. Yorkton International Seed Co.* (1974), 5 N.R. 383 (S.C.C.). See *Moore v. Ontario Investment Assn.* (1888), 16 O.R. 269 (H.C.), with which contrast *Carom v. Bre-X Minerals Ltd.* (1998), 41 O.R. (3d) 780 (Gen. Div.), which rejected the U.S. "fraud on the market theory".

relied on it, in which event it may be considered that the maker of the statement has directly affected such a third party.

It would appear that once it is proved that the defendant made a misrepresentation calculated to induce the plaintiff to act to his or her detriment and that the plaintiff suffered loss consistent with his or her having acted on the misrepresentation, the onus will then be on the defendant to establish that the plaintiff did not in fact rely on the misrepresentation.[16]

What the law requires is that the plaintiff establish that the false statement caused the plaintiff to act in such a way as to result in suffering loss or damage. The plaintiff's reliance on the statement must be the material cause of the plaintiff's loss.

Hence if the plaintiff knew the true state of affairs, it may not be possible to establish the crucial reliance.[17] However there is a distinction between the plaintiff's actual knowledge of the truth and the situation where the plaintiff has the means of acquiring such knowledge but does not do so. The fact that the party to whom the statement was made could have verified its accuracy but did not, even if that party was careless in not doing so, will not excuse the fraudulent party from liability for deceit. There is no defence of contributory negligence on the part of the plaintiff to an action for deceit.[18]

However, the plaintiff's reaction to or conduct in reliance upon the false statement must be conduct that would be expected to result from the sort of untrue statement that is involved. If it is not, then there will be no liability for deceit. The damage that results must be damage that flows from the ordinary course of events from the kind of untrue statement that has been made to the plaintiff as the direct and natural consequence of the plaintiff's belief in and reliance upon the misrepresentation.

6. RECOVERABLE DAMAGES

Damages for deceit are at large. In an action in tort for deceit those damages are meant to compensate the plaintiff for actual loss attributable to the deceit, unlike the situation if the plaintiff is suing for rescission of a contract and damages for fraudulent misrepresentation when the damages may include loss of profit that might have been made if the statement had been true. In a tort action the plaintiff is entitled to be put back into the position in which he or she would have been if the representation had not been made, not into the position in which the plaintiff would have been if the statement had been true. But consequential damages, for example, for physical inconvenience and disruption and possibly mental disturbance, may also be awarded in a tort action,[19] as may aggravated or exemplary

---

16 *Sidhu Estate v. Bains* (1996), 25 B.C.L.R. (3d) 41 (C.A.).

17 *Modern Livestock Ltd. v. Elgersma* (1989), 69 Alta. L.R. (2d) 20 (Q.B.).

18 *Central Railway of Venezuela v. Kisch* (1867), L.R. 2 H.L. 99; *Ambico Ltd. v. Loeb Inc.* (1993), 13 O.R. (3d) 423 (C.A.).

19 *Mafo v. Adams*, [1970] 1 Q.B. 548; *Doyle v. Olby Ironmongers Ltd.*, [1969] 2 Q.B. 158.

damages in appropriate instances, for instance if the defendant's conduct offended against community standards.[20]

[20] *Goldstar Management Ltd. v. Varvis* (1995), 34 Alta. L.R. (3d) 74 (Q.B.).

Chapter 20

INJURIOUS FALSEHOOD

1. A MODERN TORT

An action for slander of title was recognized by the common law some centuries ago.[1] That action lay when one person falsely and intentionally denied that another was the owner of certain property. Like defamation it involved a false statement of fact (hence the use of the term "slander"). However, unlike defamation it did not involve an attack upon another person's character, but an attack upon another's claim to property. In this respect it resembled the tort of deceit, since the statement was intended to deceive. However, deceit was committed when the defendant intended to deceive the plaintiff to the plaintiff's detriment. Slander of title was concerned with statements intended to deceive third parties to the detriment of the plaintiff.

It was not until a series of English decisions in the 19th century[2] that it was accepted that an action would lie not only for "slander of title" but also where someone published to a third party an untrue statement about the plaintiff that did not reflect upon the character of the plaintiff, and so was not a libel, but nonetheless caused that other economic loss. These culminated in the decision in *Ratcliffe v. Evans*[3] in 1892. The false statement in that case was to the effect that the plaintiff had gone out of business. The result of this was that previous customers, believing the statement to be true, ceased patronizing the plaintiff's business to his or her economic detriment. For the plaintiff's loss the defendant was liable. Subsequently other decisions[4] held that an action would lie if the false statement did not attack the plaintiff's title to property but attacked or "disparaged" the quality of the plaintiff's property or goods, thereby causing the plaintiff to incur economic loss.[5] These various decisions were later followed in Canada.[6]

---

1 Prosser, "Injurious Falsehood: The Basis of Liability" (1959) 59 Col. L.R. 425.

2 *Pitt v. Donovan* (1813), 1 M. & S. 639; *Wren v. Weild* (1869), L.R. 4 Q.B. 730; *Western Counties Manure Co. v. Lawes Chemical Manure Co.* (1874), L.R. 9 Ex. 218; *Riding v. Smith* (1876), 1 Ex. D. 91.

3 [1892] 2 Q.B. 524.

4 See, *e.g.*, *White v. Mellin*, [1895] A.C. 154; *Barrett v. Associated Newspapers Ltd.* (1907), 23 T.L.R. 666; *Royal Baking Powder Co. v. Wright, Crossley & Co.* (1900), 18 R.P.C. 95.

5 Wood, "Disparagement of Title and Quality" (1942) 20 Can. Bar Rev. 296.

6 *Gordon v. McGibbon* (1875), 16 N.B.R. 49; *Cormier v. Bourque* (1894), 32 N.B.R. 283; *Smith v. Dun* (1911), 19 W.L.R. 518; *Sheppard Publishing Co. v. Press Publishing Co.* (1905), 10 O.L.R. 243; *Manitoba Free Press Co. v. Nagy* (1907), 39 S.C.R. 340.

As a result of this development the expression "slander of title", which described the medieval action, ceased to be apposite. In its place courts and writers coined the term "injurious falsehood" to denote the various ways in which false statements, other than those which qualified as defamation or deceit, could cause economic loss.

In the modern law of torts there are two versions of this action: slander of title, the old action based on an attack upon the plaintiff's title to property; and slander of goods, when the attack is on the quality of the plaintiff's property. These, together with the action for passing-off, which will be discussed in the succeeding chapter,[7] are the means whereby, before the creation of statutory wrongs such as infringement of copyright, infringement of patent and conduct that is in breach of the *Trade-marks Act*,[8] the common law attempted to deal with unfair competition between traders. This development came about because, in the words of an Australian judge,[9] the law of torts "values competitive conduct between traders to bring down prices and improve products".

2. SLANDER OF TITLE

This variety of the tort of injurious falsehood occurs when oral or written aspersions[10] are cast upon the plaintiff's ownership of land by reason of which the plaintiff is prevented from selling or leasing it. Similarly, a false claim that the defendant has a chattel mortgage over goods belonging to the plaintiff may be slander of title, if the requisite intention is established, because by so doing the defendant is asserting that the plaintiff's title is not free from encumbrances, which may affect the plaintiff's ability to sell or otherwise dispose of the goods.[11] Such potential liability, it appears, has not been affected by the enactment of a provincial *Personal Property Security Act* which replaces the old law of chattel mortgages by a new system of registration of security interests.[12] Slander of title may also be committed by a false claim of a lien over someone else's property.[13]

A mere assertion of a rival title will not amount to slander of title unless it is made falsely and with the requisite intention to harm the plaintiff.[14] However if the defendant registers a certificate of *lis pendens* against a plaintiff's title to land this may not constitute slander of title. By such a certificate the defendant may be alleging some defect in the plaintiff's title. But the defendant may

---

7 Below p. 177.

8 R.S.C. 1985, c. T-13. Below p.

9 *Camponar Sociedad Limitada v. Nike Int. Ltd.* (2000), 169 A.L.R. 677 at 679 (H.C.A.) *per* Gleeson C.J.

10 This is another difference between slander of title and slander amounting to defamation, since the latter is committed only when the statement is oral not written: above p. 136.

11 *Siopiolosz v. Taylor*, [1944] 2 D.L.R. 92 (Ont. C.A.).

12 *Osman Auction Inc. v. Murray* (1994), 16 Alta. L.R. (3d) 292 (Q.B.).

13 *Garrett v. Ayr Ventures Inc.* (1995), 21 O.R. (3d) 407 (Gen. Div.).

14 *Cf. Manitoba Free Press v. Nagy* (1907), 39 S.C.R. 340.

simply be indicating that he or she has a claim against the plaintiff without at the same time throwing doubt on the plaintiff's title. Some cases suggest that the conduct of the defendant in such circumstances may be absolutely privileged because such a certificate is issued by a court. This, however, is not entirely clear.[15]

3. SLANDER OF QUALITY

This variety of injurious falsehood involves a slanderous accusation about or the disparagement of the quality of the plaintiff's goods or land which has the result of persuading a third party not to enter into any sort of transaction regarding such land or goods with the plaintiff. Because of the way in which the tort has developed, it would appear not to matter from the point of view of liability, whether the behaviour of the defendant should properly be considered to be slander of title or slander of goods, as long as the essential elements of the tort can be established.

A leading Canadian case in this respect is *Manitoba Free Press v. Nagy*.[16] The defendant newspaper reported that the plaintiff's house, which the plaintiff wanted to sell, was haunted. This was an injurious falsehood, though whether it amounted to slander of title or slander of quality was never resolved but, in any event, was immaterial. What was relevant was the issue of malice, that is, whether, in order to succeed, the plaintiff had to establish not only that the defendant intentionally published an untrue statement, but also whether it was made in bad faith.[17]

To qualify as a slander or disparagement of quality of property the offending statement must amount to more than "puffing" of the defendant's property in comparison with that of the plaintiff (which would be the equivalent of "vulgar abuse" in defamation). There must be a statement that misleads, misrepresents and deceives, for example, by a comparison which relies upon, or suggests, something that is untrue about the plaintiff's goods.[18] However, some more recent decisions suggest that injurious falsehood may be an appropriate action to bring in circumstances analogous to but not actually constituting slander or

---

15 See and contrast *Tersigni v. Fagan*, [1959] O.W.N. 94 (C.A.); *Geo. Cluthe Manufacturing Co. v. ZTW Properties Inc.* (1995), 23 O.R. (3d) 370 (Div. Ct.); *James v. Alcock* (1996), 143 Nfld. & P.E.I.R. 106 (Nfld. T.D.). Note also the effect of a deed of rectification: *Eagle Const. v. Thistle* (1984), 50 Nfld. & P.E.I.R. 97 (Nfld. T.D.), with which contrast *Almas v. Spenceley* (1972), 25 D.L.R. (3d) 653 (Ont. C.A.), and a caution on the plaintiff's title, *Captain Developments Ltd. v. Nu-West Group Ltd.* (1982), 37 O.R. (2d) 697 (H.C.), reversed on appeal (1984), 6 D.L.R. (4th) 179 (Ont. C.A.).

16 (1907), 39 S.C.R. 340.

17 In this respect recklessness sufficed.

18 *Acme Silver Co. v. Stacey Hardware Co.* (1891), 21 O.R. 261 (H.C.). See also *Alberta Geophysical Products Ltd. v. Geo. E. Failing Supply Co.* (1963), 43 D.L.R. (2d) 681 (Alta. T.D.).

disparagement of goods, for example, where the statement accused the defendants of fraud which led to the loss of a sale by the defendants.[19]

4. THE ELEMENTS OF LIABILITY

The statement in issue must be false, untrue. Unlike defamation, however, in which once the statement is published it is presumed to be untrue and the defendant is obliged to allege and prove that it is true,[20] in both versions of the tort of injurious falsehood there is no such presumption. The plaintiff must prove that the statement was false.[21] The plaintiff must also prove that the statement was intended to refer to the plaintiff,[22] just as in defamation the plaintiff must show that reasonable people believed that the defamatory statement referred to the plaintiff.[23]

Next there is the question of malice. One view is that the element of "malice" entails that all the plaintiff has to prove is publication of the statement in the knowledge that it was false and with the intent that it should cause the plaintiff harm. From this the inference could be drawn that the publication was without just cause or excuse and so supported liability. Another view is that "malice", here as in other areas of the law, such as malicious prosecution,[24] means that bad faith or an absence of good faith on the part of the defendant must be established by the plaintiff. The issue was left open by the contradictory reasons given at various levels in *Manitoba Free Press v. Nagy*.[25] In the Supreme Court of Canada it was held that once the plaintiff proved that the false statement was made with reckless disregard for its consequences, lack of good faith was established and liability could follow.

Both the relevance of malice and the meaning of the term have been the subject of conflicting decisions. However it is suggested that the majority of the decisions support the view that malice is essential,[26] especially where a defendant pleads some kind of privilege to publish the statement (unless the privilege is "absolute"),[27] and that it refers to bad faith or the absence of good faith on the

---

19 *First Choice Canadian Communications Corp. v. Terra Cable Ltd.* (1993), 133 N.B.R. (2d) 115 (Q.B.); *Procor Ltd. v. U.S.W.A.* (1989), 71 O.R. (2d) 410 (H.C.), additional reasons at (1990), 71 O.R. (2d) 410 at 434 (H.C.).

20 Above p. 131.

21 *Vulcan Industrial Packaging Ltd. v. C.B.C.* (1979), 23 O.R. (2d) 213 (Master).

22 *Unitel Communications Inc. v. Bell Canada* (1994), 17 B.L.R. (2d) 63 (Ont. Gen. Div.).

23 Above p. 133.

24 Below p. 154.

25 (1907), 39 S.C.R. 340.

26 *Langdon's Coach Lines Ltd. v. Toronto Transit Commission*, [1956] O.R. 45 (H.C.); *Captain Developments Ltd. v. Nu-West Group Ltd.* (1982), 37 O.R. (2d) 697 (H.C.), reversed on other grounds (1984), 6 D.L.R. (4th) 179 (C.A.); *Simpson v. Chiropractors' Assn. (Saskatchewan)* (1999), 185 Sask. R. 7 (Q.B.), proof of intent to injure necessary (reversed on other grounds (2001), 203 Sask. R. 231 (C.A.)); *Hein v. Canadian Fairbanks Morse Co.*, [1938] 4 D.L.R. 63 (N.B.C.A.); *Siopiolosz v. Taylor*, [1944] 2 D.L.R. 92 (Ont. C.A.).

27 Above p. 173.

part of the defendant. This might be proved by showing that the defendant was reckless whether the statement was true or false, as in the case of deceit.[28] This means that injurious falsehood, like deceit, is not a tort that can be committed negligently.

Since the modern action for injurious falsehood derives from the older action on the case for words, and in actions on the case damage was the gist of the action, the plaintiff must also prove that the falsehood caused him or her actual or special damage. Alleging general damages will not suffice: the plaintiff must plead and prove particulars of special damage suffered as a result of the falsehood.[29] However in Ontario, by the *Libel and Slander Act*,[30] in actions for slander of title, slander of goods or other malicious falsehood, the plaintiff does not have to allege and prove special damage where the published words are calculated to cause pecuniary damage and are published in writing or other permanent form.

---

28 Above p. 167.

29 See, *e.g.*, *Hein v. Canadian Fairbanks Morse Co.*, [1938] 4 D.L.R. 63 (N.B.C.A.); *Petten v. E.Y.E. Marine Consultants* (1994), 120 Nfld. & P.E.I.R. 313 (Nfld. T.D.); *Glo-Ken Distributors Ltd. v. B.C. Chemicals Ltd.* (1959), 19 D.L.R. (2d) 635 (B.C.C.A.). Once such damages have been proved the plaintiff can then claim for a general loss of business as well as the special loss set out in the claim: *Alberta Geophysical Products Ltd. v. Geo. E. Failing Supply Co.* (1963), 43 D.L.R. (2d) 681 (Alta. T.D.).

30 R.S.O. 1990, c. L.12, s. 19; see *Almas v. Spenceley* (1972), 25 D.L.R. (3d) 653 (Ont. C.A.).

Chapter 21

PASSING-OFF

1. AN EXPANDED TORT

The tort of passing-off, which, as will be explained later, has undergone important development in recent years, is another tool employed by the common law, like the tort of injurious falsehood, to cope with unfair competition that is based upon lies and deception. Indeed it has been said that passing-off is a branch of injurious falsehood.[1] Whereas injurious falsehood was committed by falsely stating that property did not belong to the plaintiff, or that the plaintiff's goods were somehow defective, passing-off involves giving the false impression that the defendant's merchandise or business is not the defendant's but the plaintiff's.

Passing-off is a tort concerned only with misconduct that impinges upon another party's commercial activity.[2] Like deceit, from which it developed, it involves the essential element of misrepresentation. Unlike deceit, however, it does not necessarily involve a deliberate intention to defraud.[3] In its classical form, prior to recent expansion of the scope of this tort, it dealt with situations arising out of the sale of goods or the carrying on of a business in such a way as to mislead the public into believing that the goods being sold or the business in question were the goods or business of another.[4] In essence the defendant was attempting to thrive through the reputation of another person, the plaintiff. It involved creating confusion: it was a form of false description. It was unfair trading. The common law tort of passing-off is still of importance even though various provisions of the *Trade Marks Act*[5] also cover misconduct that might also qualify as passing-off, with the result that liability is frequently imposed under that statute than under the common law, or, sometimes, both at common law and under the statute.

---

1 *Consumers Distributing Co. v. Seiko Time Canada Ltd.* (1984), 10 D.L.R. (4th) 161 (S.C.C.) at 171 *per* Estey J.

2 *Young v. Scot Young Ltd.*, [1972] 3 O.R. 638 (H.C.); *Polsinelli v. Marzalli* (1987), 60 O.R. (2d) 712 (H.C.), affirmed (1987), 61 O.R. (2d) 799 (Div. Ct.).

3 *Eli Lilly & Co. v. Novopharm Ltd.* (1997), 147 D.L.R. (4th) 673 (Fed. T.D.), affirmed (2000), 195 D.L.R. (4th) 547 (Fed. C.A.), leave to appeal refused (2001), 275 N.R. 200*n*.

4 *Westfair Foods Ltd. v. Jim Pattison Industries Ltd.* (1990), 68 D.L.R. (4th) 481 (C.A.); *Ayerst, McKenna & Harrison Inc. v. Apotex Inc.* (1983), 146 D.L.R. (3d) 93 (C.A.).

5 R.S.C. 1985, c. T-13, s. 7.

2. CLASSICAL PASSING-OFF

Simple old-fashioned passing-off, as it was termed in 1984,[6] required proof of the following factors: (a) the acquisition of a distinctive reputation for his or her goods or services by the plaintiff, the result of which was that, in association with a trade name or a trade mark, he or she had built up a property right in goodwill and reputation; (b) actual or probable confusion between the goods or services of the plaintiff and those of the defendant; (c) misrepresentation by the defendant leading to deception of the public; and (d) actual or threatened damage to the goodwill or property of the plaintiff.

A plaintiff may acquire the requisite distinctive reputation as a consequence of use of a name, phrase or mark that, on its face or because of a secondary meaning, gives what the plaintiff does or provides exclusivity.[7] This, in turn, leads or is likely to lead to confusion on the part of the public between the plaintiff's goods or business and those of the defendant when he or she uses a name, phrase or mark that closely resembles that of the plaintiff. This may occur by the use of his or her own name by the defendant; or by the way the defendant's goods or services are packaged or presented to the public; or by the use of a label like that of the plaintiff.[8] Whether such confusion has occurred or is likely is a question of fact to be determined by a court on the basis of the evidence. As previously noted, an intent to deceive is not required, although, if such an intent is proved it will be more easily determined that deception and confusion have been established.[9] In the absence of any such intent it is important to prove that those who deal in such goods or services are likely to be confused or deceived by what the defendant has done. But it is not essential that the parties be involved in a similar business activity, as long as the defendant's activity can legitimately be mistaken to be that of the plaintiff.[10]

For damages to be awarded actual loss must be proved by the plaintiff. For the plaintiff to obtain an injunction to restrain the defendant from use of the offending name, phrase or mark, the plaintiff must prove the possibility of such loss. If the plaintiff seeks an interlocutory injunction pending the determination

---

6 *Joseph v. Lee* (1984), 78 C.P.R. (2d) 159 (Ont. Co. Ct.) at 164-166.

7 *Ray Plastics Ltd. v. Dustbane Products Ltd.* (1990), 75 O.R. (2d) 37 (H.C.), affirmed (1994), 57 C.P.R. (3d) 474 (Ont. C.A.); *Oxford Pentaflex Canada Ltd. v. Korr Marketing Ltd.* (1979), 23 O.R. (2d) 545 (H.C.), affirmed (1980), 27 O.R. (2d) 760 (C.A.), affirmed (1982), 134 D.L.R. (3d) 271 (S.C.C.). Contrast *Walt Disney Productions v. Triple Five Corp.* (1994), 17 Alta. L.R. (3d) 225 (C.A.) with *Walt Disney Productions v. Fantasyland Hotel Inc.* (1994), 20 Alta. L.R. (3d) 146 (Q.B.), affirmed (1996), 38 Alta. L.R. (3d) 441 (C.A.).

8 *Hurlburt Co. v. Hurlburt Shoe Co.*, [1925] S.C.R. 141; *Saskatoon Star Phoenix Group Inc. v. Noton* (2001), 206 Sask. R. 106 (Q.B.); *Reckitt & Colman Products Ltd. v. Borden Inc.*, [1990] 1 All E.R. 873.

9 *Cadbury Schweppes Property Ltd. v. Pub Squash Co. Property*, [1981] 1 All E.R. 213.

10 *Mountain Shadows Resort Ltd. v. Pemsall Enterprises Ltd.* (1973), 9 C.P.R. (2d) 172 (B.C.S.C.). *Cf. Krouse v. Chrysler Canada Ltd.* (1973), 1 O.R. (2d) 225 (C.A.), where the plaintiff failed to prove the necessary connection between the parties. In this case a claim for "appropriation of personality", an aspect of privacy (above p. 147) failed. Contrast *Athans v. Canadian Adventure Camps Ltd.* (1977), 17 O.R. (2d) 425 (H.C.).

of an action for passing-off, the plaintiff must prove a *prima facie* case of passing-off, that irreparable damage not capable of being adequately compensated by an award of damages would follow if the injunction were not granted, and that, on the balance of convenience such an injunction should be issued.

3. EXPANSION: MODERN VIEWS

Change came through a number of English cases leading to the decision of the House of Lords in *Warnink (E.) B.V. v. J. Townend & Sons (Hull) Ltd.*[11] Earlier cases had held that the terms "Champagne", "Scotch whisky" and "sherry" could be protected, since they denoted that the goods in question possessed certain qualities or characteristics. The same was held in the *Warnink* case with respect to the word "advocaat". In other words the tort of passing-off would lie when the deception and confusion related to the product's recognizable and distinctive qualities.

A similar approach may be seen in a Canadian case, *Institut national des appellations d'origine des vins et eaux-de-vie v. Andres Wines Ltd.*,[12] which was also concerned with use of the name "champagne", where the claim for passing-off failed because there was no misrepresentation, an element required in both classical and modern versions of the tort. The necessary misrepresentation was also absent in *Consumers Distributing Co. Ltd. v. Seiko Time Canada Ltd.*[13] This concerned the defendant's conduct in importing into Canada and selling certain watches although the defendant had not been appointed an authorized dealer. The action failed because there was no evidence of possible confusion of the public. Nor was there any misdescription of the watches. In a later case, *Ciba-Geigy Canada Ltd. v. Apotex Inc.*[14] the Supreme Court of Canada introduced a new idea into the law of passing-off. The classical tort was designed to protect traders from unfair competition, or the "pirating" of intellectual property that damaged another trader's goodwill. To the court, however, the law of passing-off also protected consumers. It was designed to promote "commercial morality". This approach, it is suggested, while seemingly based upon the ideas promulgated in the *Warnink* and *Seiko* cases, goes beyond them. It may mark an important development in the evolution of this tort.

---

11 [1979] 2 All E.R. 927.

12 (1987), 60 O.R. (2d) 316 (H.C.), affirmed (1990), 74 O.R. (2d) 203 (C.A.).

13 (1984), 10 D.L.R. (4th) 161 (S.C.C.).

14 (1992), 95 D.L.R. (4th) 385 (S.C.C.).

Chapter 22

CONSPIRACY

1. INTRODUCTION

The torts considered in the previous chapters involved some sort of fraud or deception, whether direct or indirect. Those to be discussed in this and the succeeding chapters do not necessarily involve deception, although the use of fraud or deceit may occur in the course of their commission. What is much more pertinent in such instances is the intent to cause injury to the plaintiff by indulging in the proscribed conduct. Whether this common factor permits the conclusion that wherever there is an intent to injure there will be liability in tort, in the absence of some lawful justification or excuse, is another question. Recent *dicta*, if not decisions, suggest that there may emerge a more general principle along such lines. It is too soon to state with definition and certainty the nature and scope of such principles.

The law of torts draws an important distinction between acts done by one person alone and those done by two or more people acting in combination. Generally speaking, the kinds of misconduct which have been discussed previously, as well as those which will be the subject of later chapters, usually involve only one wrongdoer. There may, of course, be more than one, either acting in concert or independently. Each will be liable accordingly for his or her part in the commission of the appropriate tort and the damage attributable to their particular acts or omissions. Sometimes one person will be liable vicariously for the torts of another, even though the person thus responsible has committed no tort.[1] Where there is more than one wrongdoer there may also be some form of contribution between them in respect of the damage incurred by the victim.[2] In some situations, however, the fact that two or more wrongdoers have acted together may constitute a conspiracy that is actionable as a tort quite apart from any other tort committed by them singly or together. Moreover, the fact of conspiracy can provide the basis of a distinct, independent form of tortious liability, even where no other tortious conduct is perpetrated by the conspirators. In the former situations, the commission of the tort of conspiracy is normally ignored by the victim, and indeed may be regarded by the courts as an otiose allegation. The victim can and usually does sue for the appropriate tort

---

1 Above p. 31.

2 Below p. 210.

committed by the conspirators.[3] In the other instances, however, there is either an actionable conspiracy, or no tort has been committed. The victim must establish that the tort of conspiracy has occurred in order to obtain redress, in the form of an injunction to restrain the conspirators from continuing to commit acts which may cause injury, or damages in respect of the economic loss already sustained in consequence of the conspiracy.

2. THE MEANING OF CONSPIRACY

A conspiracy may result in criminal as well as tortious liability. Historically the latter grew out of the former, which was largely concerned with conduct that involved the abuse of legal process.[4] The idea underlying both the crime and the tort is that something done by two or more persons acting together in concert may be more harmful than something perpetrated by one person acting alone. Where the crime of conspiracy is involved the conspirators must intend to commit a criminal act. In the case of the tort, as will be seen, the conspirators may not intend to commit criminal acts. The scope of the tort of conspiracy is wider. However, unlike the crime, in which the agreement to combine is criminal even though nothing has been done and no harm has been caused to anyone, in the case of the tort of conspiracy, which originally was remediable by an action on the case, damage is an essential element. Unless some damage has been suffered by the victim no action will lie. Such damage may be physical in nature, in which event, as already noted, it may be more appropriate for the victim to sue in respect of the tort that has caused the physical damage, such as trespass. However, more usually in modern times a conspiracy may, or may be intended to, cause economic harm. Where this is the case there has been much controversy over the nature of the acts perpetrated or intended to be perpetrated by the conspirators that will entitle a court to hold that an actionable tort has been committed. In recent years, in England and Canada, the character of those acts and, consequently, the circumstances in which the tort of conspiracy will be committed, have been the subject of discussion and redefinition.

The problem has been that earlier statements about the meaning and scope of the tort of conspiracy appear to have led to the conclusion that what was lawful when done by one person would automatically become unlawful, that is actionable, if the performance of such an act was the subject of a combination on the part of two or more persons. At the same time that approach suggested that a bad

---

3 *Ward v. Lewis*, [1955] 1 W.L.R. 9 at 11 *per* Lord Denning. A claim in conspiracy should not normally be conjoined with a claim in respect of a specific tort, even if the tort has been committed by two or more persons acting in concert: *Greenhalgh v. Mallard*, [1947] 2 All E.R. 255; *Elliott v. C.B.C.* (1993), 108 D.L.R. (4th) 385 (Ont. Gen. Div.), affirmed (1995), 125 D.L.R. (4th) 534 (Ont. C.A.); *Private Equity Management Co. v. Vianet Technologies Inc.* (2000), 48 O.R. (3d) 294 (S.C.J.). However, the conspiracy is not merged with the specific tort: *Hunt v. T & N plc*, [1990] 2 S.C.R. 959; *Horn Abbott Ltd. v. Reeves* (2000), 1 C.C.L.T. (3d) 236 (N.S.C.A.).

4 Burns, "Civil Conspiracy: An Unwieldy Vessel Rides a Judicial Tempest" (1982) 16 U.B.C.L.R. 229.

motive could turn an otherwise lawful act into an unlawful, that is actionable, one, a proposition that ran counter to the basic idea that lawful conduct will not become tortious merely because it is perpetrated for an improper motive.[5]

3. THE MODERN CONCEPT OF CONSPIRACY

The foundations of the modern tort of conspiracy were laid down in the "great trilogy" of cases decided by the House of Lords at the turn of the 19th century: *Mogul S.S. Co. v. McGregor, Gow & Co.*;[6] *Allen v. Flood*;[7] *Quinn v. Leathem*.[8] Prior to this, conspiracy was said to be involved where there was "an agreement of two or more to do an unlawful act, or to do a lawful act by unlawful means"[9] or where the object of a combination was "unlawful or, if lawful, it was obtained by unlawful means".[10] In a subsequent decision, *Sorrell v. Smith*,[11] the House of Lords held that a combination to injure another person in his or her trade would be actionable, even if no specific unlawful acts or means were employed by the conspirators to attain that object. That is to say, the combination *per se* made that which otherwise was lawful unlawful and actionable if the combination was intended simply to injure another person's trade. However, the House of Lords held, if the purpose of the combination was not just to injure another's trade but to forward or defend the trade of the conspirators such conspiracy or combination was not actionable (unless unlawful acts, *i.e.*, crimes or torts, were or were intended to be employed for such purpose).

That decision was limited to actions intended to promote, advance, or defend legitimate trade interests. In *Crofter Hand Woven Harris Tweed Ltd. v. Veitch*[12] the House of Lords extended this to cover other legitimate interests, such as those of a trades union, as involved in that case. Hence, after that decision, apart from combinations to perform criminal or tortious acts, the case law in England and Canada appeared to have accepted the proposition that a conspiracy or combination *per se* was the employment of "unlawful means", within the earlier definitions of conspiracy. Therefore, unless "privileged" by reason of the legitimacy of the end to be attained by the combination, which was discussed but not defined or restricted by the *Crofter* case, the combination would be an actionable conspiracy justifying an action for damages if damage to the victim resulted or an injunction if such damage were threatened. For example, in one instance,[13] where the purpose of the conspiracy was to break down a colour bar so as to

---

5 *Mayor of Bradford v. Pickles*, [1895] A.C. 587. But this may not always be the case: see above p. 161 in relation to nuisance.

6 [1892] A.C. 25.

7 [1898] A.C. 1.

8 [1907] A.C. 495.

9 *Mulcahy v. R.* (1868), L.R. 3 H.L. 306 at 317 *per* Willes J.

10 *Gibbons v. Metcalfe* (1905), 1 W.L.R. 139 at 141 *per* Dubuc C.J.

11 [1925] A.C. 700.

12 [1942] A.C. 435.

13 *Scala Ballroom (Wolverhampton) Ltd. v. Ratcliffe*, [1958] 3 All E.R. 220.

prevent discrimination, no action would lie. In contrast, where the purpose was to avenge an insult or slight perpetrated by the victim of the conspiracy towards one of the conspirators, this was not a legitimate purpose and liability resulted.[14]

This was changed, in England, by the decision of the House of Lords in *Lonrho Ltd. v. Shell Petroleum Co.*[15] This involved a combination to break a statutory provision which made trading with Rhodesia, as it was then, illegal, at the time when, prior to the end of colonial rule of Rhodesia, the unilateral declaration of independence of Rhodesia by the white settlers was in question. Although a criminal breach of statute was being committed, the legislation gave no right of civil action to anyone particularly affected or harmed by such breach. Hence no single conspirator could have been sued by the victim of the combination. In such circumstances the issue arose whether the mere fact of combination gave rise to liability for the tort of conspiracy. In this respect it was important that the purpose of the combination was not to injure the victim, though this was its effect, but the protection of the interests of the combiners. It was held that, in the absence of a predominant intent to injure the victim, in the event of which there would be liability, what was not actionable when done by one party acting alone could not be made actionable, as a conspiracy, when it was done together by those combining. Thus in England a conspiracy involves a combination to commit unlawful acts or to commit lawful, that is not actionable, acts with the predominant intent to injure another.

Although the Supreme Court of Canada cited and relied upon this decision in *Canada Cement LaFarge Ltd. v. B.C. Lightweight Aggregate Ltd.*,[16] the way that Court defined what was an actionable conspiracy differed significantly from the approach taken by the House of Lords. The Canadian Court introduced into the definition of civil conspiracy the idea of a "constructive intent" to injure another as an alternative to situations where the conspirators were imbued with an "actual" intent to injure. For the Canadian Court a conspiracy was committed either: (a) when two or more persons combined to use lawful or unlawful means for the predominant purpose of causing injury to the plaintiff; or (b) when their conduct was unlawful and was directed towards the plaintiff and the defendant conspirators should know that injury to the plaintiff was likely and did in fact result.[17] The distinction between these two "scenarios" lies in the fact that: (1) in the second the conduct has to be unlawful; (2) injury to the plaintiff does not have to be the predominant purpose of the combination; and (3) injury to the plaintiff should have been foreseen as a likely consequence of the defendants' actions.

Thus whereas in England an express intent to cause injury to the victim of a conspiracy is essential, in Canada such intent may not be necessary as long as the conspirators act unlawfully and their conduct can be interpreted as amounting to a "constructive" intent to cause such injury, derived from their knowledge

---

14 *Huntley v. Thornton*, [1957] 1 All E.R. 234; see also *Hammer v. Kemmis* (1956), 7 D.L.R. (2d) 684 (B.C.C.A.).

15 [1981] 2 All E.R. 456.

16 (1983), 145 D.L.R. (4th) 385 (S.C.C.).

17 *Ibid.*, at 393-399. For examples, see *Surrey (District) v. Marall Homes Ltd.* (1988), 48 C.C.L.T. 70 (S.C.C.); *Knoll Estate v. Jon Picken Ltd.* (1991), 83 D.L.R. (4th) 447 (Ont. C.A.).

that, in the circumstances, such injury was likely. In Canada, therefore, the scope of the tort of conspiracy is wider than in England.[18]

4. ESSENTIALS OF LIABILITY FOR CONSPIRACY

Based on what has been set out above with respect to the scope of liability for conspiracy in Canada, the following elements are essential and must be established as existing before any such liability can *prima facie* be imposed upon the alleged conspirators. These are: (a) an agreement between two or more persons; (b) an actual or "constructive" intent to injure the plaintiff; (c) the commission of unlawful acts or the employment of unlawful means, where the intent to injure is "constructive"; (d) damage to the plaintiff (or threatened damage, which requires an injunction to restrain the defendants from carrying out their intent, on the ground that a later award of damages would not adequately compensate the plaintiff).

Knowledge that there is a conspiracy and even acquiescence in what the other parties are doing will not suffice, nor will a common intention between several persons.[19] There must be an actual agreement, a meeting of the minds of the parties, though this need not take the form of a contract.[20] Such an agreement may exist between corporations, or between a corporation and its directors,[21] but not, usually, between a corporation and its servants or agents acting under orders from their employer.

The requirement of an intent to injure means that conspiracy cannot be committed negligently or accidentally. The parties must know and intend what they are doing. That intent must be to injure the plaintiff as the predominant purpose of the combination. Hence if it can be shown that the conspirators really intended to assist a native band by picketing the plaintiff's customers,[22] or to benefit a company's creditors and shareholders,[23] or improve a union's situation,[24] the necessary intent will be lacking. Evidence that the defendants acted out of self-interest may also disprove the requisite intent.[25] Where "constructive" intent is involved, lack of awareness that the defendants' conduct would cause the plaintiff harm will defeat an action for conspiracy based on the employment of unlawful acts or means.

---

18 *Lehndorff Canadian Pension Properties Ltd. v. Davis & Co.* (1987), 39 C.C.L.T. 196 (B.C.S.C.).

19 *Posluns v. Toronto Stock Exchange & Gardiner* (1964), 46 D.L.R. (2d) 210 (Ont. H.C.), affirmed (1966), 53 D.L.R. (2d) 193 (Ont. C.A.), affirmed [1968] S.C.R. 330; *Maguire v. Calgary*, [1983] 4 W.W.R. 342 (Alta. C.A.).

20 *Polimeni v. Danziger* (1995), 105 Man. R. (2d) 91 (Q.B.), affirmed (1997), 113 Man. R. (2d) 304 (C.A.).

21 *Hall-Chem Inc. v. Vulcan Packaging Inc.* (1994), 12 B.L.R. (2d) 274 (Ont. Gen. Div.).

22 *Daishowa Inc. v. Friends of the Lubicon* (1998), 158 D. L. R. (4th) 699 (Ont. Gen. Div.).

23 *Liu v. Sung* (1997), 37 B.C.L.R. (3d) 158 (C.A.).

24 *Garry v. St. Eloi* (1989), 77 Sask. R. 187 (Q.B.).

25 *Beaudoin v. Waters* (1997), 52 Alta. L.R. (3d) 158 (Q.B.); *923087 N.W.T. Ltd. v. Anderson Mills Ltd.*, [1997] N.W.T.R. 212 (S.C.).

Where such unlawful conduct is pertinent to liability, what is meant is more often than not the perpetration of a crime, a tort, a breach of contract or a breach of statute. It can include the breach of a fiduciary obligation.[26] The commission of a conspiracy that is outlawed by the *Criminal Code* will not suffice for this purpose,[27] but conduct that otherwise is contrary to that Code or infringes provincial legislation will.[28] An agreement to act in concert to commit such torts as inducing a breach of contract, nuisance, defamation, fraud, or intimidation will also fall within the ambit of the tort of conspiracy.[29] It has also been held[30] that unlawful acts or means includes a breach of the *Competition Act*,[31] the breach of a statute that does not entitle someone to bring a civil action but can involve other proceedings, and a breach of the rules of natural justice.[32] Whatever acts or means are involved must be central, and not incidental, to the attainment of the object or purpose of the conspiracy.

Damage, that is pecuniary loss, caused by the conspiracy must be suffered by the plaintiff if an action for damages is to be maintained.[33] This means actual loss. Once this has been proved to have occurred the damages awarded may include foreseeable consequential loss, as well as punitive or exemplary damages.[34]

5. DEFENCES TO, OR LIMITATIONS ON LIABILITY FOR, CONSPIRACY

In Ontario and Saskatchewan[35] legislation, copying an earlier English Act,[36] protects trade union members from liability if the acts alleged to support an action were done "in contemplation or furtherance of a trade dispute",[37] as long as such acts would not be actionable if committed without any agreement or com-

---

26 *Levy-Russell Ltd. v. Tecmotiv Inc.* (1994), 13 B.L.R. (2d) 1 (Ont. Gen. Div.).

27 R.S.C. 1985, c. C-46; *Lokos v. Manfor Ltd.* (1990), 67 Man. R. (2d) 296 (Q.B.), affirmed (1994), 97 Man. R. (2d) 283 (C.A.).

28 *Korte v. Deloitte, Haskins & Sells* (1993), 8 Alta. L.R. (3d) 337 (C.A.).

29 See, *e.g.*, *Hammer v. Kemmis* (1956), 7 D.L.R. (2d) 684 (B.C.C.A.); *Elliott v. C.B.C.* (1993), 108 D.L.R. (4th) 385 (Ont. Gen. Div.), affirmed (1995), 125 D.L.R. (4th) 534 (Ont. C.A.); *Royal Bank v. Holoboff* (1998), 221 A.R. 192 (Q.B.); *Shaw v. Lewis*, [1948] 2 D.L.R. 189 (B.C.C.A.). Knowledge that the acts in question are unlawful may not have to be proved if the parties intended to use the acts: *Churchill v. Walton*, [1967] 2 A.C. 224.

30 *Westfair Foods Ltd. v. Lippens Inc.* (1989), 64 D.L.R. (4th) 335 (Man. C.A.); *Apotex Inc. v. Hoffman-LaRoche Ltd.* (2000), 195 D.L.R. (4th) 244 (Ont. C.A.).

31 R.S.C. 1985, c. C-34.

32 *Mark Fishing Co. v. U.F.A.W.* (1972), 24 D.L.R. (3d) 585 (B.C.C.A.), affirmed 38 D.L.R. (3d) 316 (S.C.C.); *Evaskow v. B.B.F.* (1968), 9 D.L.R. (3d) 715 (Man. C.A.).

33 *Brideau v. Boucher* (1994), 156 N.B.R. (2d) 178 (Q.B.).

34 *Claiborne Industries Ltd. v. National Bank of Canada* (1989), 59 D.L.R. (4th) 533 (Ont. C.A.); *McKinnon v. F.W. Woolworth Co.* (1968), 70 D.L.R. (2d) 280 (Alta. C.A.).

35 *Rights of Labour Act*, R.S.O. 1990, c. R.33, s. 3(1); *Trade Union Act*, R.S.S. 1978, c. T-17, s. 28.

36 *Trade Disputes Act*, 1906, 6 Edw. 7, c. 47, s. 1. This has been amended by subsequent legislation.

37 There is no statutory definition of these terms in England or Ontario, although "trade dispute" is defined in the Saskatchewan Act.

bination. This means that certain conspiracies, otherwise actionable if entered into by non-union members, will not lead to liability on the part of trade union members acting only for the purposes of a trade dispute. However, if the acts in question would be actionable on some other ground than conspiracy, for example, trespass or intimidation, the legislation will not afford protection even to union members.

At common law, however, the only possible way to avoid liability is by establishing that the combination was justified. There can be no justification of a conspiracy to commit unlawful acts in order to attain the conspirators' purpose or object. If their conspiracy is a conspiracy to injure, without the commission of unlawful acts, it is possible that it can be "justified". This will be the case if the object of the conspiracy, as previously mentioned,[38] is legitimate or justifiable. There is no judicial definition or delimitation of what is a legitimate or justifiable purpose. It was the subject of much inconclusive discussion by the House of Lords in the *Crofter* case.[39] Nor was there by the Supreme Court of Canada in the *Canada Cement* case.[40] Nor, in the former decision, could the various members of the House of Lords agree whether it was for the plaintiff, as part of the plaintiff's case, to disprove a legitimate or justifiable purpose or for the defendant, by way of defence, to plead that their combination was for such a purpose. Only if the latter were true would justification be a defence. Inconclusive decisions in Canada,[41] by courts lower than the Supreme Court, following the *Canada Cement* case appear to support the proposition that justification, while possible, is not a defence since it is for the plaintiff to establish that the predominant purpose or object of the defendants was to injure the plaintiff. Thus it is open to the highest court to determine this issue at some later date.[42]

---

38 Above p. 183.

39 [1942] A.C. 435.

40 (1983), 145 D.L.R. (3d) 385 (S.C.C.).

41 Inconclusive because some of them were reversed on appeal: see, for example, *Thorvaldson v. Saskatchewan* (1990), 82 Sask. R. 257 (Q.B.), reversed (1991), 93 Sask. R. 22 (C.A.).

42 See, generally, Heydon, "The Defence of Justification in Cases of Intentionally Caused Economic Loss" (1970) 20 U.T.L.J. 138.

Chapter 23

INTIMIDATION

1. ORIGINS

The history of the law of torts discloses that the idea that a threat to cause harm may be unlawful and give rise to liability is not new. If such threats are directed towards a particular individual so as to cause that person to fear the possibility of personal physical injury, the tort of assault will have been committed. If such threats are directed against a third party with the intention of forcing that person to act to the detriment of the plaintiff, who is the true intended victim of the defendant's conduct, cases stretching back to the 17th century have recognized that an action will lie at the suit of such ultimately intended victim. For example, to threaten potential students at a school with harm so that they stayed away, to the detriment of the schoolmaster, was held wrongful in *Garret v. Taylor*.[1] To fire at potential traders with the plaintiff, thereby threatening them with physical injury, in order to prevent their attending the plaintiff's ship to trade, was actionable in *Tarleton v. M'Gawley*.[2] Sometimes liability could be founded on conspiracy or nuisance, the threats being merely evidence of the wrongfulness of the actions of the defendant or defendants.[3] In all such instances the ultimate justification of liability was not that physical injury might occur to the plaintiff, but that the plaintiff incurred economic loss or harm as a result of the defendant's actions vis-à-vis a third party or third parties.

2. THE MODERN FOUNDATION OF THE TORT

It was not until 1964, in the case of *Rookes v. Barnard*,[4] that the House of Lords formally recognized the existence of a distinct tort of intimidation. That the law in Canada also acknowledges this tort was subsequently accepted by the Supreme Court of Canada in *Central Canada Potash Co. v. Saskatchewan (Attor-*

---

1 (1620), Cro. Jac. 567.

2 (1793), 1 Peake 270.

3 See, *e.g.*, *Vulcan Iron Works v. Iron Moulders Union, Winnipeg Local 174* (1911), 21 Man. R. 473 (C.A.); *United Mine Workers of America, Local Union No. 1562 v. Williams & Rees* (1919), 59 S.C.R. 240.

4 [1964] A.C. 1129.

ney-General),[5] as well as by various provincial courts,[6] even where, on the facts of a particular case, liability was denied. However, although the tort of intimidation can now be said to be firmly enshrined, there are many unresolved aspects of the tort, and many problems created by its recognition. These stem from *Rookes v. Barnard* itself as well as later exposition and discussion of what was said therein.

The defendants were officers of a trades union the members of whom were employed by B.O.A.C. The plaintiff was also employed by B.O.A.C. The defendants sought the dismissal of the plaintiff by threatening B.O.A.C. that they would bring their members out on strike, which would have involved the breach both of the collective agreement made with B.O.A.C. and of the union members' individual contracts of employment. Rather than face the prospect of a strike B.O.A.C. terminated the plaintiff's employment not by instant, and wrongful, dismissal but by giving him the appropriate length of notice as required under his contract of employment. Hence, as will be explained in a later chapter, no action would lie against the defendants for inducing or procuring a breach of contract. The House of Lords held that the defendants could be made liable for intimidation. This was because, by the use of the threat to strike in breach of various contracts, the defendants had caused detriment to the plaintiff, namely the loss of his employment.

Although this form of liability in tort was not regarded by the House of Lords as novel, but as established by earlier case law to which reference has been made, the exposition of this tort made clear, for the first time, that there were two varieties of intimidation.

One would occur where the defendant forced the plaintiff directly to act to the plaintiff's detriment, for example, by getting the plaintiff to abandon a lucrative contract with a third party. This is referred to as "two-party" intimidation. If the means adopted by the defendant were unlawful, such as the use or threat of violence or the making of false and fraudulent misrepresentations, an action for intimidation might be unnecessary. Only if the method invoked by the defendant to get the plaintiff to act to his or her own detriment did not entail such clearly criminal or tortious conduct might it be necessary for the plaintiff to resort to the tort of intimidation to obtain compensation for his or her loss.

The second version of intimidation, which was involved in *Rookes v. Barnard*, was "three-party" intimidation, where the defendant intimidated a third party in order to force such third party to act to the detriment of the plaintiff. This may also entail detriment to the third party, for example if the result is that the third party breaks a contract with the plaintiff which not only harms the plaintiff but also brings loss to the third party. However, as *Rookes v. Barnard* exemplifies, there is no need for the defendant to intimidate the third party into committing a wrongful act with respect to the plaintiff for the tort of "three-party" to be committed.

---

5 (1978), 88 D.L.R. (3d) 609 (S.C.C.).

6 *Mintuck v. Valley River Band No. 63A* (1977), 75 D.L.R. (3d) 589 (Man. C.A.); *Boychuk v. Northwest Territories Housing Corp.* (1985), 33 C.C.L.T. 28 (N.W.T.S.C.); *Gershman v. Manitoba Vegetable Producers' Marketing Board*, [1976] 4 W.W.R. 406 (Man. C.A.).

Since 1964, therefore, both versions of this tort may be committed in appropriate situations. Whether it is "two-party" or "three-party" intimidation, the elements of the tort appear to be the same.

3. WHAT MUST BE PROVED FOR LIABILITY

The following are essential features of this tort.[7] First, coercion by the defendant of another person to do or refrain from doing an act. Second, the use of a threat to compel that other person. Third, the threat in question must be a threat to use unlawful means. Fourth, the person threatened must accede to the demand of the defendant. Fifth, the defendant must intend to harm or injure the person threatened. Sixth, the person so threatened must incur damage or loss.

The fundamental rationale of the tort is that it is wrongful intentionally to make unlawful threats that have the effect of interfering with the freedom of the threatened person to act. This is a tort that can only be committed intentionally, not either accidentally or negligently. Various Canadian decisions since 1964 illustrate the distinction between threats that are intended to produce injury to another and those which are made with another intent in mind, even though the result is that someone, that is the plaintiff, also suffers harm in consequence.[8]

There will only be liability if the threats have the desired effect. Hence if the person threatened does not conform to the threat but resists and refuses to accede to it, the tort will not be committed.[9]

Only an unlawful threat will generate liability. One who threatens to do what he or she may lawfully do will not be guilty of this tort[10] (though if such person acts in combination with another person or other persons, they may be guilty of conspiracy).[11] Threatening to commit criminal or tortious acts will be unlawful for this purpose. So will threatening to strike[12] or threatening a work stoppage,[13] when the strike or work stoppage would be illegal.

In *Central Canada Potash Co. v. Saskatchewan (Attorney-General)*,[14] Disbery J. held that "two-party" intimidation had occurred when the Government of

---

7 *Daishowa Inc. v. Friends of the Lubicon* (1996), 27 O.R. (3d) 215 (Gen. Div.) at 231 *per* Corbett J.

8 *Cheticamp Fisheries Co-Operative Ltd. v. Canada* (1995), 123 D.L.R. (4th) 121 (N.S.C.A.); *Mintuck v. Valley River Band No. 63A* (1977), 75 D.L.R. (3d) 589 (Man. C.A.); *Boychuk v. Northwest Territories Housing Corp.* (1985), 33 C.C.L.T. 28 (N.W.T.S.C.).

9 See, *e.g.*, *Poulos v. Matovic* (1989), 47 C.C.L.T. 207 (Ont. H.C.); *Roth v. Roth* (1991), 4 O.R. (3d) 740 (Gen. Div.).

10 *Allen v. Flood*, [1898] A.C. 1; *Sandy Ridge Sawing Ltd. v. Norrish* (1996), 140 Sask. R. 146 (Q.B.); *No. 1 Collision Repair & Painting (1982) Ltd. v. Insurance Corp. of B.C.* (1998), 4 C.C.L.I. (3d) 135 (B.C.S.C.), affirmed (2000), 21 C.C.L.I. (3d) 1 (B.C.C.A.).

11 Above p. 184.

12 *Huntley v. Thornton*, [1957] 1 W.L.R. 321.

13 *Canadian Ironworkers Union No. 1 v. Int. Association of Bridge, Structural & Ornamental Ironworkers Union, Local No. 97* (1970), 73 W.W.R. 172 (B.C.C.A.), affirmed [1972] S.C.R. 295.

14 (1975), 57 D.L.R. (3d) 7 (Sask. Q.B.).

Saskatchewan used the threat of the imposition of certain *ultra vires* legislation on the plaintiffs if they did not adhere to policies desired by that government, even though to have done so would have caused the plaintiffs the loss of considerable sums of money. This was reversed by the Court of Appeal[15] on the ground that the legislation was not *ultra vires*, so no unlawful threat had been used, and by the Supreme Court of Canada[16] on the ground that the official who uttered the threat had no intent to injure the plaintiffs. Hence the original decision by Disbery J. on the effect of a threat to apply *ultra vires* legislation remains unresolved. Another case in which there was a threat involving legislation is *Roman Corp. v. Hudson's Bay Oil and Gas.*[17] There it was argued that an unlawful act was employed when the defendants, the Prime Minister and other Ministers, threatened to introduce into Parliament and ensure the passage of legislation to make illegal and impossible the sale of Canadian companies to foreigners. The argument failed because the Court held that the defendants were not acting unlawfully, because they were entitled, even obliged, to advise the Crown on matters of policy and to effect such policy by the enactment of appropriate legislation.

Controversy has centred around the question whether a threat to break a contract can amount to an unlawful act, the use of which to convince someone to act or refrain from acting in a certain way can support an action for intimidation.

4. THE EFFECT OF A THREAT TO BREAK A CONTRACT

The decision in *Rookes v. Barnard* suggests that where "three-party" intimidation is involved a threat by the defendant to break his or her contract with the third party will constitute the use of unlawful means. As far as "two-party" intimidation is concerned, there is no decision that settles the matter. However in an English case[18] it was suggested that such a threat, for example if a debtor threatened that he would not pay his creditor what was owed unless the creditor agreed to accept a lesser sum in settlement of the debt, could lead to liability for intimidation. A similar view was expressed, also by way of *obiter dictum*, as in the English case, by Disbery J. in *Central Canada Potash.*[19] Neither the Saskatchewan Court of Appeal nor the Supreme Court of Canada appear to have repudiated that view, even though, as seen above, the decision of Disbery J. was reversed by both courts on various grounds.

The problem is that recognition of a threat to break a contract for this purpose may blur or eliminate the distinction between liability for breach of contract and

---

15 (1977), 88 D.L.R. (3d) 203 (C.A.).

16 (1978), 88 D.L.R. (3d) 609 (S.C.C.).

17 [1973] S.C.R. 820.

18 *D. & C. Builders Ltd. v. Rees*, [1966] 2 Q.B. 617 at 625 *per* Lord Denning.

19 (1975), 57 D.L.R. (3d) 7 (Sask. Q.B.) at 120-123.

liability in tort, and may affect the law relating to privity of contract.[20] As far as the first objection is concerned, since a party can now sue for breach of contract or in tort where the facts will support either action,[21] it would not seem to matter whether an intimidated plaintiff in a "two-party" situation chooses to sue the intimidator for an anticipated breach of contract[22] or for the tort of intimidation, as long as the plaintiff makes an election and is not compensated twice over for the same wrongful act. Nor is the doctrine of privity of contract[23] interfered with by permitting an action for "three-party" intimidation based upon a threat by the intimidator to break a contract. The action is not founded upon the intimidator's breach of a contract with the third party (to permit which would infringe the privity of contract doctrine). It is based upon the intentional infliction of harm by the intimidator upon the plaintiff. The latter's action is unconnected with, and not founded upon the contract. It is pure tort. In this respect it resembles the action for inducing or procuring a breach of contract, which has never been suggested, at least in modern times, to affect or impinge upon the doctrine of privity.

The conclusion is that the views expressed by the House of Lords in *Rookes v. Barnard* and by Disbery J. in *Central Canada Potash* correctly reflect the law relating to what can amount to an unlawful act for the purposes of this tort.

---

20 See, *e.g.*, Hoffman, "Rookes v. Barnard" (1965) 81 L.Q.R. 116; Wedderburn, "Torts Out of Contract: Transatlantic Warnings" (1970) 33 Mod. L.R. 309; Stevens, "Interference with Economic relations — Some Aspects of Turmoil in the Intentional Torts" (1974) 12 Osgoode Hall L.J. 595.

21 Fridman, *The Law of Contract in Canada*, 4th ed. (Toronto: Carswell, 1999), pp. 735-741.

22 *Ibid.*, pp. 638-661.

23 *Ibid.*, pp. 187-190.

Chapter 24

INDUCING BREACH OF CONTRACT

1. THE SCOPE OF THE TORT

Forty years before the House of Lords began to give shape to the modern law of conspiracy, it was held in England, in *Lumley v. Gye*,[1] that any intentional, deliberate conduct to procure, induce or otherwise cause someone to break a contract of service with a third party was actionable at the suit of such third party who had suffered damage as a consequence. The defendant was the manager of an opera house in London. He persuaded a famous singer, who had contracted to perform at a rival opera house owned by the plaintiff, to sing at the defendant's opera house not that of the plaintiff. In the action that ensued the plaintiff recovered damages for the loss he incurred when the defendant caused the singer to break her contract with the plaintiff.

The basis for allowing this action for inducing the breach of a contract for the provision of personal services was the law that emerged in medieval England following the devastation of the Black Plague. This led to a loss of population causing in turn a reduction in the labour force. The *Statute of Labourers* was enacted in consequence to prevent the "stealing", as it were, of workers by one employer from another. The theory of the medieval approach to this issue was that it was a tort against property to interfere with the relationship of master and servant. By the 19th century, when *Lumley v. Gye* was decided, the idea that a master had a proprietary interest in a servant who worked for him under a contract of service was outmoded. Nevertheless the majority of the court in that case held that the master or employer had a sufficient interest in the performance of the contract with the servant, the employee, to justify making it tortious to bring about the breach of such contract.

Initially the tort was committed when there was interference with the provision of services over an extended period and where the defendant acted from malice, in the sense of spite or ill-will. Subsequent English cases,[2] which, like *Lumley v. Gye* have been followed in Canada,[3] held that the tort could be

---

[1] (1853), 2 E. & B. 216: on which see Waddams, "Johanna Wagner and the Rival Opera Houses" (2001), 117 L.Q.R. 431.

[2] *Bowen v. Hall* (1881), 6 Q.B.D. 333; *Temperton v. Russell*, [1893] 1 Q.B. 715; *Quinn v. Leathem*, [1901] A.C. 495; *South Wales Miners' Federation v. Glamorgan Coal Co.*, [1905] A.C. 239.

[3] *Krug Furniture Co. v. Berlin Union of Woodworkers* (1903), 5 O.L.R. 463 (K.B.); *Brauch v. Roth* (1904), 10 O.L.R. 284 (C.P.); *Posluns v. Toronto Stock Exchange & Gardiner* (1964), 46 D.L.R. (2d) 210 (Ont. H.C.), affirmed (1966), 53 D.L.R. (2d) 193 (Ont. C.A.), affirmed (1968), 67 D.L.R. (2d) 165 (S.C.C.); *Slade & Stewart Ltd. v. Haynes* (1969), 5 D.L.R. (3d) 736 (B.C.S.C.).

committed when the contract the defendant induced or procured to be broken was not only a contract for the provision of service or services but any contract whatever its nature.[4] Furthermore it was held that malice, in the sense of spite or ill-will, did not have to be proved, as long as the causing of the breach was intended and was unjustified.[5] The requirement of an intention to cause a breach of contract and the issue of justification for causing such a breach have both undergone some development in more recent times.[6]

Two essential ingredients of this tort have not changed.

First, there must have been a binding, enforceable contract between the plaintiff and a third party.[7] Hence if their relationship was not, or was not yet, contractual, or the contract between them was invalid for some reason, no tort wll be committed by someone who induces the third party not to perform his or her intended, illusory or imagined obligations towards the plaintiff.

Second, there must have been a breach of the contract as a whole or of a term or terms of such contract, even if such term does not, or such terms do not, go to the root of the contract.[8] As will be seen in the next chapter, however, modern developments have now accepted that it can be tortious to interfere with the performance of a contract, or with the economic relations between two other parties, even though no actual breach of contract has occurred.[9]

However, the tort will not be committed if the person who induces or procured the breach of contract is the servant, agent, or director of one of the parties to such contract and the servant, agent or director acted within the scope of his or her employment or authority, as long as he or she acted in good faith, for the benefit of the employer, principal, or company, not out of malice in order only to injure the plaintiff.[10] One explanation of this was said to be that the one who caused the breach was the *alter ego* of the employer, principal, or company, with the consequence that such employer, principal or company, a contracting party, not the servant, agent, or director, was the one who caused the breach. Another was that a servant, agent, or director who acted in good faith for the benefit of the employer, principal, or company was justified and so was not acting tortiously.

---

4 *National Phonograph Co. v. Edison-Bell Phonograph Co.*, [1908] 1 Ch. 335; *Browning-Ferris Industries Ltd. v. Smithrite Disposal Ltd.* (1985), 8 C.P.R. (2d) 228 (B.C.S.C.).

5 *Quinn v. Leathem*, [1901] A.C. 495 at 510 *per* Lord Macnaghten.

6 Below p. 199.

7 *Colborne Capital Corp. v. 542775 Alberta Ltd.* (1995), 30 Alta. L.R. (3d) 127 (Q.B.), varied (1999), 69 Alta. L.R. (3d) 265 (C.A.).

8 *Ken Toby Ltd. v. B.C. Buildngs Corp.* (1997), 34 B.C.L.R. (3d) 263 (S.C.), reversed (1999), 62 B.C.L.R. (3d) 308 (C.A.); *Porta-Flex Products (P.E.I.) Ltd. v. Bank of Montreal* (1993), 108 Nfld. & P.E.I.R. 221 (P.E.I.T.D.); *U.F.C.W. Local 1252 v. Cashin* (1996), 149 Nfld. & P.E.I.R. 112 (Nfld. T.D.).

9 Below p. 201.

10 *Said v. Butt*, [1920] 3 K.B. 497; *McFadden v. 481782 Ontario Ltd.* (1984), 47 O.R. (2d) 134 (H.C.); *Polimeni v. Danziger*, [1996] 1 W.W.R. 305 (Man. Q.B.), affirmed (1997), 113 Man. R. (2d) 304 (C.A.).

2. REQUIREMENTS OF LIABILITY

The existence of a contract and the occurrence of its breach have previously been noted as essential ingredients of liability for this tort. What remains to be considered are first the knowledge and intention of the defendant and second the nature of the inducement that causes the breach. [11]

Clearly a defendant can be liable when he or she acts with actual knowledge of the contract in existence between the plaintiff and a third party and the terms of such contract.[12] The question is whether anything short of such actual knowledge will suffice. It has been held that the requisite knowledge may be assumed from the defendant's knowledge of the surrounding circumstances.[13] In one English case,[14] however, it was suggested that it was unnecessary to prove that the defendant had actual knowledge of the contract or of the term or terms that were ultimately breached, as long as the defendant had the means to obtain such knowledge and did not care whether his or her conduct led to a breach of contract. That would mean that a defendant could be liable where the defendant acted recklessly, with indifference to the possibility that harm could be caused to the plaintiff. Given the need to establish that the defendant had the intention to cause a breach of contract, it seems illogical to accept that what might be called "constructive knowledge" of the existence of a contract should satisfy the requirement of knowledge.

Besides the defendant's knowledge of the contract or the relevant term or terms the plaintiff must also prove that the defendant intended to cause, induce or procure its, or their, breach. This is a tort that is committed intentionally. That should mean that a defendant who acts negligently, and so brings about a breach of the plaintiff's contract with a third party, ought not to be liable for this tort,[15] although, as noted elsewhere,[16] in certain situations such negligent conduct might lead to the defendant's liability to the third party. However in one Canadian case[17] it was held that liability for inducing a breach of contract could be imposed on a defendant who did not intend to harm the plaintiff by causing such

---

[11] Damage to the plaintiff must also be proved: *Posluns v. Toronto Stock Exchange & Gardiner* (1964), 46 D.L.R. (2d) 210 (Ont. H.C.), affirmed (1966), 53 D.L.R. (2d) 193 (Ont. C.A.), affirmed (1965), 67 D.L.R. (2d) 165 (S.C.C.). Hence if the contract is not binding no damage will have been incurred by the plaintiff: *L.M. Rosen Realty Ltd. v. D'Amore* (1984), 7 D.L.R. (4th) 285. Damages are at large: *Exchange Telegraph Co. Ltd. v. Gregory & Co.*, [1896] 1 Q.B. 147. If an injunction is sought to restrain the defendant the belief that damage will be suffered will suffice: *Daishowa Inc. v. Friends of the Lubicon* (1996), 27 O.R. (3d) 215 (Gen. Div.).

[12] Hence lack of knowledge will negate liability: *Superior Propane Inc. v. Nanegkam Housing Corp. of Prince Edward Island* (1993), 105 Nfld. & P.E.I.R. 230 (P.E.I. C.A.); *Z Mark Int. Inc. v. Leng Novak Blais Inc.* (1996), 12 O.T.C. 33 (Gen. Div.), affirmed (1999), 122 O.A.C. 341.

[13] *Posluns v. Toronto Stock Exchange & Gardiner* (1964), 46 D.L.R. (2d) 210 (Ont. H.C.), affirmed (1966), 53 D.L.R. (2d) 193 (Ont. C.A.), affirmed (1968), 67 D.L.R. (2d) 165 (S.C.C.).

[14] *Emerald Construction Co. v. Lowthian*, [1966] 1 W.L.R. 691 (H.L.) at 700-701 *per* Lord Denning.

[15] *Lineal Group Inc. v. Atlantis Canadian Distributors Inc.* (1998), 42 O.R. (3d) 157 (C.A.).

[16] Above p. 82.

[17] *Thermo King Corp. v. Provincial Bank of Canada* (1981), 130 D.L.R. (3d) 256 (Ont. C.A.).

breach but had acted when it was a foreseeable and necessary consequence of the defendant's conduct that such breach would occur. Other Canadian cases seem to repudiate this and hold that mere negligence will not suffice for the commission of this tort,[18] although, in England, it has been held that recklessness as to the foreseeable consequences of one's acts may render a defendant liable.[19] However recklessness as regards consequences must be differentiated from recklessness as to whether the defendant's acts are lawful or unlawful.

The defendant must desire, or believe, that a breach of contract, and injury to the plaintiff, will ensue as a result of the defendant's behaviour. Hence if the defendant's object or intent was not to bring about a breach of contract but, for example, to exercise the defendant's rights under a contract with the third party then, even though such exercise led to a breach of the third party's contract with the plaintiff, this will not entail that the defendant is liable to the plaintiff for this tort.[20] In such circumstances, as in others involving, for instance, the right of the defendant to fulfil a statutory duty,[21] it can also be said that the defendant is not liable because the defendant's conduct was "justified".[22]

In *D.C. Thomson & Co. v. Deakin*[23] the English Court of Appeal recognized that the inducement required for the commission of this tort could be either direct or indirect. That enlargement of the scope of the tort has been accepted in Canada.

Direct inducement will occur when the defendant persuades or otherwise makes the third party break that party's contract with the plaintiff. Persuasion or pressure must be distinguished from mere advice.[24] What is required is some act on the part of the defendant that in effect compels the third party to break the contract.[25] Clearly the employment of, or threat to commit, criminal or tortious acts will amount to such conduct. But the defendant's conduct need not be criminal or tortious. For example, a threat by the defendant to break his or her contract with the third party if the latter does not break his or her contract with the plaintiff will suffice. So will a threat to do something lawful. So will the making of a contract with the third party that is inconsistent with such party's contract with the plaintiff.[26] It has also been held that if the defendant does something with respect to the third party that makes it impossible for the party to perform his or her contract with the plaintiff the defendant will be guilty of this tort. That happened when the defendant, unknown to the third party, replaced

---

18 *Lineal Group Inc. v. Atlantis Canadian Distributors Inc.* (1998), 42 O.R. (3d) 157 (C.A.); *McLaren v. B.C. Institute of Technology* (1978), 94 D.L.R. (3d) 411 (B.C.S.C.), with which contrast *Nicholls v. Richmond (Township)* (1983), 145 D.L.R. (3d) 362 (B.C.C.A.).

19 *Emerald Construction Co. v. Lowthian*, [1966] 1 W.L.R. 691 (H.L.), at 704 *per* Diplock L.J.

20 *Dirassar v. Kelly, Douglas & Co.* (1966), 59 D.L.R. (2d) 452 (B.C.C.A.), affirmed (1967), 64 D.L.R. (2d) 456 (S.C.C.).

21 *Atcheson v. College of Physicians & Surgeons (Alberta)* (1994), 148 A.R. 395 (C.A.).

22 *Cf.* below p. 199.

23 [1952] Ch. 646.

24 *Ibid.*, at 686 *per* Evershed M.R.; *Fabbi v. Jones* (1972), 28 D.L.R. (3d) 224 (S.C.C.).

25 *Roman Corp. v. Hudson's Bay Oil & Gas Ltd.*, [1973] S.C.R. 820.

26 *Sefton v. Tophams Ltd.*, [1964] 3 All E.R. 876, affirmed [1965] Ch. 1140, reversed on other grounds, [1967] 1 A.C. 50.

tires on a car which the third party had agreed with the plaintiff would be displayed bearing the plaintiff's tires.[27]

Indirect inducement can also take many forms. What is generally involved is conduct by the defendant with respect to X that induces X to act upon Y in such a way that causes Y to break Y's contract with the plaintiff.[28] It is a question of causation, of proving the direct connection between X's act and the ultimate breach.[29] For such conduct to involve the defendant in liability to the plaintiff for this tort it must be shown that it was the defendant's conduct, not the independent action of Y that caused the breach of Y's contract with the plaintiff, and that the defendant employed unlawful means[30] to make X act on Y to induce Y's breach of the contract with the plaintiff. The use of lawful means to such end will not amount to indirect inducement for this purpose. Among the unlawful means that have attracted such liability are breach of statute, [31] secondary picketing[32] and misrepresentation.[33] Unlawful means appears to refer to any act that the defendant was not at liberty to commit.[34]

3. THE DEFENCE OF JUSTIFICATION

When the defendant acts lawfully, not illegally, with the unintended consequence that the plaintiff's contract with a third party is broken, it has been seen[35] that the defendant cannot be held liable for inducing such breach. In such circumstances the defendant's conduct may be said to be justified. Alternately it has been said that the defendant has a privilege to act in such way.[36] One such situation has been held to arise when the defendant acts out of the desire to further his or her own legitimate self-interest, and not with the object of injuring the plaintiff, provided that the defendant does not act illegally but in pursuance of a right to act as he or she has done.[37]

---

27 *G.W.K. Ltd. v. Dunlop Rubber Co.* (1926), 42 T.L.R. 376.

28 *Garry v. Sherriff Gordon Mines Ltd.* (1987), 42 C.C.L.T. 241 (Sask. C.A.) at 262-263 *per* Cameron J.A.

29 *D.C. Thomson & Co. Ltd. v. Deakin*, [1952] Ch. 646 at 679 *per* Evershed M.R.

30 *E.g.*, a threat to commit a tort: *Orchard v. Tunney*, [1957] S.C.R. 436.

31 *Int. Brotherhood of Teamsters v. Therien*, [1960] S.C.R. 265; *Mark Fishing Co. v. United Fishermen & Allied Workers' Union* (1972), 24 D.L.R. (3d) 585 (B.C.C.A.), affirmed 38 D.L.R. (3d) 316 (S.C.C.).

32 *Western Stevedoring Co. v. Pulp, Paper & Woodworkers of Canada* (1975), 61 D.L.R. (3d) 701 (B.C.C.A.); *Daishowa Inc. v. Friends of the Lubicon* (1996), 27 O.R. (3d) 215 (Gen. Div.).

33 *Air Canada v. Desmond* (1990), 96 N.S.R. (2d) 256 (N.S. Co. Ct.).

34 *Torquay Hotel Co. v. Cousins*, [1969] 2 Ch. 106 at 139 *per* Lord Denning.

35 Above p. 198.

36 *Posluns v. Toronto Stock Exchange & Gardiner* (1964), 46 D.L.R. (2d) 210 (Ont. H.C.), affirmed (1966), 53 D.L.R. (2d) 193 (Ont. C.A.), affirmed (1968), 67 D.L.R. (2d) 165 (S.C.C.), at 270 *per* Gale C.J.

37 *Dirassar v. Kelly, Douglas & Co.* (1966), 59 D.L.R. (2d) 452 (B.C.C.A.), affirmed (1967), 64 D.L.R. (2d) 456 (S.C.C.); *Franklin Supply Co. v. Midco Supply Co.* (1995), 33 Alta. L.R. (3d) 362 (C.A.). Contrast the earlier view expressed in *Klein v. Jenoves*, [1932] O.R. 504.

However, the scope of this defence of justification or privilege is by no means clear. It has rarely been raised with success. Among the factors that, at various times, and in different cases, have been said to support a plea of justification have been: promotion of the public interest, as long as the defendant acted from impersonal motives;[38] a superior contractual right;[39] the exercise of a statutory right;[40] and the advancement of morality or social policy.[41]

Although it has been said that the defence is flexible and ought not to be defined or applied too narrowly,[42] the idea that the inducement of a breach of contract can be justified and therefore not tortious raises problems. In the first place, for the law to excuse what otherwise would be actionable seems to be inconsistent with the notion that conduct perpetrated intentionally and causes damage or harm that is foreseeable as a likely consequence should give rise to liability. Second, to excuse such conduct on the ground that the defendant acted out of a good, and not a bad, motive seems to contradict the notion that actions are not to be judged by the motive of the actor. A bad motive does not by itself normally make a lawful act unlawful, nor does a good motive normally make an unlawful act lawful.[43] Admittedly there are, or appear to be, exceptions to this.[44] Nonetheless the irrelevance of motive may be considered a fundamental proposition of the law of torts, as it is of the criminal law. Hence it may be difficult for a defendant to justify conduct that has the effect of inducing the breach of a valid, binding contract.

---

38 See, *e.g.*, *Bank of Nova Scotia v. Gaudreau* (1984), 27 B.L.R. 101 (Ont. H.C.) at 144-146 *per* Sutherland J.

39 *Rogers Cable TV Ltd. v. 373041 Ontario Ltd.* (1996), 69 C.P.R. (3d) 85 (Ont. Gen. Div.).

40 *Atcheson v. College of Physicians & Surgeons (Alberta)* (1994), 148 A.R. 395 (C.A.).

41 *Brimelow v. Casson*, [1924] 1 Ch. 302.

42 *Greig v. Insole*, [1978] 3 All E.R. 449 at 493 *per* Slade J.

43 *Mayor of Bradford v. Pickles*, [1895] A.C. 587; *Allen v. Flood*, [1898] A.C. 1.

44 For example, in cases of nuisance and conspiracy; pp. 61, 183, 187.

Chapter 25

INTERFERENCE WITH ECONOMIC INTERESTS

1. THE EXTENSION OF LUMLEY V. GYE

As explained in the previous chapter, the principle derived from the decision in *Lumley v. Gye*[1] was restricted in its application, for more than a century, to conduct that resulted in the breach of a contract. If anything less than a breach was the consequence there would be no liability on the part of the defendant on the basis of the 1853 decision, even if the defendant acted intentionally to cause the plaintiff harm,[2] unless the defendant, to achieve his or her object, perpetrated some other tort, or acted with others, which might give rise to liability for conspiracy.[3] In the 19th century there were some judicial statements suggesting that to act maliciously, without lawful justification or excuse, with the purpose or motive of inflicting economic harm upon another might be actionable even if no conspiracy was involved.[4] This so-called "leading heresy" was rejected by courts which stressed the importance of establishing that some nominate tort, such as inducing a breach of contract, before liability could ensue as a result of the defendant's deliberate unjustified interference with the economic interests or relations of the plaintiff.

In the United States, however, there developed what became known as the "*prima facie* tort" doctrine, by which any injury to a lawful business, even if it did not come within the scope of some defined tort, would be *prima facie* actionable unless it could be justified or excused on the ground that it was the inevitable result of a lawful effort on the part of the defendant.[5] This evolution

---

1 (1853), 3 E. & B. 216.

2 *D.C. Thomson & Co. v. Deakin*, [1952] Ch. 646; *Stratford & Son Ltd. v. Lindley,* [1965] A.C. 307.

3 Above p. 183.

4 *Mogul S.S. Co. v. McGregor, Gow & Co.* (1889), 23 Q.B.D. 598 at 613 *per* Bowen L.J.; *Quinn v. Leathem*, [1901] A.C. 495 at 510 *per* Lord Macnaghten.

5 Hale, "Prima Facie Torts, Competition and Non-Feasance" (1946) 46 Columbia L.R. 196; Note: "The Prima Facie Tort Doctrine" (1952) 52 Columbia L.R. 503; Forkosch, "An Analysis of the 'Prima Facie Tort' Cause of Action" (1957) 42 Cornell L.Q. 465; Brown, "The Rise and Threatened Demise of the Prima Facie Tort Principle" (1959) 54 Northwestern U.L.R. 563. The classic case was *Tuttle v. Buck* (1909), 107 Minn. 145, which concerned rival barbers located adjacent to each other. The classic description of the basis of such liability was the concept of "disinterested malevolence" employed by Holmes J. in *American Bank & Trust Co. v. Federal Reserve Bank of Atlanta* (1921), 256 U.S. 350.

permitted American courts to give greater protection to various forms of unfair business competition, hence the description of this form of liability as the "competitive tort".[6]

In 1966 the Australian High Court, in *Beaudesert Shire Council v. Smith*,[7] propounded the idea that "a person who suffers harm or loss as the inevitable consequence of the unlawful, intentional and positive acts of another is entitled to recover damages from that other". Under that principle any damaging interference with another person's contract, even if a breach did not ensue, would give rise to liability to the one whose contract had been affected, as long as the interferer acted unlawfully and intentionally. However, the *Beaudesert* doctrine was criticized and has now been repudiated by the court that first gave it voice.[8] However, following some remarks made by Lord Denning in 1969[9] about the scope of the doctrine of *Lumley v. Gye*, based upon the notion that each party to a contract has a right to the performance of it, such that it was wrongful not only to bring about the breach or non-performance of such contract but also to interfere with its execution without causing a breach, later English,[10] Australian[11] and New Zealand[12] decisions began to recognize a tort of unlawful interference with trade or business that could be committed despite the fact that the defendant's conduct did not induce the breach of a contract between the plaintiff and a third party. The same view has been taken by courts in Canada,[13] which have indicated that the elements of this tort are: (1) interference with the plaintiff's trade or business; (2) by the use of unlawful means; (3) with the intent to injure the plaintiff; and (4) and with the result that the plaintiff suffers damage or loss.[14]

By way of distinguishing this new tort from the older tort of inducing or procuring a breach of contract, courts have referred to it as "interference with contractual relations" or "interference with economic relations".[15]

---

6 Callman, "What is Unfair Competition?" (1940) 28 Geo. L.J. 585; Note: "Developments in the Law: Competitive Torts" (1964) 77 Harvard L.R. 880.

7 (1966), 120 C.L.R. 145.

8 *Northern Territory of Australia v. Mengel* (1995), 185 C.L.R. 307.

9 In *Torquay Hotel Co. v. Cousins*, [1969] Ch. 106 at 138.

10 *Marina Shipping Ltd. v. Laughton*, [1982] Q.B. 1127; *R.C.A. Corp. v. Pollard*, [1983] 1 Ch. 135; *Merkur Island Shipping Corp. v. Laughton*, [1983] 2 A.C. 570; *Lonrho plc v. Fayed*, [1990] 2 Q.B. 479, reversed on other grounds [1992] A.C. 448; *Hadmor Productions Ltd. v. Hamilton*, [1983] 1 A.C. 191.

11 *Ansett Transport Industries (Operations) Pty Ltd. v. Australian Federation of Air Pilots* (1989), 95 A.L.R. 211. Note the denial of any such action by the High Court in *Sanders v. Snell* (1998), 196 C.L.R. 329 at 346.

12 *Emms v. Brad Lovett Ltd.*, [1973] 1 N.Z.L.R. 282; *Van Camp Chocolates Ltd. v. Aulsebrooks Ltd.*, [1984] 1 N.Z.L.R. 354.

13 See, *e.g.*, *Westfair Foods Ltd. v. Lippens Inc.* (1989), 61 Man. R. (2d) 282 (C.A.); *Thorvaldson v. Saskatchewan* (1990), 82 Sask. R. 257 (Q.B.), reversed on other grounds (1991), 93 Sask. R. 22 (C.A.); *Daishowa Inc. v. Friends of the Lubicon* (1998), 158 D.L.R. (4th) 699 (Ont. Gen. Div.). Contrast *Merchants Consolidated Ltd. (Receiver of) v. Ince Holdings Ltd.* (1996), 92 Man. R. (2d) 253 (C.A.) at 258 *per* Twaddle J.A.

14 Fridman, "Interference with Trade or Business" (1993) 1 Tort L.R. 19, 99.

15 *Ontario Store Fixtures Inc. v. MMMuffins Ltd.* (1989), 70 O.R. (2d) 42 (C.A.).

2. INTERFERENCE WITHOUT BREACH OF CONTRACT

One way in which this tort can be committed is if the defendant directly and intentionally interferes with the performance or execution of a contract between the plaintiff and another person. This would occur if the defendant's acts prevented or hindered one party to the contract from fulfilling its terms even though such non-performance did not amount to a breach of the contract. This is what happened in *Torquay Hotel Co. v. Cousins*,[16] where the conduct of the union presided over by the defendant made it impossible for one party to a contract to deliver oil to a hotel to do so. Such non-delivery was not a breach of the contract because of the provisions of an exemption clause in the contract. Similarly, in *Gershman v. Manitoba Vegetable Producers' Marketing Board*[17] this tort could be committed when, by reason of the defendant's acts, an existing employment contract between the plaintiff and a third party was not renewed or continued as it could have been under the terms of such contract. In *Martin v. International Maple Leaf Springs Water Corp.*[18] the interference caused the loss of the plaintiff's opportunity to continue to earn his living or practise his chosen vocation. As these and other cases make clear, it is the intent to injure that triggers liability.

This tort can also be committed if the defendant's acts indirectly cause the interference. However, if the allegation is that the defendant's acts indirectly caused interference with, but no breach of, the plaintiff's contract with a third party, then the acts of the defendant must have been unlawful *per se*, such as harassment[19] or intimidation,[20] or making untrue and inflammatory remarks about the plaintiff.[21] A defendant acts unlawfully, it has been suggested,[22] when he or she is not at liberty to do what he or she has done. In all such cases it is the unlawful character of what the defendant has done that is the basis of liability.[23]

3. INTERFERENCE NOT INVOLVING EXISTING CONTRACTS

The law can now be said to accept the possibility for interference with an existing contract whether the result is a breach of the contract or merely prevention or hindrance of its performance in circumstances when this will not constitute a

---

16 [1969] Ch. 106.

17 (1975), 65 D.L.R. (3d) 181 (Man. Q.B.), affirmed (1976), 69 D.L.R. (3d) 114 (Man. C.A.).

18 (1998), 38 C.C.E.L. (2d) 128 (Ont. C.A.).

19 *Mintuck v. Valley River Band No. 63A* (1977), 75 D.L.R. (3d) 589 (Man. C.A.).

20 *Boychuk v. Northwest Territories Housing Corp.* (1985), 33 C.C.L.T. 28 (N.W.T. S.C.).

21 *Braunfel Engineering & Construction Ltd. v. Sanger*, [1997] B.C.J. No. 886 (B.C.S.C.) (QL).

22 *Volkswagen Canada Ltd. v. Spicer* (1978), 91 D.L.R. (3d) 42 (N.S.C.A.).

23 See also *Yellow Submarine Deli Inc. v. AGF Hospitality Associates Inc.* (1995), 106 Man. R. (2d) 51 (Q.B.); *Royal Bank v. Wilton* (1995), 165 A.R. 261 (C.A.), which raises the question of "justification" in relation to this tort, as uncertain in this context as it is in the context of inducing a breach of contract: above p. 199.

breach. *Lumley v. Gye* has been extended so far. The question is whether the principle underlying that case can be extended further, so as to cover situations where the defendant prevents the making of a contract between the plaintiff and a third party or otherwise harms the economic interests of the plaintiff.

It has been seen, in an earlier chapter,[24] that if the prevention of the making of a contract is brought about by what has been termed "injurious falsehood" liability may follow. Some Canadian cases which might be thought to have involved liability for this tort, appear to have been decided on the basis that the conduct of the defendant amounted to unlawful interference with contractual relations. In the cases in question the defendant falsely claimed to be the owner of a vehicle which the plaintiff was intending to sell to a third party,[25] or published false advertising to obtain a market away from the plaintiff.[26] In another instance the conduct of the defendant was held to be not only unlawful interference with trade or business but also the intentional infliction of nervous shock and an invasion of privacy.[27] Hence it would appear to have been unnecessary for the court to invoke this tort to make the defendant liable.

However, apart from such decisions, there are dicta in a number of Canadian cases, many of which have been referred to earlier, which support the idea that it is actionable in tort intentionally to cause economic harm by unlawful means, even though no inducement of the breach of an existing contract, nor any interference with its due performance, is involved. There are also decisions which recognize the possibility of such liability, but deny it on the facts of the cases in question on the ground that the defendant did nothing unlawful, or did not act in bad faith, or had no intent to injure the plaintiff.[28] It would seem to be reasonable and legitimate to conclude, therefore, that in Canada the evolution of the *Lumley v. Gye* principle has gone so far as to extend potential liability to cover situations where one person acts unlawfully with the intent to cause economic harm to another however this is accomplished, whether by causing the breach or disruption of that person's contract with a third party or injuriously affecting that person's economic interests or relations with others.

---

24 Above p. 171.

25 *Paragon Properties (Finance) Ltd. v. Del Swan Trucking Inc.* (1998), 68 Alta. L.R. (3d) 165 (C.A).

26 *Mead Johnson Canada v. Ross Pediatrics* (1996), 31 O.R. (3d) 237 (C.A.).

27 *Tran v. Financial Debt Recovery Ltd.* (2000), 193 D.L.R. (4th) 168 (Ont. S.C.J.).

28 See, *e.g.*, *Daishowa Inc. v. Friends of the Lubicon* (1998), 158 D.L.R. (4th) 699 (Ont. Gen. Div.); *Gerrard v. Manitoba* (1990), 71 Man. R. (2d) 219 (Q.B.), affirmed (1992), 81 Man. R. (2d) 295 (C.A.); *Cheticamp Fisheries Co-Operative Ltd. v. Canada* (1995), 139 N.S.R. (2d) 224 (C.A.).

PART III:
ANCILLARY MATTERS

Chapter 26

MULTIPLE WRONGDOERS

1. VARIOUS SITUATIONS

More than one person may have been involved in causing the plaintiff's damage or injury. Unless any one of them has a valid defence that can be raised to a possible action, each may be liable to the plaintiff. The extent of any such liability, and the rights, if any, that may arise as between the different wrongdoers will depend upon the manner in which they are involved in what happened. There are three possible situations: (1) the acts of the defendants are independent in character and time and cause different kinds of damage or injury to the plaintiff; (2) the acts of the defendants are independent but occur at the same time and combine to cause damage or injury to the plaintiff; and (3) the defendants act together, in the same way and at the same time, to commit damage or injury to the plaintiff.

Defendants in situation (1) are usually described as "successive" tortfeasors, although they have also been described as non-concurrent several tortfeasors. Those in situation (2) are "several" tortfeasors, because their acts may be said to be severed from each other. Defendants in situation (3) are "joint" tortfeasors because they have acted jointly to cause harm.[1] In modern terminology defendants who come within situations (2) and (3) are sometimes also called "concurrent" tortfeasors[2] because their acts occur simultaneously even though, in situation (2) those acts are distinct and independent.[3] Defendants in situation (1) are treated differently from those who are either several or joint tortfeasors within situations (2) and (3).

2. SUCCESSIVE TORTFEASORS

An example of a situation involving such tortfeasors would be if one were, by negligent driving, to run down the plaintiff and break his or her leg, and, later, while the plaintiff was lying on the ground, a second person were to drive negli-

---

[1] For different uses and meanings of these various terms see *Report on Contribution Among Wrongdoers and Contributory Negligence*, Ontario Law Reform Commission, 1988; *Inglis Ltd. v. South Shore Sales & Service Ltd.* (1979), 104 D.L.R. (3d) 507 (Ont. C.A.).

[2] *Fletcher v. Hand* (1994), 21 Alta. L.R. (3d) 346 (C.A.).

[3] But see *Inglis Ltd. v. South Shore Sales & Service Ltd.* (1979), 104 D.L.R. (3d) 507 (Ont. C.A.).

gently and hit and kill the plaintiff. In such cases there are no interdependent rights or responsibilities between the different tortfeasors. The issue that arises is to determine whose act caused which damage. The individual tortfeasor will be liable only for the damage caused by, and traceable to, him or her, and will be exonerated from liability for all later damage. For example, if various defendants have caused independent nuisances which cumulatively cause inconvenience to the plaintiff, the court will have to divide the plaintiff's loss between them according to the proportion of the plaintiff's inconvenience for which each defendant is responsible.[4] In the example given above, the defendant who caused the breaking of the plaintiff's leg will be liable for that, not for the plaintiff's death. Nor will the first defendant be excused from liability because the later death of the plaintiff meant that the plaintiff did not suffer much loss as a result of the breaking of his or her leg.

How to evaluate the damages payable by the first defendant in such an instance was discussed by the House of Lords in *Baker v. Willoughby*.[5] A "devaluation" principle or method of apportionment was applied. The first defendant was held liable for a general reduction in the plaintiff's capacity to earn money or enjoy life. The second defendant was liable only for additional devaluation. This approach has been applied[6] and rejected[7] in Canada. In its place the British Columbia Court of Appeal[8] dealt with the problem by apportioning the plaintiff's loss on a percentage basis between the two causes that brought about that loss. In view of this difference of opinion between Canadian courts, as well as doubts expressed by the House of Lords in 1982, the matter will have to be determined, eventually, by the Supreme Court of Canada.[9]

3. JOINT AND SEVERAL TORTFEASORS

(a) The Distinction

Joint tortfeasors act in concert, in furtherance of a common intent or design,[10] for example, where two or more persons driving separate cars both deliberately or negligently run down the plaintiff at the same time. Conspirators are joint tort-

---

4 *Ibid.*, at 510.

5 [1970] A.C. 467.

6 *Long v. Thiessen* (1968), 65 W.W.R. 577 (B.C.C.A.); *Hicks v. Cooper* (1973), 41 D.L.R. (3d) 454 (Ont. C.A.); *Cormier v. Fraser* (1989), 93 N.B.R. (2d) 91 (C.A.).

7 In *Pryor v. Bains* (1986), 69 B.C.L.R. 395 (C.A.). See also *Borque v. Wells* (1991), 82 D.L.R. (4th) 574 (N.B.C.A.).

8 *Pryor v. Bains*, *ibid.*

9 Although that Court refused leave to appeal the *Borque* case: (1992), 87 D.L.R. (4th) vii (S.C.C.).

10 *The Koursk*, [1924] P. 140; *Bains v. Hofs* (1992), 76 B.C.L.R. (2d) 98 (C.A.). But merely agreeing on a common action, such as hunting together, will not make defendants joint tortfeasors where both shoot and one, which being unknown, accidentally hits the plaintiff; *Cook v. Lewis*, [1951] S.C.R. 830.

feasors.[11] So are master and servant or employer and employee, when the master or employer is vicariously liable for the conduct of the servant or employee.[12] Several tortfeasors act independently, not in concert, even though their combined acts result in the damage or loss suffered by the plaintiff. Thus if a servant or employee tortiously harms the plaintiff by conduct which is not within the scope of the employee's employment, so that no vicarious liability ensues, but the employer is independently negligent and that negligence helped to bring about the plaintiff's injury, the servant or employee and the employer will not be considered to be joint, but will be several, tortfeasors.[13]

(b) Consequences

At common law the distinction between joint and several tortfeasors was very important and had vital consequences. Thus joint or several tortfeasor could be sued individually for all the loss suffered by the plaintiff. Joint, but not several, tortfeasors could be sued together. If joint tortfeasors were sued jointly, the court could find all, or only one or some, responsible. But there could be no apportionment of liability between them. If the plaintiff sued one joint tortfeasor and obtained a judgment against that one, the plaintiff could not later sue a second or other joint tortfeasor, even if the prior judgment had not been satisfied. This was because there was only one cause of action against all the joint tortfeasors and this was disposed of by, or "merged" in, the judgment.[14] The rule did not aply to several tortfeasors because there was not one, but several distinct causes of action. A judgment against one several tortfeasor was for the loss that tortfeasor caused. Consequently judgment against that tortfeasor did not affect the plaintiff's cause of action against others in resect of the damage they caused.

This has been altered by statute, at least in some provinces.[15] Where such a statute is in force, a plaintiff can now sue each tortfeasor, whether joint or several, together or *seriatim*, until satisfaction has been obtained or all are proved unable to pay. A tortfeasor actually sued can bring into the action, or pursue separately in a distinct action, other tortfeasors, whether joint or several, whom he or she alleges was also partly responsible for the original plaintiff's loss or damage. A judgment against one tortfeasor will not bar an action against others.

If the plaintiff releases one tortfeasor from liability, for example, by some settlement of the plaintiff's claim on the basis of a payment (but not by a covenant not to sue),[16] this would preclude an action against another joint tortfeasor but not an action against another several tortfeasor. This common law doctrine has been abolished in Ontario,[17] where a release of one joint tortfeasor will no

---

11 Above p. 182.

12 Above p. 31.

13 *Q. v. Minto Management Ltd.* (1985), 49 O.R. (2d) 531 (Q.B.), affirmed (1986), 57 O.R. (2d) 781 (C.A.).

14 *Brinsmead v. Harrison* (1872), L.R. 7 C.P. 547.

15 See, *e.g.*, *Courts of Justice Act*, R.S.O. 1990, c. C.43, s. 43; *Law and Equity Act*, R.S.B.C. 1996, c. 253, s. 53(2).

16 *Duck v. Mayeu*, [1892] 2 Q.B. 511.

17 *Courts of Justice Act*, R.S.O. 1990, c. C.43, s. 139.

longer operate to bar an action against another joint tortfeasor. Equivalent reform of the law has not taken place in other provinces.

The common law, for reasons never made clear, also prohibited the recovery of any contribution or indemnity by one tortfeasor from any other, whether they were joint or several tortfeasors.[18] This has now been abolished by legislation in all the common law provinces.

(c) Contribution and Indemnity

Under the relevant statutory provisions,[19] unless the right to contribution has been excluded by an express or implied contract between the parties,[20] one tortfeasor may be able to recover either some contribution or a complete indemnity in respect of damages paid or payable to the plaintiff.

There are two possible situations giving rise to a claim for contribution or indemnity. In the first place, the tortfeasor from whom contribution or indemnity is sought may be someone "found at fault", that is someone who has been sued and held liable to the victim or someone who has settled with the victim after having admitted liability. Hence if such tortfeasor has been held not liable, either on the merits of the case or for some technical reason, such as that the claim is statute-barred under the provisions of a *Limitations Act*, no contribution or indemnity is recoverable.[21]

Second, a claim for contribution or indemnity can also be made against a tortfeasor who could have been sued by, and would have been held liable to, the victim. However recovery of contribution or indemnity will be possible from a tortfeasor who has never been sued, even if, at the time contribution or indemnity is sought, an action against him or her by the victim would have been statute-barred. Time only begins to run against a tortfeasor from whom contribution or indemnity is sought when the proceedings for such recovery are instituted, not when the original cause of action by the victim arose.[22]

All joint and several tortfeasors are liable to make contribution or indemnify each other to the degree in which they are found to be at fault or negligent, which is a question of fact.[23] If that determination is factually impossible, the parties will be deemed equally at fault or negligent. It has not been decided whether the basis for determination of liability in this context is to be based upon causation or culpability. However for a complete indemnity to be recovered by one tortfeasor from another the former must probably be entirely inno-

---

18 *Merryweather v. Nixan* (1799), 8 T.R. 186; *The Koursk*, [1924] P. 140.

19 See, *e.g.*, *Negligence Act*, R.S.O. 1990, c. N.1.

20 *Laing Property Corp. v. All Seasons Display Inc.* (2000), 79 B.C.L.R. (3d) 199 (B.C.).

21 *Inglis Ltd. v. South Shore Sales & Service Ltd.* (1979), 104 D.L.R. (3d) 507 (Ont. C.A.); *Parkland v. Stetar* (1974), 50 D.L.R. (3d) 376 (S.C.C.). In Ontario the other tortfeasor must be made a party to the action either by the victim or by third party proceedings issued by the tortfeasor claiming contribution: *Cohen v. S. McCord & Co.*, [1944] O.R. 568 (C.A.).

22 *Nesbitt v. Beattie*, [1955] O.R. 111 (C.A.): *British Columbia Hydro & Power Authority v. Kees van Western*, [1974] 3 W.W.R. 20 (B.C.S.C.).

23 *Ingles v. Tutkaluk Construction Ltd.*, [2000] 1 S.C.R. 298 at 338; *Martin v. Listowel Memorial Hospital* (2001), 192 D.L.R. (4th) 250 (Ont. C.A.).

cent of any blame, and merely liable to the victim on some technical basis. Such would be the case of one who is an "innocent" converter, who has committed the wrongful act in reliance on the statement of another party, the true converter since he or she knows that the chattel in question did not belong to him or her.[24] Hence, also, an employer or principal who is vicariously liable even though innocent of any personal wrongdoing[25] may also be able to recover a full indemnity from the tortious employee or agent. Indeed such complete indemnity may be recovered from the employee or agent in contract on the ground that the employee or agent, by negligently injuring the victim, has broken an express or implied term of the contract under which he or she is employed, requiring the employee or agent to act with reasonable care and skill.[26]

---

24 Above p. 126.

25 Above p. 31.

26 *Lister v. Romford Ice & Cold Storage Co.*, [1957] A.C. 555: with which contrast *Harvey v. R.G. O'Dell*, [1958] 2 Q.B. 78.

Chapter 27

DAMAGES

1. THE PRINCIPAL REMEDY AND ITS ALTERNATIVES

The payment of money in the form of damages was, and remains, the principal means whereby the common law dealt with loss or injury caused by tortious conduct. The chief aim of the law, as discussed earlier,[1] is to compensate the victim. As far as possible the victim is to be given an amount that will replace what has been lost. This is not really possible in the case, for example, of loss of life or amputation of a limb. The law can only attempt to monetize the harm suffered, to express it in some financial terms. Damages in tort cases are "at large", that is to say they are calculated on the basis of the value placed by the court on the kind of loss suffered by the plaintiff. In cases of personal injury such damages cover a range of incidents flowing from the infliction of such injury.[2] In addition to such compensatory damages, however, additional sums may be awarded as either "aggravated" or "punitive" damages.[3]

In certain situations other remedies may be available to a victim at common law. These include self-help, specific restitution of a chattel, restitution of the specific amount lost by the plaintiff by reason of the tort committed by the defendant. The equitable remedy of an injunction is now also available even though the acts of the defendant constitute a wrong originally only actionable at common law.

As noted in earlier chapters,[4] at common law a plaintiff, without seeking the assistance of a court, may do various things by way of remedying the wrong done by the defendant. A plaintiff may abate a nuisance; repossess land or a chattel that has been wrongfully taken by the defendant; or seize and detain cattle found trespassing on the plaintiff's land. There are dangers inherent in the employment of such self-help. If the plaintiff goes too far he or she may in turn be guilty of a tort against the defendant. In cases of detinue,[5] instead of damages the plaintiff may seek and may be awarded specific restitution of the goods detained by the defendant. This is a discretionary remedy and will not be granted when the chattel is an ordinary article of commerce and damages

1 Above p. 8.
2 Below p. 217.
3 Below p. 216.
4 Above pp. 52, 54, 66, 120.
5 Above p. 130.

would adequately compensate the plaintiff. Recovery of land wrongfully taken by the defendant may also be awarded in an action for trespass to land.

The common law also recognized an alternative claim for money in certain torts which involved economic loss, such as conversion, trespass to goods or deceit. The plaintiff was permitted to elect whether to sue in tort or to bring an action for money had and received. When this occurred the plaintiff was said to "waive" the tort. This did not mean that the plaintiff forgave the defendant for the wrong the latter committed. It meant that the plaintiff chose to forgo his or her cause of action in tort for damages at large and sue for the specific amount of money lost by the plaintiff, and gained by the defendant at the plaintiff's expense, through what was originally treated as a quasi-contractual action. Waiver of tort may still occur, but the action is now regarded as a claim for unjust enrichment or restitution.[6]

Courts of equity could issue injunctions to force someone to refrain from a certain course of action or perform a specific act. This remedy was of particular importance in the context of the tort of nuisance.[7] Under modern legislation, which follows an English statute of 1858,[8] injunctions can now be issued by all courts either instead of or in addition to an award of damages. The remedy is still equitable in nature and therefore, unlike damages, which are obligatory if the plaintiff establishes a cause of action, it is discretionary. An injunction will not be granted where damages would provide adequate compensation and to grant an injunction would be oppressive to the defendant.[9] Injunctions may be "interlocutory", where their purpose is to restrain the defendant pending the trial of an action to determine whether the defendant is committing or has committed a tort, for example, a nuisance;[10] or "perpetual", when the issue has been determined and the defendant is ordered either to refrain forever from committing the nuisance, when it is termed "prohibitory", or to do something specific, such as close a factory that is committing a nuisance, when it is termed "mandatory". There is also a "*quia timet*" injunction, which may be issued before a defendant has done something but is threatening to do it and, if done, the action would involve commission of a nuisance. Since damages can be awarded in place of such an injunction, the curious and anomalous situation arises in which a party may obtain damages for a tort that has not yet been committed.[11]

---

6 See Fridman, *Restitution*, 2nd ed. (Toronto: Carswell, 1992), pp. 355-367.

7 Above p. 66.

8 *Chancery Amendment Act*, 1858, 21 & 22 Vict., c. 27: see, *e.g.*, *Courts of Justice Act*, R.S.O. 1990, c. C.43.

9 *Shelfer v. City of London Electric Lighting Co.*, [1895] 1 Ch. 287.

10 Fridman, *The Law of Contract in Canada*, 4th ed. (Toronto: Carswell, 1999), pp. 848-852.

11 *Leeds Industrial Co-Operative Society v. Slack*, [1924] A.C. 851: but only when the damage caused would be irreparable; *Mendez v. Palazzi* (1976), 12 O.R. (2d) 270 (Co. Ct.).

2. CATEGORIES OF DAMAGES

There are three major categories of damages that may be awarded at common law: compensatory; aggravated; and punitive or exemplary.

(a) Compensatory Damages

These, as the name would indicate, are designed to recompense the plaintiff for the value of what the plaintiff has lost as a result or consequence of the tortious act for which the defendant is responsible in law. Such damages may be divided into two subcategories: "nominal" and "substantive".

If the plaintiff has really lost nothing, has suffered no or only trivial damage, the plaintiff's damages will be nominal, recognizing the fact that a right with which the plaintiff is invested has been wrongly infringed by the defendant. Usually such damages are awarded when the plaintiff has a cause of action that does not depend upon proof that he or she has incurred damage or loss, for example, trespass to land, goods, or the person of the plaintiff,[12] or slander that is actionable *per se*.[13] Sometimes, indeed, the claim of the plaintiff is so undeserving of merit, even though it has a proper foundation in law, that the court will award what are termed "contemptuous" damages, a sum so small that it gives official recognition to the fundamental invalidity of the plaintiff's complaint (and may also result in the costs of the action, on both sides, having to be paid by the "successful" plaintiff).

Both in actions which do not require proof that damage has been suffered, such as trespass, and in those in which proof of damage is an essential ingredient in the liability of the defendant, such as negligence, conspiracy, or slander which is not actionable *per se*, once the plaintiff has established that damage or loss has been incurred, whether it be physical harm or economic loss or both, the plaintiff will be entitled to substantive damages. These also may be divided into two subcategories: "special" and "general".

The former are particular, specific, items of damage, not normally presumed to have occurred as a matter of law. These need to be alleged specially. They are calculated in advance, in respect of expenses actually incurred by the plaintiff as a legally recoverable consequence of the defendant's tort. Examples of these are: medical expenses and fees; loss of rent that would have been earned from a chattel unlawfully detained by the defendant; amounts paid to a housekeeper when a wife has been put into hospital by the defendant's trespass or negligence; salary or wages lost to the plaintiff by reason of his or her incapacity to work as a consequence of the defendant's tort;[14] the expense of hiring a replacement ve-

---

12 Above pp. 40, 50, 52.

13 Above p. 136.

14 No deductions are to be made from any such award in respect of income tax: *R. v. Jennings*, [1966] S.C.R. 532, not following *British Transport Commission v. Gourley*, [1956] A.C. 185. As regards *other* deductions, *e.g.*, pensions payable under accident insurance policies, see *Parry v. Cleaver*, [1970] A.C. 1; *Boarelli v. Flannigan*, [1973] 3 O.R. 69 (C.A.); *Canadian Pacific Ltd. v.*

hicle because of the damage to, or destruction of the plaintiff's car or truck. Such special damages are usually, but not necessarily, agreed between the parties in the litigation.

All other compensatory damages are general. Over and above the special damages, if any, courts can, and do, award a more general sum to compensate the plaintiff for those losses which fall within the scope of the defendant's liability. In this respect it is necessary to determine whether the loss or damage claimed by the plaintiff to have been suffered is too remote a consequence of the defendant's tortious act to be compensable by the defendant. This may depend upon whether the plaintiff's claim is in negligence, in respect of a tort of strict liability, or for conduct which was intentionally committed in order to harm the plaintiff.[15] The issue of remoteness is normally one that is connected with the issue of the defendant's liability rather than with that of the assessment, in monetary terms, of the plaintiff's loss. Once the question of remoteness has been decided in the plaintiff's favour so as to involve the defendant in liability, the question of assessment arises.[16]

(b) Aggravated Damages

Such damages are also intended to compensate the plaintiff, although these damages frequently cover the kind of conduct that could be the subject of punitive damages.[17] However they are meant to compensate the plaintiff for aggravated damage he or she has suffered. This can occur if the defendant's act has caused the plaintiff to feel significantly worse than might normally be expected to be the result of the act in question. They take into account any further harm caused to the feelings of the plaintiff as a consequence of some outrageous conduct on the part of the defendant.[18] Although theoretically such damages may be awarded over and above compensatory damages whatever the tort committed by the defendant, it should be noted that they are rarely awarded in actions for negligence causing personal injury.

(c) Punitive or Exemplary Damages

The purpose of such damages is not to compensate the plaintiff, for they represent nothing which the plaintiff has lost by reason of the defendant's conduct. Their aim is to punish the defendant, to make an example of him or her, and so to deter others from such behaviour, so as to make it clear the court thinks that the defendant has behaved in an intolerable, inexcusable, outrageous manner. The Supreme Court of Canada explained in *Manning v. Hill*[19] that punitive damages were to be awarded when the defendant's conduct was to be regarded as

---

Gill, [1963] S.C.R. 654; *Ratych v. Bloomer* (1990), 69 D.L.R. (4th) 25 (S.C.C.); *Cunningham v. Wheeler* (1994), 113 D.L.R. (4th) 1 (S.C.C.).

15 See, *e.g.*, above, pp. 82, 114, 168.

16 Below

17 *Vorvis v. Insurance Corp. of British Columbia* (1989), 58 D.L.R. (4th) 193 (S.C.C.) at 200.

18 *Manning v. Hill* (1995), 126 D.L.R. (4th) 129 at 183 (S.C.C.).

19 (1995), 126 D.L.R. (4th) 129 (S.C.C.).

vicious, high-handed or arrogant, thereby meriting that the defendant be penalized.

Usually such damages are awarded in respect of torts that depend upon proof of an intent to injure, malice, or the deliberate infliction of harm on the plaintiff. This would exclude cases of negligence. However, there have been some decisions in which punitive damages were awarded in an action for negligence involving personal injury. In such instances there was evidence that the defendant was conscious of the consequences of carelessness but was indifferent to the danger involved. The defendant disregarded the rights of the plaintiff.[20]

3. DAMAGES FOR NEGLIGENCE CAUSING PERSONAL INJURY

While, as previously explained, the general nature of such damages is to compensate the plaintiff for the harm done so as to put the plaintiff back into the position in which he or she was prior to the commission of the wrong by the defendant, what may be awarded to a plaintiff by way of compensatory damages depends upon the wrong that has been committed and upon the kind of damage that has been inflicted. Some account of what is recoverable in respect of any particular tort may be found in the appropriate chapter.[21] So, too, what may be recovered by way of damages where a plaintiff dies as a result of the commission of a tort is considered in the next chapter.[22] What is to be discussed here is the assessment of compensatory damages where, as a result of negligence, the plaintiff has incurred non-fatal personal injury.

Reference has been made earlier to "special" damages comprising medical and similar expenses, and loss of income or earnings prior to the trial of the action. All other damages are "general", and are intended to compensate the plaintiff for all other pecuniary and non-pecuniary losses.

Pecuniary losses include the future loss of earnings or income caused by the plaintiff's inability or reduced ability to work because of his or her injuries[23] and the cost of providing the plaintiff with future care. This may cover the period of the plaintiff's recovery: it may extend to the remainder of the plaintiff's life. In the latter event various factors have to be taken into consideration: (a) the appropriate standard of care; (b) deductions for free or subsidized care; (c) the plaintiff's life expectancy; (d) the normal contingencies of life; (e) no duplication with loss of future earnings; (f) the rate of return on the capital sum

---

20 See and compare: *Coughlin v. Kuntz* (1987), 42 C.C.L.T. 142 (S.C.C.); *Shobridge v. Thomas* (1999), 47 C.C.L.T. (2d) 73 (S.C.C.); *DiDomenicantonio v. Finnigan* (1988), 49 D.L.R. (4th) 342 (S.C.C.); *McBeth v. Boldt* (1998), 164 D.L.R. (4th) 247 (S.C.C.).

21 See, *e.g.*, pp. 66, 114, 137.

22 Below Chapter 28.

23 On deductions see above p. 215, note 14.

awarded the plaintiff; and (g) future inflation. Such pecuniary losses are fully compensated.[24]

Non-pecuniary losses, however, are subject to restriction. The dollar limit of such losses (originally $100,000) will change to take into account the effects of inflation. What is comprehended within the scope of such losses are pain and suffering, loss of expectation of life, and loss of amenities. The calculation of what should be awarded for loss of amenities, which refers to the plaintiff's enjoyment of life, has been a source of difficulty where the plaintiff, although alive, has been rendered senseless, a "vegetable", that is incapable of appreciating what has happened, as a result of the defendant's negligence. In *H. West & Son v. Shepherd*[25] the House of Lords held that an objective test was to be applied: a victim was entitled to damages for loss of amenities even though unable to appreciate what had been lost. This was followed and accepted by the Supreme Court of Canada in *R. v. Jennings*.[26] However, the House of Lords later appears to have been critical of its earlier decision,[27] the High Court of Australia rejected that earlier decision in *Skelton v. Collins*,[28] and the Supreme Court's adoption, in *Andrews v. Grand & Toy Alberta Ltd.*,[29] of the Australian court's "functional" approach to non-pecuniary losses, and comments in the later case of *Lindal v. Lindal*[30] suggest that it may ultimately reject the English "objective" view.

Once the court has assessed the amount that is recoverable by the plaintiff it is payable as a lump sum.[31] The plaintiff will receive a capital sum of money which may be invested to produce interest that will compensate the plaintiff, *inter alia*, for loss of income and the cost of future care. Because such interest may exceed the rate of inflation, the courts apply a "discount factor", based on the real rate of return the plaintiff should expect to receive on the damage award,[32] thereby preventing an unjust enrichment of the plaintiff at the expense of the defendant. Periodic payments, unless authorized by a statute such as the Ontario *Courts of Justice Act*, s. 116,[33] cannot be ordered,[34] although the introduction of such payments has often been urged on the ground that the situation of the plaintiff may alter long after the date of judgment.

---

24 *Andrews v. Grand & Toy Alberta Ltd.* (1978) 83 D.L.R. (3d) 452 (S.C.C.); *Arnold v. Teno* (1978), 83 D.L.R. (3d) 609 (S.C.C.); *Thornton v. Board of Trustees of School District No. 57 (Prince George)* (1978), 83 D.L.R. (3d) 480 (B.C.C.A.).

25 [1964] A.C. 326.

26 [1960] S.C.R. 532.

27 *Lim Poh Choo v. Camden & Islington Area Health Authority*, [1980] A.C. 174.

28 (1966), 115 C.L.R. 94.

29 Above note 24.

30 (1981), 129 D.L.R. (3d) 263 (S.C.C.).

31 *Andrews v. Grand & Toy Alberta Ltd.* (1978), 83 D.L.R. (3d) 452 (S.C.C.).

32 *Lewis v. Todd* (1980), 115 D.L.R. (3d) 257 (S.C.C.).

33 R.S.O. 1990, c. C.43.

34 *Lewis v. Todd* (1980), 115 D.L.R. (3d) 257 (S.C.C.).

4. MITIGATION

In respect of all damages, whether special or general, and whether the claim is for personal injuries,[35] damage to property or economic loss, the victim is under a duty at common law to mitigate his or her damages, by acting in a reasonable way to reduce the loss which he or she would otherwise suffer in consequence. This does not mean that the victim or her must incur expense to avoid expense or loss, nor that he or she must go out of his or her way to prevent untoward loss. Thus an injured victim is not obliged to limit his or her expenditure on medical and other treatment in order to reduce the ultimate liability of the defendant. The victim may not seek extravagant or unnecessary treatment, but he or she need spare no reasonable expense in the search for adequate medical aid and assistance to obtain his or her recovery from the effects of the defendant's wrongdoing. However, if the victim has incurred extra expense in an attempt to reduce his or her loss, as a result not of the defendant's wrongdoing, but because of some extrinsic factor such as the victim's own impecuniosity, making it more difficult and expensive for him or her to obtain alternative means of carrying on his or her business when the defendant's negligence brought about a disruption, and possible heavy financial loss if the work were not continued, then such expense may not be attributable to the defendant's negligence. Mitigation is one thing, but doing something which produces a consequence which is not caused by the defendant and is therefore a remote consequence of the defendant's tort, is quite another. There is no obligation to compensate a victim for damage or loss which is the product of some factor not brought about, or into operation by the wrongdoing of the defendant. Nor is there any obligation on the defendant to compensate the victim in respect of any loss which could have been avoided or lessened by some reasonable action on the part of the victim.[36] In a sense this is a question of causation, but it goes not to the issue of responsibility so much as to the question of assessment or compensation of damages.[37]

---

35 See, *e.g.*, *Kozak v. Funk* (1995), 136 Sask. R. 12 (Q.B.), with which contrast *Khalil v. Gunn* (1999), 254 A.R. 238 (Q.B.).

36 Such as the plaintiff's refusal to undergo medical treatment that might cure him or her: *Janiak v. Ippolito* (1985), 16 D.L.R. (4th) 1 (S.C.C.).

37 Note also apology as a form of mitigation of damages in cases of defamation: above p. 142.

Chapter 28

DEATH

1. AT COMMON LAW

A tort could not be committed against a dead person.[1] The law of torts was concerned with living persons. The dead had no rights.[2] One consequence of this was that if someone who had an accrued right of action in tort against another died the cause of action died with his or her death. The maxim of the common law was: *actio personalis moritur cum persona*. A personal action died when the plaintiff died. Nor did it matter whether the potential plaintiff was killed immediately by the defendant's tortious act or was only injured but died subsequently. It has never been clear what was the basis for this doctrine, which emerged early in the 19th century,[3] became enshrined in the law,[4] and gave rise to the maxim that it was "cheaper to kill than to maim". Another consequence of the maxim was that, if the defendant died before judgment, the claim against him or her also ended and could not be brought or continued against the defendant's estate.[5]

Legislation was necessary to effect a change in the law. In 1846, in England, by the *Fatal Accidents Act*,[6] where someone was killed by the wrongful act of another person, or later died, certain dependents of the deceased were given a right of action to recover compensation for the loss they suffered by reason of such death. Fatal Accidents Acts have since been enacted in the common law provinces of Canada.[7] The effect of such enactments is to create an action for "wrongful death". Later English legislation, also emulated in Canada,[8] provides that actions in tort, with certain exceptions, such as actions for defamation or malicious prosecution, can be brought or continued by the deceased's executors

---

1 Hence it was not possible, and remains impossible, to bring an action for defamation of a deceased person.

2 But certain wrongdoing against a dead person, such as grave-robbing or desecration of a corpse, may be crimes.

3 *Baker v. Bolton* (1808), 1 Camp. 493.

4 See *Osborn v. Gillett* (1873), L.R. 8 Ex. 88; *Admiralty Commissioners v. S.S. Amerika*, [1917] A.C. 38; *Monaghan v. Horn* (1882), 7 S.C.R. 409.

5 This was not the situation where the cause of action was for breach of contract: Fridman, *The Law of Contract in Canada*, 4th ed. (Toronto: Carswell, 1999), at p. 731.

6 Which has been replaced by more modern legislation.

7 Note, however, the different provisions of the Ontario *Family Law Act*: below p. 223.

8 See, *e.g.*, *Trustee Act*, R.S.O. 1990, c. T.23; *Survival of Actions Act*, R.S.A. 2000, c. S-27; *Estates Administration Act*, R.S.B.C. 1996, c. 122.

or administrators, depending on whether the deceased died testate or intestate, and can be brought against the estate of a deceased defendant.

2. WRONGFUL DEATH

The situation in Ontario must be differentiated from that in the other common law provinces.

In the latter the effect of the provincial *Fatal Accidents Act* is to create a cause of action for wrongfully, that is by reason of any wrongful act, neglect or default, causing the death of a "relative", as defined in the legislation. That cause of action is distinct from any cause of action that can be brought by the deceased's estate under the survival of actions legislation discussed later. However, like such causes of action it, too, is based upon a right to sue the defendant that had accrued to the deceased prior to his or her death.[9] Thus, for example, if the deceased had already settled with the defendant and been compensated, or there was some bar to such an action by the deceased, no action can be brought by those who might otherwise have been allowed to sue for wrongful death.[10]

The rationale for allowing an action to "dependents" in such circumstances is that, by reason of the death of the deceased, the dependants have been deprived of financial support. In this respect this legislation created another,[11] in this instance statutory, exception to the rule that there could be liability only to a plaintiff to whom injury was a foreseeable consequence of negligence or other wrongful act on the part of the defendant. As with the other exceptions, it was not necessary that the loss incurred be foreseeable by the defendant.[12]

The dependants who can claim under this legislation vary from province to province, but usually they include spouses, parents, children, grandchildren, and stepchildren, even illegitimate or adopted children. Their claim is based upon the fact that they had a reasonable expectation of deriving pecuniary benefit from the deceased.[13] However "pecuniary benefit" is interpreted widely.[14] Such loss, however, must result from a familial, not a contractual relationship between the deceased and the claimant.[15]

---

9 Hence it can be affected by contributory negligence on the part of the deceased (or the dependants who are claiming): *Larney Estate v. Friesen* (1986), 38 C.C.L.T. 106 (Man. C.A.); *Littley v. Brooks*, [1932] S.C.R. 462.

10 *B.C. Electric Railway Co. v. Gentile*, [1914] A.C. 1034.

11 The others are the actions for loss of services and, formerly, though this has now gone, the action for loss of consortium.

12 Remoteness of damage is also not relevant: *Vaiman v. Yates* (1987), 41 D.L.R. (4th) 186 (S.C.C.).

13 *Adkins v. Mintz* (1973), 7 O.R. (2d) 102 (C.A.).

14 *Vana v. Tosta*, [1968] S.C.R. 71. See *Reeves v. Croken* (1985), 22 D.L.R. (4th) 272 (S.C.C.). On the calculation of the loss see *Lewis v. Todd* (1980), 115 D.L.R. (3d) 257 (S.C.C.). Aggravated damages, on which see above p. 216, cannot be recovered.

15 *Katz v. Little* (1963), 38 D.L.R. (2d) 515 (Man. Q.B.). But see *Mensink v. Duek* (1979), 9 C.C.L.T. 149 (B.C.S.C.) for an exceptional instance where the loss of the "brains" of a one-man company caused financial loss to family members who were employees.

The Ontario *Family Law Act*[16] replaced the older *Fatal Accidents Act* for that province. This new statute, unlike the other provincial statutes, applies to fatal and to non-fatal injuries suffered by someone by reason of the defendant's tortious conduct, although, as is the case under them, the action will not lie if the deceased or injured person would have been able to sue.[17] The definition of "dependant" includes men and women not married to the deceased or injured person, as long as they cohabited for at least three years, if they are the natural or adopted parents of a child. The claimant must have been eligible as the appropriate family member at the time of the relevant incident.[18] Neither punitive nor aggravated damages can be recovered in an action under this Act. What is recoverable is specified in the statute. These include damages for loss of "guidance, care and companionship", a phrase that has caused difficulty.[19]

3. SURVIVAL OF ACTIONS

The second important statutory reform of the law that has taken place since the 19th century, thereby getting rid of the other effect of the *actio personalis* doctrine, is the recognition of survival of a cause of action in tort, except for defamation and malicious prosecution,[20] both for the benefit of the victim's estate and so as to make the tortfeasor's estate liable despite the death of the tortfeasor. The cause of action that becomes vested in the estate of the victim or against that of the tortfeasor is the cause of action that was originally vested in the deceased. It is not a new or distinct cause of action. Hence it can be affected by a defence that would have been available against the deceased, such as consent or contributory negligence, and it can be settled out of court by the executor or administrator of the deceased, in the same way that it could have been settled by the deceased. One important difference between the action by the deceased's estate and the action that could have been brought by the deceased is the time within which the action can be brought.[21] The limitation period for an action by a deceased person's estate in Ontario was two years from the death of the deceased.[22] It is the normal limitation period or within one year of the deceased's death (whichever is the longer) in the Yukon.[23]

In an action by the estate of a deceased victim of a tort, not all the damages that might have been recoverable had the deceased been able to sue may be recovered. Thus in various provinces some or all of the following kinds of dam-

---

16 R.S.O. 1990, c. F.3, ss. 61-63.

17 *Butler Trucking Co. v. Brydges* (1984), 10 D.L.R. (4th) 275 (Ont. C.A.).

18 Discussed in *MacIsaac v. Smith* (1987), 35 D.L.R. (4th) 451 (Ont. C.A.).

19 See *Reidy v. Mcleod Estate* (1984), 11 D.L.R. (4th) 411 (Ont. H.C.), varied as to amounts (1986), 27 D.L.R. (4th) 317 (Ont. C.A.).

20 There may be others depending on the particular province in which the cause of action arises and is being pursued.

21 On limitation of actions see below p. 226.

22 *Trustee Act*, R.S.O. 1990, c. T.23, s. 38(3). See now S.O. 2002, c. 26.

23 *Survival of Actions Act*, R.S.Y. 1988, c. 166, s. 9(2).

ages may be excluded:[24] for physical disfigurement; for loss of expectation of life; pain and suffering; and loss of amenities.[25] Everything depends on the legislation in the particular province. It is uncertain whether the estate of a deceased victim can recover, as the victim would have been able to recover had the victim sued, damages representing earnings the victim would have obtained during the years that were lost because his or her life expectancy was curtailed as a conseqence of his or her injuries. In an action by the deceased personally, certain "collateral benefits" derived from or payable to the victim as a consequence of his or her injuries,[26] may have to be brought into account, with the effect of reducing what may be claimed from the tortfeasor. In some jurisdictions the relevant legislation provides that such collateral benefits are not to be taken into account. Elsewhere, however, they may be.

---

24 For these categories of damages see p. 215.

25 So may punitive and aggravated damages: on which see p. 216.

26 See p. 215, note 14.

Chapter 29

BARS TO LIABILITY

1. ACTS OF PLAINTIFF

It has already been noted that, in certain circumstances, a plaintiff guilty of contributory negligence and a plaintiff who is *volens*, that is whose consent to being injured or assumption of risk preceded the commission of a tort, may lose the right to sue in respect of such a tort.[1] This right will also be lost if the plaintiff, after the commission of a tort, releases the wrongdoer from liability or waives his or her claim by appropriate conduct. Such release or waiver usually occurs when the parties enter into a settlement of a claim or action by a binding contract whereby the plaintiff accepts some consideration, in the form of money, in return for the plaintiff's surrender of his or her right of action. Such an agreement is usually termed an "accord and satisfaction".[2]

2. SATISFACTION

A right of action in respect of a tort is also lost by the payment of a sum of money awarded by the judgment of a court. In such circumstances the judgment is said to be "satisfied". However, the right to sue will also be lost if the plaintiff has obtained a judgment in his or her favour even though that judgment has not been "satisfied". The cause of action merges in the judgment. Hence the judgment will bar any further action on the same facts between the same parties, even one that is based upon a different cause of action or involves different consequences. Thus a judgment will bar any subsequent proceedings in respect of the same kind of damage, *e.g.*, personal injury, even though different heads of damage are involved. It will also bar a later action for entirely different damage, or entirely different acts or consequences, as long as these result from the same wrong. This is not the rule in England, where it was held, in *Brunsden v. Humphrey*,[3] that different sorts of damage, for example, to a chattel as contrasted with to the person of the plaintiff, gave rise to distinct actions. The Supreme

---

1 Above pp. 90-95.

2 On which see Fridman, *The Law of Contract in Canada*, 4th ed. (Toronto: Carswell, 1999), pp. 587-589.

3 (1884), 14 Q.B.D. 141, but see *Conquer v. Boot*, [1928] 2 K.B. 336.

Court of Canada rejected this in *Cahoon v. Franks*[4] and preferred to treat the different kinds of damage as belonging to the same cause of action, a more practical, if possibly less logical, attitude. The Canadian view was that the different kinds of damage were part of the factual situation supporting a claim, they were yardsticks useful in measuring the extent of the damage caused by the tort. Hence the rule is that the plaintiff can only sue once in respect of a particular tort.[5] However this will not prevent a plaintiff from suing separately in respect of each time he or she is affected, when the tort is a continuing one, such as trespass to land or nuisance, or where the tort has been committed more than once.[6]

3. LIMITATION OF ACTIONS

A right of action may be barred or lost where the victim has neglected to pursue his or her action within the appropriate period of time. The subject of limitation is governed by statutory provisions, which will be found in all the common law provinces. The different statutes lay down different limitation periods for various torts, and while there are some similarities between provinces, it cannot be said that there is any general degree of uniformity.[7] Hence it is necessary to examine the precise provisions of the statute in a given province in order to ascertain the applicable limitation period for each case, *i.e.*, each tort in each jurisdiction.

The essential idea behind the notion of limitation is very simple. A party should not be able to delay indefinitely the bringing of his or her action. It is unfair to the wrongdoer — who is left in suspense as to whether or not he or she is liable, and if so, the extent of the liability. It may result in witnesses dying or leaving and becoming inaccessible, or forgetting what they heard or saw. It would mean that disputes would be left for many years without resolution. Hence the need to put some limit upon the time within which the victim may sue. Because different situations and different causes of action involve different limitation periods, it can be a matter of some considerable importance for the victim to identify his or her cause of action correctly, and bring the appropriate suit. Hence some problems with respect to the availability of a tort action in cases of breach of contract whether an action is properly one of trespass or negligence, or one for slander or upon the case for words.[8]

---

4 [1967] S.C.R. 455.

5 Cf. above p. 218 in relation to a lump-sum award of damages for personal injuries and the refusal of the common law to allow awards for the periodic payment of such damages.

6 See, *e.g.*, *Konskier v. B. Goodman Ltd.*, [1928] 1 K.B. 421; *Truro (Town) v. Archibald* (1901), 31 S.C.R. 380. Or where the plaintiff sues in different capacities: *Randolph v. Tuck*, [1962] 1 Q.B. 175.

7 See, *e.g.*, R.S.O. 1990, c. L.18 and, in 2004, S.O. 2002, c. 24; R.S.A. 2000, c. L-15.1; R.S.B.C. 1996, c. 266. Note also that other statutes may apply to specific situations, *e.g.*, actions by the estate of a deceased victim, under, *e.g.*, the *Trustee Act*, R.S.O. 1990, c. T.23, s. 38(3) or in respect of claims against public authorities: *Public Authorities Protection Act*, R.S.O. 1990, c. P.38, s. 7(1): six months.

8 *Cf.* the judgment of Laskin J.A. in *Schwebel v. Telekes*, [1967] 1 O.R. 541 (C.A.).

An important issue whenever a question of limitation arises is the date from which the limitation period runs. Ordinarily, this will be when all the elements of the tort have occurred on the basis of which the victim can maintain an action. Thus, in a case of trespass to the person, it will be when the assault or battery takes place; in a case of conversion it will be when the act constituting the denial of the plaintiff's title occurs; in a case of defamation, when the defamatory matter is published to a third person; in a case of detinue, when the wrongdoer refuses to return the chattel, where he or she has no justification in law for so refusing. In negligence actions, however, the cause of action only arises when the damage on which the action is based, and in respect of which it is brought, is suffered by the plaintiff. In all such cases, it would appear, the cause of action can arise without the victim knowing that it has done. Hence the enactment in British Columbia[9] that the cause of action will not arise until the plaintiff discovers, or with "reasonable diligence" could have discovered that damage was suffered. Where the tort is a continuing one, *e.g.*, a trespass resulting from leaving chattels on the land of another, or a nuisance emanating from the maintenance of a factory which continues to produce smoke or fumes that harm the health of the adjoining landowner, the period of limitation runs from each day; in other words the plaintiff can sue in respect of all damage caused during the appropriate statutory period immediately preceding the issuance of his or her writ.

The limitation statutes, however, usually contain special provisions for victims who are under some legal disability, *viz.*, infancy or insanity, at the time that the cause of action first arises.[10] Such provisions only apply to a disability at the time of the cause of action. Disability during the passage of the period of limitation, however, will not have any effect. Time will continue to run, and the operation of the statutory provisions will not be suspended. In some jurisdictions, *e.g.*, Alberta,[11] there may be a suspension of the period if the cause of action is concealed by fraud on the part of the defendant. Fraud in this context would appear to mean not only conduct which is fraudulent in the common law sense, but also any unconscionable behaviour which precludes true appreciation of the situation on the part of the victim.

---

9 R.S.B.C. 1996, c. 266, s. 6(3), (4). *Cf.* S.O. 2002, c. 24, s. 5. See also in relation to damage to property and financial loss, *Central & Eastern Trust Co. v. Rafuse* (1986), 31 D.L.R. (4th) 481 (B.C.C.A.).

10 *E.g.*, R.S.A. 2000, c. L-15.1, s. 5; S.O. 2002, c. 24, ss. 6, 7.

11 R.S.A. 2000, c. L-15.1, s. 4.

Chapter 30

POSSIBLE PROSPECTIVE OR EMERGING TORTS

1. THE FLEXIBILITY OF THE LAW

Torts, as stated in the quotation cited in the first chapter,[1] are "infinitely various". Some that have been part of the law for centuries have been modified to fit new situations. Others have been introduced to provide a remedy where none existed previously. Such developments point to the flexibility and adaptability of the law of torts. The process of development has not ceased, as may be seen, for example, in the way the law has begun to acknowledge liability for wrongful interference with trade or business even though a breach of contract has not been induced[2] or acceptance of liability for the negligent infliction of "pure" economic loss.[3] More and more conduct that results in harm to others is gradually coming within the scope of the law of torts. Some kinds of misconduct, however, even when they cause harm to another party, are not yet treated as being tortious, for example, causing harm by the commission of perjury.[4] In such situations writers and judges speak of *damnum sine injuria*, that is, damage resulting from no wrongful, therefore actionable, behaviour.

Although it is unlikely that the law will ever accept that whenever conduct causes damage, loss or harm, liability will ensue (unless some justification or lawful excuse for such conduct can be asserted), the range or scope of tortious liability may continue to evolve by the creation or acceptance of new forms of liability, that is, new torts. Two different, but not necessarily distinct, lines of development may be suggested. One is the inclusion of certain forms of liability, hitherto not considered as types of tortious liability, within the ambit of the law of torts. The other is the determination that certain other kinds of conduct, previously regarded as instances of *damnum sine injuria*, although upon occasion a judge has been unwilling to make a definite determination to such effect where a defendant has sought to have a cause of action struck out as being unknown to

---

1 Above p. 3, note 1.

2 Above p. 203.

3 Above p. 81.

4 *Hargreaves v. Bretherton*, [1959] 1 Q.B. 45.

the law,[5] should ultimately be accepted as giving rise not only to liability but to tortious liability.

In the first category are: breach of confidence; breach of fiduciary duty; spoliation; discrimination; and, possibly, what might be termed "constitutional" torts. In the second are: invasion of privacy; harassment; and acting in bad faith.

2. INCLUSION AS TORTS?

The types of conduct that are included in the first category are all instances in which the party guilty thereof at the present time, and as the law now is, will be liable, on some basis, to someone injuriously affected by such conduct. To the latter a remedy is available. For breach of confidence and breach of fiduciary duty there will be an action for damages and/or for an accounting of the profits made by such breach.[6] For spoliation, the destruction or concealment of vital evidence, there exist procedural remedies.[7] Where discrimination occurs there are administrative remedies created by statutes[8] that may be invoked by the person subjected to the discrimination.[9] If the wrongdoing in question takes the form of conduct that infringes a person's rights under the *Canadian Charter of Rights and Freedoms*,[10] it is provided by section 24 that a court may grant the victim such remedy as the court deems appropriate, which includes an award of damages.[11]

Thus it is not that such conduct goes unpunished or that the victim of such conduct is bereft of any relief or remedy. That being so, it might be considered unnecessary to treat such conduct as being tortious so as to give rise to an action for damages, or some other remedy, distinct from whatever remedy is now available at common law, in equity or under statute. However there are decisions and dicta indicating that some Canadian judges have thought that at least some

---

5 For example, *Whittaker v. Sanders* (1975), 9 O.R.(2d) 238 (H.C.), where children attempted to sue a man who had disrupted their family life by engaging in a love affair with their mother with the result that she left home. On the trial of a preliminary issue of law, the action was not struck out. The judge was unsure whether there was an action for what might be called "loss of a mother" (unless the situation fell within the *Family Law Act*, above p. 223).

6 *Cadbury Schweppes Inc. v. FBI Foods Ltd.* (1994), 93 B.C.L.R. (3d) 318 (Q.B.), affirmed (1996), 23 B.C.L.R. (3d) 326 (C.A.), affirmed (1999), 167 D.L.R. (4th) 577 (S.C.C.); *Canson Enterprises Ltd. v. Boughton & Co.*, [1991] 3 S.C.R. 534.

7 *Endean v. Canadian Red Cross Society* (1998), 157 D.L.R. (4th) 465 (Ont. C.A.); *Spasic Estate v. Imperial Tobacco Ltd.* (1998), 42 O.R. (3d) 391 (S.C.), reversed (2000), 49 O.R. (3d) 699 (C.A.). See also above Chapter 17, p. 158 note 12.

8 *E.g.*, *Human Rights Code*, R.S.O. 1990, c. H.19; R.S.B.C. 1996, c. 210; *Human Rights Act*, R.S.P.E.I. 1988, c. H-12.

9 *Board of Governors of Seneca College of Applied Arts and Technology v. Bhaduria*, [1981] 2 S.C.R. 181.

10 *Constitution Act, 1982*, Part I, which is Schedule B of the *Canada Act, 1982*, c. 11 (U.K.).

11 Pilkington, "Damages as a Remedy for Infringement of Charter" (1984) 62 Can. Bar Rev. 517.

of the forms of misconduct referred to above may also be regarded as torts.[12] Moreover breach of confidence has been considered to be a tort by writers in other jurisdictions (though not, as yet, by any Canadian judge).[13] Canadian writers and judges have not yet accepted the concept of a "constitutional tort", which appears to exist in the United States.[14] However, the fact that the Charter recognizes the possibility of an action for damages for its infringement, which may be likened to the action for breach of statutory duty brought by an individual particularly damaged by a breach of a statute, suggests that acceptance of the notion of a constitutional tort may not be too far distant.

3. RECOGNITION AS TORTS?

The kinds of conduct that are included in the second category raise different issues. Thus, as noted in Chapter 15, the common law has not yet accepted that all "invasions of privacy" should be treated as tortious.[15] Some can be dealt with as specific torts such as trespass to land, or what has come to be known as "appropriation of personality".[16] It was the failure of the common law to recognize that any invasion of privacy should be a tort that led to the passage of legislation in several, but not all provinces.[17] Perhaps, in time, the fact that at least some invasions of privacy are tortious at common law, and many others are actionable under statute, may lead to the general conclusion that there is a sufficient "interest" in the protection of a person's privacy to justify treating all, or at least all serious attacks or invasions thereon as tortious and therefore actionable.

Harassment has also been the subject of judicial (and in England legislative)[18] notice in recent years. The decision of the Alberta Court of Appeal in *Motherwell v. Motherwell*,[19] which was followed in some later English cases involving allegations of harassment[20] and subsequently criticized and rejected by the

---

12 See, *e.g.*, *Sfarzer v. Chodos* (1986), 54 O.R. (2d) 663 (S.C.), affirmed (1989), 66 O.R. (2d) 350 (C.A.); *Copperview Haven Ltd. v. Waverley Park Estates Ltd.* (1984), 55 B.C. L. R. 230 (C.A.); *Burke v. Cory* (1959), 19 D.L.R. (2d) 252 (Ont. C.A.) at 261 *per* Schroeder J.A.; *Robb Estate v. St. Joseph's Health Care Centre* at first instance, which was reversed on appeal (1998), 166 D.L.R. (4th) 158 (Ont. Div. Ct.); *Coriale (Litigation guardian of) v. Sisters of St. Joseph of Sault Ste Marie* (1998), 41 O.R. (3d) 347 (Gen. Div.); *Spasic Estate v. Imperial Tobacco Ltd.* (2000), 49 O.R. (3d) 699 (C.A.); *Smith v. New Brunswick Human Rights Commission* (1996), 137 D.L.R. (4th) 76 (N.B.Q.B.), but this was reversed on other grounds (1997), 143 D.L.R. (4th) 251 (N.B.C.A.).

13 Todd *et al.*, eds., *The Law of Torts in New Zealand*, 2nd ed. (Wellington: Brooker's, 1997), pp. 800-817; North, "Breach of Confidence: Is There a New Tort?" (1972) 12 J.S.P.T.L. 149.

14 Dobbs, *The Law of Torts* (St. Paul: West Group, 2001), Vol. 1, pp. 81-94.

15 Above p. 147.

16 Above pp. 52, 147.

17 Above p. 148.

18 *Protection from Harassment Act*, 1997, c. 40.

19 (1976), 73 D.L.R. (3d) 62 (Alta. S.C.); above pp. 59, 148.

20 *Khorasandjian v. Bush*, [1993] Q.B. 727; *Burris v. Azadani*, [1995] 1 W.L.R. 1372.

House of Lords,[21] suggests that there is some inclination on the part of Canadian judges to recognize that some forms of harassment may be actionable as torts. This may be said to be borne out by other decisions that recognize that, apart from any remedies under human rights legislation, the victim of sexual harassment may be able to sue the harasser in tort.[22] If this is so, then the common law in Canada is closer to an action for the tort of harassment than it is to an action for the tort of invasion of privacy.

Finally, it has been suggested, in an Australian case,[23] that where someone is under a duty to act in good faith, the failure to do so justifies an action in tort. The judge who determined this relied on various American cases which, as subsequently pointed out,[24] were later repudiated as giving rise to any general tort of bad faith. There appears to be one Canadian case, *Dillon v. Guardian Insurance Co.*,[25] in which the wrongful refusal by an insurance company to settle a valid claim could be treated as a tort. This, however, does not seem to be acceptable in view of the House of Lords decision[26] that, while a failure to deal in good faith might give rise to certain remedies, more contractual than tortious in nature, it would not constitute a tort for the commission of which damages could be awarded. Recent Canadian decisions to the effect that punitive damages can be awarded for certain breaches of contract, including the improper refusal of an insurance company to honour its policy and compensate the victim of a destructive fire,[27] suggest that there may be no need to invoke the law of torts to cope with such misconduct. However, that is not to say that the views expressed in the Australian case and the *Dillon* case referred to above may not one day come to be accepted as part of the law.

---

21 *Hunter v. Canary Wharf Ltd.*, [1997] A.C. 655.

22 *Champagne v. Kapuskasing Plumbing & Heating Ltd.* (1996), 30 O.R. (3d) 403 (Gen. Div.); *Lajoie v. Kelly*, [1997] 3 W.W.R. 181 (Man. Q.B.).

23 *Gibson v. Parkes District Hospital* (1991), 26 N.S.W.L.R. 9 (S.C.N.S.W.).

24 Fleming, "Insurer's Breach of Good Faith—A New Tort?" (1992) 108 L.Q.R. 357. See also Handford, "A Good Faith Tort" (1993) 1 Tort Law Rev.

25 (1984), 2 C.C.L.I. 227 (Ont. S.C.).

26 *Banque Financière de la Cité SA v. Westgate Insurance Co.*, [1991] 2 A.C. 249.

27 *Vorvis v. Insurance Corp. of British Columbia*, [1989] 1 S.C.R. 1085; *Whiten v. Pilot Insurance Co.* (2002), 209 D.L.R. (4th) 257 (S.C.C.).

INDEX

V

W